"For any English teacher who wonders why she teaches, this book will keep you afloat in both challenging educational times and those times when you feel understood. It is a book that I will read again and again, revisiting its pages like a trusted friend. This book informs the practicalities of a rich teaching life: it supports our classroom endeavors, encouraging and reflecting best practices, while simultaneously nurturing the heart of why we began teaching in the first place. Here's a book to 'read,' in the words of C.S. Lewis, 'to know we are not alone.'"

—Denise Maltese, middle school English teacher, Onteora, NY, and winner of the 2008 NCTE James Moffett Award for K–12 Teaching

"At a time when all the discussion about teachers seems so critical, here comes this book that brings some light into my world, reminding me as nothing else has lately what it means to be a teacher, and an English teacher in particular. It is enough that this book restores my pride in our profession; that the book also offers examples of great teaching and expands my conception of my own practice—well, that just makes this book all the more of a gift to our profession."

—Jim Burke, Burlingame High School, CA, author of *I Hear America Reading* and *The English Teacher's Companion*, and founder of the English Companion Ning

"Explaining exactly what the best English teachers do by connecting congenial strains of contemporary science, psychology, and literary theory with perennial themes from both Eastern and Western philosophy, Wilhelm and Novak confirm the highest values of democratic education and offer an inspiring vision of what it truly means to put students first. They show how what really counts in the humanities classroom is the humanity we manifest in it, and how manifesting this humanity is what brings us to come to count for ourselves and for one another. The authors not only describe the future of English, but its best current practices and its deep historical legacy. This book is more than prophetic. In our increasingly dehumanized world, it's a necessity."

—Robert Inchausti, Professor of English, Cal Poly, San Luis Obispo, CA, and author of *Spitwad Sutras: Classroom Teaching as Sublime Vocation* and *Thomas Merton's American Prophecy*

"With the spirits of Matthew Arnold and John Dewey hovering over every page, Wilhelm and Novak probe the question 'What is English?' Drawing on an array of thinkers and intellectual traditions, they make the case that art, and particularly the reading of literature, can help create a 'transactional mentality'—a transcending of the narrow boundaries of 'self' to achieve an openness to others, a sense of true community, and democracy in the best sense. It is a demanding, stimulating, and hopeful journey."

—Thomas Newkirk, University of New Hampshire

"If you yearn, as I do, for an education that encourages students to come alive to themselves, to others, and to the world, you must read this book. We who teach cannot afford to fiddle with information and test scores while the planet burns. We need to help our students become grounded in true self, cultivate wisdom and generosity, and live in a way that reflects reverence for the gifts of nature and human nature. In this important book, Wilhelm and Novak point the way with stories of great teaching and learning and a powerful framework of ideas that sheds light on teaching in every discipline." —**Parker J. Palmer, author of** *The Courage to Teach, Let Your Life Speak,* **and** *Healing the Heart of Democracy*

"Education is for the renewal of life; but most schooling deadens us. I have been working in the field of educational renewal for the past quarter century. So I have been very much cheered in this dark educational time by *Teaching Literacy for Love and Wisdom,* which vividly and coherently connects the educative processes of inner renewal and community renewal with the large-scale processes of democratic and ecological renewal the world now needs. It is a reminder for all of us of what education is and what schools are for and of what we can make of ourselves by truly caring for the education of our young." —**John Goodlad, founder of the Institute for Educational Inquiry and the National Network for Educational Renewal and author of** *A Place Called School, What Schools Are For,* **and** *In Praise of Education*

"In a technologically competitive world that demands 'more math and science,' what is English for? Wilhelm and Novak reveal how reading and writing, despite being classic left-hemisphere activities, can be taught so that they develop right-hemisphere awareness. Literacy becomes a pathway to love, to wisdom, and to hope, rather than one more educational entrapment of an egocentric and instrumental culture. This is a lively, inspiring, and, literally, mind-opening book."
— **Ellen Dissanayake, University of Washington, author of** *What Is Art For?, Homo Aestheticus,* **and** *Art and Intimacy*

"Wilhelm and Novak have respectfully recovered Louise Rosenblatt's inspired use of John Dewey's transactionalism in her transactional theory of reading, and then brilliantly gone beyond it, breaking fresh ground in classroom practice for a new generation that sorely needs it. Dewey and Rosenblatt would both rejoice in their creative and timely reconstruction of their work."
—**Jim Garrison, Virginia Tech, past president of the John Dewey Society, and author of** *Dewey and Eros*

"A great strength of this book is that the authors are masterful storytellers. And in sharing their own stories—as well as those of their students, colleagues, and cooperating teachers—they provide powerful testimony to the brave vulnerability, trusting friendship, and honest meaningfulness that a humanistic education can provide. Read this book for the pleasure that it affords, and allow it to help propel you along in your *own* journey toward greater loving wisdom."
—**Megan Laverty, Teachers College, author of** *Iris Murdoch's Ethics: A Consideration of Her Romantic Vision*

LANGUAGE AND LITERACY SERIES

Teaching Literacy for Love and Wisdom: Being the Book and Being the Change
JEFFREY D. WILHELM & BRUCE NOVAK

Overtested: How High-Stakes Accountability Fails English Language Learners
JESSICA ZACHER PANDYA

Restructuring Schools for Linguistic Diversity: Linking Decision Making to Effective Programs, Second Edition
OFELIA B. MIRAMONTES, ADEL NADEAU, & NANCY L. COMMINS

Words Were All We Had: Becoming Biliterate Against the Odds
MARÍA DE LA LUZ REYES, ED.

Urban Literacies: Critical Perspectives on Language, Learning, and Community
VALERIE KINLOCH, ED.

Bedtime Stories and Book Reports: Connecting Parent Involvement and Family Literacy
CATHERINE COMPTON-LILLY & STUART GREENE, EDS.

Envisioning Knowledge: Building Literacy in the Academic Disciplines
JUDITH A. LANGER

Envisioning Literature: Literary Understanding and Literature Instruction, Second Edition
JUDITH A. LANGER

Writing Assessment and the Revolution in Digital Texts and Technologies
MICHAEL R. NEAL

Artifactual Literacies: Every Object Tells a Story
KATE PAHL & JENNIFER ROWSELL

Educating Emergent Bilinguals: Policies, Programs, and Practices for English Language Learners
OFELIA GARCÍA & JO ANNE KLEIFGEN

(Re)Imagining Content-Area Literacy Instruction
RONI JO DRAPER, ED.

Change Is Gonna Come: Transforming Literacy Education for African American Students
PATRICIA A. EDWARDS, GWENDOLYN THOMPSON MCMILLON, & JENNIFER D. TURNER

When Commas Meet Kryptonite: Classroom Lessons from the Comic Book Project
MICHAEL BITZ

Literacy Tools in the Classroom: Teaching Through Critical Inquiry, Grades 5–12
RICHARD BEACH, GERALD CAMPANO, BRIAN EDMISTON, & MELISSA BORGMANN

Harlem on Our Minds: Place, Race, and the Literacies of Urban Youth
VALERIE KINLOCH

Teaching the New Writing: Technology, Change, and Assessment in the 21st-Century Classroom
ANNE HERRINGTON, KEVIN HODGSON, & CHARLES MORAN, EDS.

Critical Encounters in High School English: Teaching Literary Theory to Adolescents, Second Edition
DEBORAH APPLEMAN

Children, Language, and Literacy: Diverse Learners in Diverse Times
CELIA GENISHI & ANNE HAAS DYSON

Children's Language: Connecting Reading, Writing, and Talk
JUDITH WELLS LINDFORS

The Administration and Supervision of Reading Programs, Fourth Edition
SHELLEY B. WEPNER & DOROTHY S. STRICKLAND, EDS.

"You Gotta BE the Book": Teaching Engaged and Reflective Reading with Adolescents, Second Edition
JEFFREY D. WILHELM

No Quick Fix: Rethinking Literacy Programs in America's Elementary Schools, The RTI Reissue
RICHARD L. ALLINGTON & SEAN A. WALMSLEY, EDS.

Children's Literature and Learning: Literary Study Across the Curriculum
BARBARA A. LEHMAN

Storytime: Young Children's Literary Understanding in the Classroom
LARWRENCE R. SIPE

Effective Instruction for Struggling Readers, K–6
BARBARA M. TAYLOR & JAMES E. YSSELDYKE, EDS.

The Effective Literacy Coach: Using Inquiry to Support Teaching and Learning
ADRIAN RODGERS & EMILY M. RODGERS

Writing in Rhythm: Spoken Word Poetry in Urban Classrooms
MAISHA T. FISHER

Reading the Media: Media Literacy in High School English
RENEE HOBBS

teachingmedialiteracy.com: A Web-Linked Guide to Resources and Activities
RICHARD BEACH

What Was It Like? Teaching History and Culture Through Young Adult Literature
LINDA J. RICE

Once Upon a Fact: Helping Children Write Nonfiction
CAROL BRENNAN JENKINS & ALICE EARLE

Research on Composition: Multiple Perspectives on Two Decades of Change
PETER SMAGORINSKY, ED.

Critical Literacy/Critical Teaching: Tools for Preparing Responsive Literacy Teachers
CHERYL DOZIER, PETER JOHNSTON, & REBECCA ROGERS

The Vocabulary Book: Learning and Instruction
MICHAEL F. GRAVES

Building on Strength: Language and Literacy in Latino Families and Communities
ANA CELIA ZENTELLA, ED.

(Continued)

LANGUAGE AND LITERACY SERIES (*continued*)

Powerful Magic: Learning from Children's Responses
to Fantasy Literature
NINA MIKKELSEN

New Literacies in Action:
Teaching and Learning in Multiple Media
WILLIAM KIST

Teaching English Today: Advocating Change in the
Secondary Curriculum
BARRIE R.C. BARRELL, ROBERTA F. HAMMETT,
JOHN S. MAYHER, & GORDON M. PRADL, EDS.

Bridging the Literacy Achievement Gap, 4–12
DOROTHY S. STRICKLAND & DONNA E. ALVERMANN, EDS.

Crossing the Digital Divide: Race, Writing, and
Technology in the Classroom
BARBARA MONROE

Out of This World: Why Literature Matters to Girls
HOLLY VIRGINIA BLACKFORD

Critical Passages: Teaching the Transition to College
Composition
KRISTIN DOMBEK & SCOTT HERNDON

Making Race Visible:
Literary Research for Cultural Understanding
STUART GREENE & DAWN ABT-PERKINS, EDS.

The Child as Critic: Developing Literacy Through
Literature, K–8, Fourth Edition
GLENNA SLOAN

Room for Talk: Teaching and Learning in a
Multilingual Kindergarten
REBEKAH FASSLER

Give Them Poetry! A Guide for Sharing Poetry with
Children K–8
GLENNA SLOAN

The Brothers and Sisters Learn to Write
ANNE HAAS DYSON

"Just Playing the Part"
CHRISTOPHER WORTHMAN

The Testing Trap
GEORGE HILLOCKS, JR.

School's Out!
GLYNDA HULL & KATHERINE SCHULTZ, EDS.

Reading Lives
DEBORAH HICKS

Inquiry Into Meaning
EDWARD CHITTENDEN & TERRY SALINGER, WITH ANNE M. BUSSIS

"Why Don't They Learn English?"
LUCY TSE

Conversational Borderlands
BETSY RYMES

Inquiry-Based English Instruction
RICHARD BEACH & JAMIE MYERS

The Best for Our Children
MARÍA DE LA LUZ REYES & JOHN J. HALCÓN, EDS.

Language Crossings
KAREN L. OGULNICK, ED.

What Counts as Literacy?
MARGARET GALLEGO & SANDRA HOLLINGSWORTH, EDS.

Beginning Reading and Writing
DOROTHY S. STRICKLAND & LESLEY M. MORROW, EDS.

Reading for Meaning
BARBARA M. TAYLOR, MICHAEL F. GRAVES,
& PAUL VAN DEN BROEK, EDS.

Young Adult Literature and the New Literary Theories
ANNA O. SOTER

Literacy Matters
ROBERT P. YAGELSKI

Children's Inquiry
JUDITH WELLS LINDFORS

Close to Home
JUAN C. GUERRA

On the Brink
SUSAN HYNDS

Life at the Margins
JULIET MERRIFIELD, ET AL.

Literacy for Life
HANNA ARLENE FINGERET & CASSANDRA DRENNON

The Book Club Connection
SUSAN I. MCMAHON & TAFFY E. RAPHAEL, EDS., WITH VIRGINIA
J. GOATLEY & LAURA S. PARDO

Until We Are Strong Together
CAROLINE E. HELLER

Writing Superheroes
ANNE HAAS DYSON

Opening Dialogue
MARTIN NYSTRAND, ET AL.

Just Girls
MARGARET J. FINDERS

The First R
MICHAEL F. GRAVES, PAUL VAN DEN BROEK, &
BARBARA M. TAYLOR, EDS.

Teaching Writing as Reflective Practice
GEORGE HILLOCKS, JR.

Talking Their Way into Science
KAREN GALLAS

The Languages of Learning
KAREN GALLAS

Partners in Learning
CAROL LYONS, GAY SU PINNELL, & DIANE DEFORD

Social Worlds of Children Learning to Write in an
Urban Primary School
ANNE HAAS DYSON

Inside/Outside
MARILYN COCHRAN-SMITH & SUSAN L. LYTLE

Whole Language Plus
COURTNEY B. CAZDEN

Learning to Read
G. BRIAN THOMPSON & TOM NICHOLSON, EDS.

Engaged Reading
JOHN T. GUTHRIE & DONNA E. ALVERMANN

Teaching Literacy
for
Love and Wisdom

BEING THE BOOK and BEING THE CHANGE

TOURO COLLEGE LIBRARY
Kings Hwy

Jeffrey D. Wilhelm
Bruce Novak

Foreword by Sheridan Blau

Teachers College, Columbia University
New York and London

National Council of
Teachers of English
Urbana, Illinois

National Writing Project
Berkeley,
California

Published simultaneously by Teachers College Press, 1234 Amsterdam Avenue, New York, NY 10027; National Council of Teachers of English, 1111 W. Kenyon Road, Urbana, IL 61801-1096; and the National Writing Project, 2105 Bancroft Way, Berkeley, CA 94720-1042.

The National Writing Project (NWP) is a professional development network of more than 200 university-based sites, serving teachers across disciplines and at all levels, early childhood through university. The sites work in partnership with surrounding school districts across all 50 states, the District of Columbia, Puerto Rico, and the U.S. Virgin Islands. The NWP focuses the knowledge, expertise, and leadership of our nation's educators on sustained efforts to improve writing and learning for all learners.

Grateful acknowledgment is made to reprint the following:

"Writing in the Dark" by Denise Levertov, from CANDLES IN BABYLON, copyright ©1982 by Denise Levertov. Reprinted by permission of New Directions Publishing Corp.

Student poems appearing in Figure 3.2 from *Creating Re-Creations: Writing from the Source* by Gabriele Rico (Absey Press, 2002). Reprinted with permission.

Excerpts in Chapter 5 from Peter Elbow, *What is English?* (New York: Modern Language Association, 1990). Reprinted by permission of the Modern Language Association of America.

Library of Congress Cataloging-in-Publication Data

Wilhelm, Jeffrey D., 1959–
  Teaching literacy for love and wisdom : being the book and being the change / Jeffrey D. Wilhelm, Bruce Novak ; foreword by Sheridan Blau.
    p. cm.—(Language and literacy series)
    Includes bibliographical references and index.
  ISBN 978-0-8077-5236-4 (pbk.)—ISBN 978-0-8077-5237-1 (hardcover)
    1. English language—Study and teaching—United States. 2. English teachers—United States. 3. Education, Humanistic—United States. I. Novak, Bruce. II. Title.
  LB1576.W48767 2011
  428.0071'2—dc22

                                                                            2011006204

ISBN 978-0-8077-5236-4 (paper)
ISBN 978-0-8077-5237-1 (hardcover)

NCTE Stock No. 52364

Printed on acid-free paper

Manufactured in the United States of America

18 17 16 15 14 13 12 11   8 7 6 5 4 3 2

7/18/12

How do we teach English in a way that people will stop killing . . .?

—Mary Rose O'Reilley, *The Peaceable Classroom*

Produce great Persons. The rest follows.

—Walt Whitman, *Democratic Vistas*

It took Sputnik to get Congress interested in the quality and quantity of scientific manpower. What will it take to persuade them to see that English is really fundamental?

—Herbert J. Muller, *The Uses of English*

Without an awakening, there can be no progress. To bring it about in the country, one must place some program before it.

—Gandhi

Unless there is some kind of spiritual revolution that can keep abreast of our technological genius, it is unlikely that we will save our planet. A purely rational education will not suffice.

—Karen Armstrong, *The Great Transformation*

If civilization is to survive, we must cultivate the science of human relationships.

—Franklin Roosevelt

Everything has changed . . . except the way we think. The aim [of education] must be the training of independently acting and thinking individuals, who, however, see in the service of the community their highest life problem.

—Albert Einstein

What it takes to arrest our descent into chaos is one person after another remembering who and where they really are.

—Paul Hawken, *Blessed Unrest*

Perhaps . . . the current disequilibrium is a stirring not an erasure. . . . Not only is history not dead, [it may be] about to take its first unfettered breath. . . . There are acres of Edens inside ourselves. Time does have a future. Longer than the past and infinitely more hospitable . . . to the human race.

—Toni Morrison, "The Future of Time"

Contents

Foreword *by Sheridan Blau*   xiii

Acknowledgments   xvii

Introduction: Among Schoolteachers   1

PART I   WHAT *IS* "ENGLISH"?

1 A Brief History of a Nebulous Subject   21
2 The Power of Softness: Intimations of Deepened Humanity
   from Stories of Classroom Life   36
3 Understanding the Power of Softness
   Through the Deep Prehistory of English   50

PART II   THE WAY LIFE TEACHES:
REVISITING THE THREE DIMENSIONS OF
AESTHETIC, TRANSACTIONAL RESPONSIVENESS

4 The Evocative Dimension: Story Time and Human Life   77
5 The Connective Dimension:
   Finding Love by Sharing Insight with Implied Authors   92
6 The Reflective Dimension:
   Response and Responsibility, Love and Loving Wisdom   122

PART III   READING *BEYOND* THE BOOK:
MOVING FROM A TRANSACTIONAL WORLDVIEW
TO A TRANSACTIONAL WORLD

7 Aesthetic Education:
   The Artistry of Transactional Life in Classrooms   149
8 Aesthetic Democracy: Government of People by People
   for the Shared Life of People, Writ Small and Writ Large   173
9 Aesthetic Humanity:
   The History, and Possible Future, of Wisdom   190

Conclusion: What Can "English" Become?   210

Notes   225

References   232

Index   244

About the Authors   254

Foreword

In a post-holocaust and postmodern world, it has been difficult for any of us to maintain the faith of earlier generations in the humanizing and civilizing function of literature. We do not and dare not forget that concentration camps were sometimes commanded by officers who had been devoted readers of Shakespeare and Goethe and Rilke. More recently, whole schools of literary theorists have diminished the status of literature by declaring literary texts mere artifacts of a culture, like cooking utensils and inventory records, while canonical and classic works are declared to be valuable only as cultural capital for a privileged minority. In the meantime, in the sphere of public education, assessments and policy makers who determine curriculum for public schools treat literary knowledge as information about literature and celebrate the removal of literature from classrooms in favor of "non-fiction" that can be read for information.

At a moment in cultural history, when literature looks like an endangered species of discourse, English teachers and all of us who are academic humanists have reason to suspend our characteristic skepticism and find cause for hope and even celebration in this new book by Jeff Wilhelm and Bruce Novak with the surprising and promising title, *Teaching Literacy for Love and Wisdom: Being the Book and Being the Change.* In this inspiring volume, Wilhelm and Novak take up the mantle of Sir Philip Sidney (16th century), Mathew Arnold (19th century), and F. R Leavis (20th century) in offering a twenty-first century defense of literature, yet a defense that also draws persuasively on ancient wisdom and on powerful evidence from political, literary, and educational history, including a brilliantly reconstructed history of English education in the 20th century.

In this carefully argued and wide ranging volume, Wilhelm (an icon of the field of English education for his contributions to theory and practice in the teaching of reading to adolescents) and Novak (a philosopher as well as an English teacher and a seminal figure in NCTE's intensely philosophical, theological, and educationally-progressive Assembly for Expanded Perspectives on Learning—AEPL) combine their spiritual and intellectual forces to make a compelling case that the humanities can, in fact, humanize and confer a kind of saving wisdom on this and future generations of students, if the teaching of the texts that are at the center of the curriculum is conducted in a way that is philosophically and pedagogically consistent with what they see as the enduring core values of the humanistic and spiritual traditions from which the texts arise. And they find these traditions articulated most persuasively for the modern world in the philosophical and pedagogical writing of the intellectual mother of all of us who work in the field of English education, Louise Rosenblatt, who was herself the intellectual heir of her mentor, the philosopher John Dewey.

Building on Rosenblatt and Dewey and on an impressive collection of other philosophical and pedagogical mentors, Wilhelm and Novak propose to turn literary study and the larger field of the English language arts into a discipline explicitly devoted to the acquisition of the kind of moral, ethical, and prudential wisdom that in the ancient world the study of philosophy (and, later, theology) as well as literature promised to confer. To guide teachers in how to enact such an instructional program in real classrooms, they offer numerous descriptions of model lessons and an illustrative set of vignettes or case studies of students and instructional units and inspiring texts that they themselves and teachers they have mentored have successfully taught. The measure of success in each case is the evidence that the students who experienced such teaching seem to have gained a kind of personal and spiritual growth or illumination that contrasts dramatically with the trivial and shallow knowledge usually acquired and even specified as a goal for literary instruction in typical English classes.

But what is most remarkable and surprising about this book is its grand ambition for the reconstruction beyond the English classroom of human relations and human political institutions based on a principle of engaged reading and teaching that three generations of English teachers have learned from Rosenblatt, though it is infused in the mainstream of literary criticism since Aristotle and defines the essential experience of literature that probably seduced most of us who are English teachers into our profession in the first place. That principle is expressed in Rosenblatt's insistence that the reading of literature becomes most fully capable of producing the distinctive benefits of literature for individuals and communities when it is "aesthetic reading" or reading as an "experience" into which we enter as complete persons for the sake of the experience itself and what we can learn from that experience through engaging fully in it and reflecting on it, the way we experience and learn from our dreams or the dramas of our lives in transactions with others.

The alternative model for reading that she calls "efferent" (from the Latin *effere* to carry away) is the way we read when we look up a number in a telephone book or read a science textbook in preparation for an exam. All we want is the information we can carry away from the text, information that if already possessed would make the reading of the text itself largely irrelevant. That is the stance toward literature that trivializes and perverts literary study in classrooms and that produces the correct answers about themes or style or "literary elements" that are characteristically sought by the questions typically asked on standardized tests of reading and in many standards based classrooms as well.

Wilhelm and Novak in an entirely original and profoundly important conceptual move demonstrate that the aesthetic/efferent distinction can describe the way human beings enter into all the transactions of any life, and they call for classrooms that operate on aesthetic principles and aesthetic relationships, where persons appreciate and honor each other without reading texts or other persons as commodities for use. Classrooms built on such aesthetic attention, they argue, become sites of true dialogue and true learning and models for a truly democratic community. More than that, they demonstrate how classrooms properly conceived become sites for the kind of loving and responsible relationships and saving knowledge that is currently necessary not merely for the salvation of individual human souls and local communities, but for the salvation of the planetary soul—also at risk from a modern history of efferent reading and commodification that has compromised the ecological system and produced weapons of instant holocausts that literally threaten the survival of all future readers.

This is a book that deserves a wide readership, but not of careless or superficial readers nor of readers who would read only to "overstand" and engage in the commerce of a critical discourse designed mainly to advance competing agendas. Rather it deserves the kind of reading it advocates and invites—a reading that engages responsively and responsibly with its ideas in a relationship of mutually-supportive meaning making in a democratic dialogue that values all voices and the experience of hearing them and reflecting on them to clarify, advance, and refine the understanding and wisdom of all participants in the discourse.

Sheridan Blau
Teachers College, Columbia University
March 6, 2011

Acknowledgments

We would both like to acknowledge, first, the work of Wayne Booth, George Hillocks, James Moffett, and Louise Rosenblatt, whose differing ideas of the role of humanistic education in democratic life we have sought to bring together in this work. We would also like to thank those who have helped us put this book together—sometimes having to whip *us* to whip *it* into shape: especially Meg Lemke, Danny Miller, and the four anonymous reviewers from Teachers College Press; but also Sheridan Blau, Robert Inchausti, Peter Elbow, Megan Laverty, and Jeff Kaplan, who gave generously of their time and thought and by whose words we were both buoyed and pushed onward and deeper.

From Jeff

There are more people to thank for their guidance and assistance than can possibly be named here. Nonetheless, here is a very brief attempt. First and foremost, thanks to Bruce for having the ideas that led to this project and for leading our collaboration on it over the past 2 years, which has been a great pleasure and an honor as well. Personally, my unfettered gratitude always goes to my family, especially my wife Peggy Jo and my daughters Fiona and Jasmine. Professionally, perpetual thanks to my own most influential teachers: particularly, Bill Strohm, Michael Smith, and George Hillocks. Special appreciation to my colleagues Jim Fredricksen, Deb Appleman, John Schmitt, Steve Olsen-Smith, Tanya Baker, and all of the National Writing Project fellows with whom I have worked over the years, particularly those from the Maine and Boise State Writing Projects. A respectful bow goes to my friends Willie Stewart, Mike Weber, Dale Reynolds, "Commander" Bob White, and Melissa Newell. A sincere salute goes to Boise State University for valuing and supporting my work with teachers.

From Bruce

First I need to thank the Department of Leadership, Educational Psychology, and Foundations of Northern Illinois University and the Department of Communications at Truman College for giving me the freedom to teach the courses centered on wisdom that, in the first case, led to the idea for this project, and, in the second, helped me tie it back to the teaching of literacy—and also for being the kinds of places where this kind of teaching is the norm, not the exception. I thank the University of Chicago—and my many, many great teachers there over many, many years—for being a magnet for great thinking of all kinds. And, above all, I thank all the students who suffered, often grew, and sometimes grew together through the courses I've taught at these three places. Particularly those with whom I have kept in good touch: David, Jeff, and Stephanie from the U of C; Chris, Christa, Dave, Heather, Keith, Monica, Ray, Rob, Sara, Stephen, and Tad from NIU; and Adalberto, Bayti, Carlos, Joey, and Valentino from Truman.

There are other special debts of three kinds: personal, visionary, and financial. For showing me their religious devotion to students, I thank my mother and sister, Christine Phillips, Bert Cohler, Jeanne Shaefer, George Hillocks, Nan Koob, Yvonne Hutchinson, Lisa Ruddick, Robert Inchausti, Cristy Bruns, and Jeff. For their gorgeous visions of life and its possibilities, and for mentoring me in living a life of hope and love, I thank Ron Engel, Michael Lerner and Peter Gabel, Riane Eisler and David Loye, Parker Palmer, Jane Tompkins, Dick Graves and Sherry Swain, Gene and Mary Gendlin, David Hansen, Jim Garrison, and John Goodlad. For personal succor and giving generously of their life-force, I thank, aside from all of the above, Amy Abern, Kerry Burch, Nancy Burke, Betsy Burris, John Creger, Grace Feuerverger, Regina Foehr, Tom Gage, Carlos Gutierrez, Jim Hecimovich, Libby Jones, Jeff Kälin, Joanne Kent, D'vorah Kost, Dennis McCaughan, Linda O'Neill, Nan Phifer, Shobhana Rishi, Jessica Schneider, Nanette Schorr, Dave Shernoff, Stan Scott, Edward Stein, Jim Super, Helen Walker, and, especially, Louise Smith, whose love and companionship over 13 years were indispensable both to my life and to getting this project off the ground. For their financial magnanimity, I thank my mother Lois Kneeter, the Smith Family Foundation, Teachers College Press, Ron Miller, and the Gülen Foundation—as well as the many, many friends and colleagues who have generously put me up and fed me in the seminomadic, hand-to-mouth existence I've led in the time it took to write this. Last, thanks to Jeff, again, for believing, through thick and through thin, in this, and in me.

Among Schoolteachers

Jeff has wide repertoire of favorite teaching stories. One of the great rewards of his teaching career has been the stories he's collected, and the rich human experiences and connections they reveal.

Here's a story he tells a lot. A few years ago he was back in his old hometown, where he had taught middle school for many years. He pulled into a gas station to fill up, and lo and behold, the attendant was his former seventh-grade English student, Dan Feight, now the proud co-owner of the station. Dan had always been a big kid, but now he seemed to be a strapping 7 feet tall, swathed in a brown canvas jacket with a flannel hunting cap on his head. He immediately recognized Jeff and gave him a very exuberant hello with an enthusiastic handshake. He and Jeff exchanged pleasantries as he began to fill Jeff's fuel tank. Then Dan said "I'd like to tell you that you might have been my favorite teacher. I loved your class."

On hearing this, Jeff was stunned into an awkward silence. Then he said, "Dan, my memory is that you hated my class. You hardly ever did any work. You were always goofing off! I'm surprised you passed!"

Dan laughed uproariously, to the point that he nearly unhooked the gas nozzle. "Yeah," he admitted, "that's true!" He continued to laugh and then he said, "But you never gave up on me—you just *never* gave up. And you kept being nice to me. That's what I remember. I've thought about that—like you saw some possibility in me. And even though I hated reading, you were so revved and jazzed by it that I thought there must be something to reading, too. And I guess there was, because I'm reading more now." After a pause he put in the coda: "Maybe you weren't my favorite teacher then, but you are now!"

This encounter left Jeff feeling elated but confused. He was buoyed by a sense that he had somehow succeeded in teaching Dan—something he never would have guessed before this encounter. Yet he was fairly certain that Dan was not passionately consuming *Moby Dick* at night. So what constituted that success?

What was it that Jeff had accomplished in regard to Dan? What do we teach students peripherally through our modeling and our interactions with them and what do they learn from this? And what exactly had Dan accomplished? What had he achieved, over time, that overcame, in his mind, his total lack of traditional achievement in class?

"HOW ALIVE THEY ALL ARE!"

These days Jeff is a university professor who spends most of his time working in schools. The introduction to Jeff's first book, *"You Gotta BE the Book": Teaching Engaged and Reflective Reading with Adolescents* (1997/2008), was titled *"Really* Among Schoolchildren" and told how he learned to focus his teaching, not on texts or tests, but on his students' making of meaning. He sees his current work as trying to be *"really* among school-teachers," which means focusing his work with teachers on looking for, thinking through, and continually reimagining the intricate personal and curricular processes they find to make meaning with their students so that students can eventually make more powerful kinds of meaning by themselves.

Currently he is working with several teachers as part of the Boise State Writing Project's "Rethinking Teaching Initiative" and particularly with a subgroup of teachers who are "Rethinking AP English." As part of this initiative, Jeff is coteaching an AP literature course with one of the teachers, Rachel Bear. (Jeff's youngest daughter Jasmine is in this class, which gives the whole venture a bit more zing!)

He is also coordinating a Virtual Professional Development Site Project (VPDS) to mentor preservice interns and early career teachers into the profession. As part of this project he is working quite closely with two junior high school teachers, Andrew Porter and Sarah Veigel, and two high school teachers, Rachel Bear and Sharon Hanson, as well as with the interns these teachers are inducting into the profession. Debra Smith, another high school teacher, is involved in both of these projects and is helping to lead (along with Sharon and Rachel) a National Writing Project initiative to promote literacy instruction in the content areas. Though Jeff has other teaching and school involvements, he's been especially engaged with these particular educators.

Here is a synopsis of one day of Jeff's interactions with these teachers. It was a good day, but not in any way an atypical one.

Jeff arrives at Boise's North Junior High School while it is still dark. It's raining and the streetlights glisten off Ninth Street as he crosses it. The fluorescent lights emanating from the long windows of the big brick building are eerily inviting. He climbs the steps into the school and then two more flights up to the third floor, maneuvering around groups of breathless seventh graders trying to beat the first-period bell.

He spends the first hour in Sarah's class. Sarah is a diminutive Irish-woman with fiery red hair. She is a highly accomplished and experienced teacher in her fifties and exudes an exuberant and positive energy. You can practically feel an electrical current radiating from her. Jeff has worked with Sarah for several years and he knows that she is always completely and utterly herself. She knows exactly where she begins and where she ends. She greets every student by name as they enter the classroom. She laughs and jokes with them, and tells them that Jeff is "a crazy professor who would rather be with you than at the university! That's why I like him."

Today's activity is a gallery walk. The students have created an artistic response to their favorite short story during a unit organized around the essential question, What makes the best story? They have written an artist's statement about their visual response explaining how their artwork captures and expresses their engagement with the story. They also have a short talk to give about how the chosen story exhibits their answer to the essential question. Sarah seems to be everywhere during the gallery walk. She makes sure to visit every student. She asks questions and offers ideas for extending the students' thinking. The kids are excited and very respectful of each other's work.

After class Jeff heads off down the hall to Andrew's room where he confers with the two teachers and their interns about planning an upcoming unit on *To Kill a Mockingbird*. Andrew is a younger teacher in his 6th year, once one of Jeff's undergraduate methods students. He is very dapper and always wears a tie; he's also an outdoorsman and athlete and he coaches several sports. Andrew is very organized. Jeff doesn't say much as the two teachers contextualize the upcoming unit for the interns. Here are a few of the comments Jeff recorded as they spoke:

> *Sarah*: First thing—I want the kids to leave their reading of *To Kill a Mockingbird* with hope and a social project for the future. I won't have my kids going hopeless. In some ways what we read [in the ninth grade curriculum] is depressing. But I always look for the hope. Like I ask them to find mockingbirds in our school and community and I tell them that there should always be an Atticus there, too, to help them. So we look around the community for people in need or who are silenced or oppressed and ask who are or could be the Atticus standing up for them, helping them. I want them to ask how can we be an Atticus, or maybe even more than an Atticus—that is what I want to get after. If they don't get transformed and rehearsed for right now and the problems in the school and community, then reading the book is a waste of time in my oh-so-humble opinion . . . so that is what we have to get after.

Sarah is on fire. Andrew and Jeff exchange knowing glances as she storms on.

Sarah: Here's another thing I press them on: When you know something, are you now responsible to transform yourself, to line your behavior up with what you know? Do you just shut your mouth and go on the way you already have, which is what I think usually happens, or do you challenge yourself to change your behavior? Do you think about why you behave the way you do, why you are attached to it, even in the face of how negative it could be for you and for others? If you study social groups in the school and see how some kids are mockingbirds or outcasts does it mean that now you have to sit with people you don't know, and welcome new kids into the school instead of always sitting with your friends? What does it mean to you and how you are going to be. Great books throw down challenges. I want the kids to see and take up the challenge.

Andrew: We've been really moving in our teaching from emphasizing the textual or the book itself to emphasizing the contextual—we've been moving from information to inquiry—Sarah and I keep reminding each other that the assigned text is not the main thing. We want to get after teaching the real thing—which is preparing kids for how to be in the real world dealing with real problems. And to do it with a sense of urgency. I'm always emphasizing that the stuff we are doing is way bigger than what the school district requires. I tell the kids that we are renegades going beyond, pushing the boundaries. We don't confuse the EOC [end of course exam] and ISAT [state test] with what we are really trying to do here. I might say to them, "We need to know this for the test, but we are going to use this knowledge and leverage it for higher purposes."

Sarah: I spend lots more time planning now than I did as a young teacher, and less time grading. I want to make sure that the quality of the kids' experience each day is really high, that our relationships and activities are meaningful and fun and lead to something that we all agree is important.

Jeff was impressed with the time and energy these teachers spent framing the purpose of the unit. Most of the kids will forget *To Kill a Mockingbird*, but they won't ever forget that a teacher stood up for them, or that they learned to stand up for something themselves. After about 40 minutes, Jeff glances at his watch and excuses himself. From here, he walks three blocks over to Boise High where he's co-teaching the AP English class with Rachel Bear.

The students are just finishing up a unit framed with the essential question, Whose story gets told? The class has been reading *Things Fall Apart* by Chinua Achebe and passages from *Heart of Darkness* by Joseph

Conrad as paired texts to engage in an exploration of this question. Many concepts and strategies were emphasized during this unit, but the major focus is a study of perspective. The class has been field-testing some of the instructional ideas featured in Jeff's book *Fresh Takes on Teaching the Literary Elements* (Smith & Wilhelm, 2010).

Since it was the final day of the unit, students had been asked to compose some compelling higher level thinking questions that would help facilitate student-led Socratic Seminars. They had been experimenting with a few different structures for the discussions, but this time they organized the class in such a way that the students were divided into two large circles pursuing separate conversations. Jeff and Rachel asked for a volunteer to serve as a facilitator in each group—not to control things, but to help keep the discussion flowing. Rachel and Jeff observed as teacher researchers. What happened almost immediately was absolute magic: The kids took over completely and didn't pause for more than an hour.

That night, Rachel emailed Jeff:

> There I was, sitting back, taking notes, completely uninvolved in the discussions, listening to these 17-year-old human beings talk about incredible questions of human existence. I heard them talk about the "right to write" (who is or should be allowed to tell which stories); authorial intent and can we really know it and how this intent and meaning plays out in art; author's obligations to their readers and to the world; imperialism and its consequences; silenced voices of minorities and other marginalized people and how we might better hear them; and many other topics relating to our essential question. I heard them valuing each other's perspectives. I witnessed them conversing, having a genuine dialogue and referring to specific passages from the literature and relating this to their lives. There was no hand raising or interrupting. On the contrary, they were taking turns, stepping aside for others to speak, asking questions for clarification, inviting those who had not spoken to join in, and respectfully using each other's ideas. I remember thinking then how incredibly lucky I am to have a job where I could hear such intriguing conversation—where I can assist in and witness people in the act of becoming, of outgrowing their current selves and growing into a more animated and responsible engagement with the world. This brings me so much joy that I feel my body and soul are ready to burst into blossom.

After school Jeff walks over to Alia's Coffee shop on Main Street to meet with his "Rethinking AP English" group. He talks with Debra Smith as they wait for the others to arrive. Debra is a poet and storyteller and very articulate. This year she has voluntarily given up Junior AP English/American Lit and is teaching Senior English and AP Language. "It was time for a change. Time to shake things up and make myself rethink things and come up with new units and lessons," she explains, with a bit of fatigue in her voice. Then she brightens up:

> Do you know, in all of our English curricula for the senior year, nowhere does it mention that the outcome of the hero's journey is some kind of wisdom? Are we ashamed to aim high and speak frankly? Is it false humility or lack of confidence? Have we been so influenced by postmodernism that we have no faith in our own subject matter? I mean, I know that I am teaching for civic engagement and democracy. I am teaching for wisdom. I am not afraid to say it. But I wonder if saying it makes me look a bit kooky.

After a pause to sip her coffee, she begins again.

> Wisdom. That is knowing yourself and knowing the world and knowing your relationship to the world and how you want to be in it. It is knowing what is and what could be different and being willing to work toward transformative change. Wisdom is seeing patterns where others see chaos. Wisdom is seeing distinctions where others only see sameness. Wisdom is always asking, What if it were otherwise? Wisdom is overcoming biases. . . . It is filled with tolerance and kindness and love. . . .

By now several others have sat down at our table sipping their mochas and lattes. But Debra continues on for a bit:

> There's got to be a civic purpose for education—a higher philosophical purpose. We have to be nurturing citizenship—an informed and wise citizenship. That's why I think we should host a conference on the senior project that is going to be required for graduation—to make sure that the project works to nurture active citizenship instead of becoming some stupid hoop to jump through to graduate.

The rest of the group has arrived and the conversation about teaching heats up further. Many practical ideas are exchanged, some lesson planning occurs in pairs or triads, but the group keeps coming back to their higher purposes and they wax philosophical as they talk about their teaching. There is a lot of talk about literature, about things we have read.

Jeff looks at the group and thinks, *"How alive they all are!"* Though he is tired, he is feeling more alive for being with them and he thinks how their students must feel the same way.

Whenever Jeff works with these teachers, whenever he hears them converse about teaching, whenever he sees them interact with students, and whenever he teaches with them or watches them teach, he senses that what they are doing is very much filled with love. This is true, albeit in different ways, for each of these teachers. Love for their subject, surely, and love of literature and of learning. There is also love for individual students as specific human beings, as well as for the groups they work with, in the sense that these teachers greatly enjoy the kids and their interactions with them. There is sometimes anger, but it is a hopeful and justified anger at how kids are silenced or are deprived of opportunities or don't understand their own worth and potential. There is also something being pursued that goes well beyond content. There is something present that we would have to call "passion." The teachers are alive and pulsing with it, even if they are tired or have had a hard day or a bad lesson or if they are doubting themselves somewhat.

But there is something else too—something that could be called "joy"—that animates their teaching and every interaction with the material, with individual students or the group. There is an implicit and sometimes an explicit cultivation of joy. There is a sense of the world's challenges but a positive perspective that something can and must be done, that everything we are working on together is directly related to improving our lives, the lives of others, and the world.

Finally, there is a pushing and a probing for something deep, something that a cognitive scientist might call "understanding" but we are inclined to call "wisdom." Understanding includes justifying one's knowledge and way of doing things, typically according to disciplinary standards; wisdom supersedes this by adding a layer of passion and care, compassion, and ethical consideration. These teachers have a deep sense of mission and higher calling and every day they make this same call to their students.

LITERACY *FOR* LIFE: HOW ALIVE WE *ALL* CAN AND SHOULD BE

Unfortunately, not all teachers have this kind of call, and not nearly all who have it work in circumstances where they can answer it as fully as do Rachel, Debra, Andrew, Sharon, Sarah, and the rest of Jeff's group. Though all of them work under considerable constraints and pressures, they manage to creatively follow their calling, through an artful mix of the mundane and the sublime. Sometimes needing to summon up various forms of courage, and occasionally even to subtly practice subterfuge, they all are able to give fully of themselves to their students. Certainly, all children need and deserve teachers with this open aliveness, teachers who are regularly able to fill their classrooms with joy, love, wisdom, and real purpose. And our world clearly needs to be filled with as many humans as it can get who have been consistently filled with these qualities from a young age.

This book is an attempt to help foster the kinds of teacher thinking and educational conditions through which many more educators—maybe even most of them—will be able to center their instruction around the qualities that make us alive, and that make being alive worthwhile. This should *not* have to be done through subterfuge!

Our central approach to this will be through reimagining and reconstruing the portion of the curriculum now called "Literacy," "Language Arts," or "English." Rachel, Debra, Andrew, Sharon, and Sarah all somehow understand that their classrooms do far more than provide places to convey and construct knowledge: They seek to awaken and renew, and so to transform and deepen life. And they share this understanding with many other "English" teachers from kindergartens to graduate schools. We're sure this includes many of you just now reading this book because studies indicate that the majority of these teachers actually see their teaching as life-centered rather than focused on any particular subject matter (Goodwyn, 2005; Grossman & Stodolsky, 1996). These great-hearted teachers already understand that what they do with their students has less to do with expertise in "letters" than with awakening the life within the human spirit. We seek to help them justify this life-centered practice to their students and to the public in wide-awake ways that will enable them to extend this kind of teaching through the profession.

This reconstrual of "English," though, will also serve as the basis for a reseeing of education as a whole as centered on this awakening to life. All education, even the most subject matter–centered, should seek to "draw out" life, as the etymology of *educare* implies, and as all true teachers understand, whatever it is they teach. So ultimately we seek to provide a coherent, readily communicable view of education, and of the world that education serves, that will ground and support the already-present tacit understanding of many teachers about the life-centeredness of teaching, and its importance in the renewal of human life. And through this picture, and the practical examples of these and other teachers, we seek to help education as a whole, and society as a whole, become more life-centered at a time when this transformation is sorely needed.

OVERCOMING IMPOVERISHED AND EXTERNALIZED VIEWS OF ACHIEVEMENT

For a generation now our nation has succumbed to a fear-centered systematizing of education. From the 1983 report *A Nation at Risk* through the 2002 No Child Left Behind Act and the legislated regimes of testing and teaching to the test they introduced, a generation of teachers and several generations of students have had the enlivening possibilities of learning systematically drained out of them. The results have been poor even in terms of numerically measured achievement. But in human and social terms, they have been devastating. As Diane Ravitch—once the best known professional advocate for numerically measured standards of educational accountability—has recently said,

> Testing, I realized with dismay, had become a central preoccupation in the schools and was not just a measure but an end in itself. . . . Accountability, now a shibboleth that everyone applauds, had become mechanistic and even antithetical to good education. (Ravitch, 2010, pp. 12–13)

Based on our classroom learning and teaching over the past half century, we're guessing teachers and students have never had less fun and engagement in real learning than they do now. And we know we're hardly alone in seeing this. Former NCTE president Leila Christenbury, who recently spent a term as a high school teacher again after a long career in teacher education, found her students "largely preferred not to commit to any sort of sustained intellectual engagement" and saw the classroom as "a barren way station, . . . a locale to pass the time, turn the pages, and get the credit." And she interpreted this as a very strong sign that we have become "a complacent society" in which "the promise of education is broken" (Christenbury, 2007, pp. xv–xvi).

It is high time for us to figure out a way to bring life and human substance back into education, introducing a thoroughly thought-through life-enhancing agenda to replace this systematically deadening regime. This book is an attempt to do just that. We want to clearly and publicly justify the tacit understandings that teachers like Rachel, Debra, Andrew, Sharon, Sarah, and many of you already possess about the importance, depth, joy, and possibility that lies within what we do—so that far more of our students, fellow teachers, and fellow citizens can value these things as much as we do, so that school will no longer be the "barren way station" Christenbury's recent students saw it to be, and the now-broken promise of education can be renewed. By seeing just how "English" has served over the years as a vehicle for subtly awakening and renewing the human spirit, we hope to carve out a space for a renewed version of the English curriculum at the center of an educational system that is also primarily devoted to the renewal of that spirit rather than the deadening of it.

SEEKING A RICHER, TRUER, MORE HUMAN VISION OF ACHIEVEMENT: LITERACY FOR LIFE, LOVE, AND WISDOM

Bruce has taught English at levels ranging from a remedial sixth-grade class in an impoverished public middle school to college and graduate classes at an elite private university. Yet he sees himself primarily as a philosopher, as a "lover of wisdom" and a practitioner of "loving wisdom," as two translations of the Greek *philosophia* go. Though trained as an English teacher and as a teacher of English teachers, over the past decade he has taught and written primarily in the field of philosophy of education. Over these years—teaching courses in Philosophy and Foundations of Education from the freshman to the doctoral level at Northern Illinois University—he developed a curriculum, drawing on many of the literary practices he learned as an English teacher, for evoking and developing the inner wisdom of teachers and educational leaders. And in 2008 he staged, with his colleague Stan Scott, the international conference "Reclaiming the Wisdom Tradition for Education," sponsored by the NCTE Assembly for Expanded Perspectives on Learning.

We have been great friends for many years, but that friendship turned into a collaboration when Jeff served as the respondent to Bruce's 2008 NCTE presentation "Beyond 'English' and 'Literacy'" (Novak, 2008), which sought to reconceive "English" as a sorely needed discipline for individual and collective wisdom within democratic life. That very day Jeff proposed we write this book together, and very soon afterward we agreed on the title *Literacy for Love and Wisdom*.

From that the book's basic ideas soon became clear. Jeff's book *You Gotta BE the Book: Teaching Engaged and Reflective Reading with Adolescents* (1997/2008), which Bruce had been a huge fan of, was an application of and development of Louise Rosenblatt's "transactional," "reader-response" understanding of the reading and teaching of literature. On rereading *You Gotta BE the Book* and thinking about how it connected with teaching for wisdom, Bruce quickly discovered two things that amazed him. First, the three dimensions of the response to literature that Jeff had found through teaching literature to his middle school students—the "evocative," "connective," and "reflective" dimensions of literary reading—corresponded pretty much exactly to the three topics of the book we planned to write together: "life," "love," and "wisdom." Second, they also corresponded more or less exactly to the three dimensions of human, narrative time (what below we call "story time") that the philosopher Paul Ricoeur had laid out in his magnum opus *Time and Narrative* (1984–88), which had made a huge impact on Bruce's thinking and teaching. What Bruce saw, and Jeff quickly became quite excited about, was that the power that seeing these three different dimensions of his students' experience gave to Jeff's teaching of literature could also be drawn on to help us see how to more deeply enter into, understand, and reflectively respond to the stories of life itself. "Life," in other words, was the ability to enter "evocative" story time; "love" the capacity to "connect" with others through its flow; and "wisdom," the capacity to find new "reflective" meaning and possibility in it, to keep that flow going—perhaps the very reason why the teaching of literature has so often been seen, without our quite understanding why, as a central educational means to a wisely led life.

INQUIRY FOR WISDOM:
MOVING FROM ESSENTIAL TO EXISTENTIAL QUESTIONS

About a year down the road it also became clear how this work connected to the "inquiry" methods of teaching English developed by George Hillocks, in which we were both trained, and how those methods connected, in ways that neither of us had suspected before, with Rosenblatt's "reader-response" approach. The connection between "inquiry" and "response" materialized when Jeff happened to be in Chicago and invited Bruce to visit a teacher inservice he was leading on developing inquiry units across the school curriculum. At first this didn't seem fully related to what we were doing together, but Bruce's ears perked up when Jeff began to talk to the teachers about the critical importance of precisely formulating what he called "essential questions"—the questions that would open up exciting paths of inquiry for their students: For instance, what is a responsible community? for Civics; What makes a great leader? for U.S. History; What makes and breaks relationships? for English (see Wilhelm, 2007).

As a philosopher, Bruce knew the difference between "essential" questions—questions about the way the world works in general, like the above, which are open for discussion and debate—and "existential" questions—questions about how each one of us should best live, given the unique conditions of life given to each and every one of us. The latter are questions each of us can only answer for ourselves, by the lives we choose to lead, though dialoguing with others is an essential part of finding our own paths.

When Bruce teaches Philosophy and Foundations of Education, he centers his classes on these kinds of questions. After several weeks together, each member of the class anonymously writes down several of what Rachael Kessler, in *The Soul of Education* (2000), calls "mystery questions," the deepest questions we ask of life, usually only in our most private moments. Bruce then reads the questions they've written out loud, generating a communal depth of awareness of the life of everyone in the room: for instance, "Why am I so heartless to so many people?" "Why do I feel scared and confused about becoming an adult?" "I wonder who is God, or if there is God? If there is a God, why is there so much bad on Earth?" Once the questions have all been read, the class spends the rest of the class time sitting in a circle, without even the barriers of desks between them, talking openly about the questions that they most connected with. Later, the main assignment of the class is to write a dramatic dialogue in which they live out a currently burning existential question in their teaching lives so that they can literally *see* themselves developing new wisdom.

That is what we are after here. We have come to see what we are doing as extending Hillocks's methods into Rosenblatt's territory. By expanding inquiry from essential to existential questions—bringing personal reflective insights to bear on the deep personal experiences conjured up by the evocative and connective dimensions first of literature, then of life—we think we have found a way to help us better learn how to bring such insights into the stories of the lives we lead both individually and together, to live our real-life stories with more love and more wisdom.

"BEING THE BOOK" *AND* "BEING THE CHANGE"

This re-construal of education, and life as a whole, within "story time," we hope will make Rosenblatt's "transactional theory of the literary work" central to our understanding of human literacy in general. Over the past 2 decades, a fair amount of work in the field of literacy has downplayed the importance that Louise Rosenblatt and other "reader-response" critics attributed to the power of personal "aesthetic response" on the basis that in its concern with individual meaning making it is insufficiently concerned with social action and the accomplishment of social justice (Appleman, 2006;[1] Dressman, 2004; Edelsky, 1994; Hynds & Appleman, 1997; Willinsky, 1991). This book seeks to newly clarify and newly tap into the social power of aesthetic response, and to do so by contextualizing it in ways that have only been hinted at in earlier work in the field. Berlin (1982), Hillocks (1999), and many others have made a distinction between "expressivist" and "constructivist" rhetoric—between modes of discourse that are more personal or more social in nature. What we will show is that what Rosenblatt—and before her the great democratic philosopher John Dewey, who was her teacher—called "aesthetic transaction," refers to experience that is personal, but *not* merely subjective.

Dewey, in fact, coined the philosophical term *transaction* in his very last book, *Knowing and the Known* (Dewey & Bentley, 1949), specifically to distinguish mental life that is truly alive to others and the world—seeking transformative intercourse—from "self-actional" and "interactional" conceptions of the mind that limit themselves either to pure subjectivity or to "social construction" in which subjects cooperate for mutual benefit, but without the intent of this mutual transformation.

Earlier in his career, Dewey was one of the earliest social constructivists. His seminal works *How We Think* (1910) and *Democracy and Education* (1916) gave much of what has come to be called "progressive education" an interactive, social constructivist orientation. In later works, though—particularly *Experience and Nature* (1925), *Art as Experience* (1934), and *Knowing and the Known* (1949), the works that Rosenblatt was primarily drawing on in her influential *The Reader, the Text, and the Poem: The Transactional Theory of the Literary Work* (1978)—Dewey came to what he thought was a deeper view that led him eventually to sharply distinguish transactional from merely interactional, social constructivist engagement. Thomas M. Alexander's *John Dewey's Theory of Art, Experience, and Nature: The Horizons of Feeling* (1987) is a convincing portrait of how all of Dewey's philosophy leads to, and from, his philosophy of aesthetic experience.

Deweyan and Rosenblattian transaction, when it occurs, is response with an explicit understanding of newly shared life and possibility. In Dewey's philosophical terms, "knowing" the "known" changes the transactive knower, whose own being has become enmeshed in what is known. In Rosenblatt's poetic terms, "reader" and "text" combine to form a living "poem" that transcends what either reader or text can be on its own.

Nontransactive response is mere subjective reaction: "self-action," or the defensive illusion of such, in Dewey's terms. Many reader-response theorists and teachers have sought no more than this, as an antidote to the excessive objectivism of the New Criticism that dominated all teaching of literature starting in the 1940s, and still dominates it fairly well in secondary English classrooms. But there is always more than *reaction* in *transaction*. The experience of transaction takes us out of ourselves, and thus helps us find and expand ourselves anew. It doesn't just mirror, positively or negatively, who we already are; it opens a window for us to see better selves that we can become, to entertain new possibilities that can help us outgrow our current selves and work toward the best of who we can be.

But besides being more than just personal, transaction is also more than just social. It involves the experience, not just of cooperating with others, but of *coexisting* with them: the sharing, not just of things, ideas, and actions, but of life itself, seeing and feeling how our very being is wrapped up in others' and in larger worlds than we are accustomed to think.

Dewey's *Knowing and the Known* (Dewey & Bentley, 1949) made extraordinarily large claims about the importance of spreading transactional mentality in the modern world. As opposed to "self-action" where "things are viewed as acting under their own powers" and "interaction" where "thing is balanced against thing in causal interconnection" (p. 108), "transaction" brings about "mutual understanding" and "turn[s] differences to mutual advantage" (p. v). It affords us nothing less than "the right . . . to open our eyes to see . . . together." Without it, modern life "has been and still is chaos and nothing more" (pp. 68–69, 136).

Rosenblatt brilliantly showed how to teach literature for transactional experience, but did not then contextualize, in a thorough manner and for a broad audience, how the teaching of literature and art could play a central role—could indeed be absolutely pivotal—in the achievement of the spread of transactional mentality more generally. That is what we seek to do here.

Our subtitle, "Being the Book and Being the Change," refers both to Jeff's *"You Gotta BE the Book"* and to Gandhi's famous saying, "We need to *be* the change we want to see in the world." But it also refers to—and in some ways originated in—a comment from an anonymous course evaluation Bruce received in one of his Philosophy of Education courses:

> This class has totally changed my life and my perspective and outlook on life. It has also changed the way I interact with myself and others. This has been the most difficult class for me so far, mainly because I did not want to change. But one cannot help but change or at least think about change after the experiences of this class. I'm always going to love and thank you for showing how to change or at least start the process of changing, from within first, then the world.

This is about as clear and as direct a depiction of the educative power of transactional mentality as one can get. And we think it puts into words what Dan Feight could have said to Jeff about what happened to him in Jeff's class. Transactional mentality in general converts the power art and literature can have for the betterment of our lives into power for the betterment of life itself. It converts the power of "being the book" into the power of "being the change," the renewing and renewable energy of art into the renewing and renewable energy of humanely lived life. That is why it is so critically important for us to learn, and to teach, how to tap into this hitherto largely buried energy—because in it lies our own largely buried life and much of our capacity for our own betterment.

TRANSACTION BEYOND LITERATURE:
RESPONSE AND RESPONSIBILITY

What we will seek to show in this book is how the dynamics of transaction apply, first to the experience and teaching of art and literature, but then also, and more importantly, to human experience as a whole—as we take in and respond to the story of life itself.

The experience of literature, and art more generally, enables this transformation to take place in a relatively pure manner, unobstructed by what Rosenblatt called the external "efferent" exigencies of life, which tend to dominate our view of the many practical situations—such as the carrying out of recipes and surgical operations—where we need to precisely control the results. In our concern for outside efferent effects, we tend to overlook the aesthetic, affective, internal dimensions of our experience. The "aesthetic" originally referred to "feeling," not "beauty"—a sense still retained in its antonym "anaesthetic" but now generally lost to common parlance. Alexander Gottlieb Baumgarten, the eighteenth-century German philosopher who founded the field of aesthetics, saw it as the study of "what vivifies us" (Baumgarten, 2007/1750 & 1758). Dewey and Rosenblatt both use "aesthetic" in this sense. To understand the dynamics of transactional experience is thus to understand the dynamics of human feeling and human flourishing, and, most importantly, how we can tap into those dynamics to help one another flourish.

Our book has three main parts. The first is a history of, and an initial vision of a new future for, the century old curricular discipline called "English." We will show how it got its name; how its practice, over time, has come to be deeply contested; and how we might come to reconceive and even rename this discipline once we get a clearer understanding of the vivifying properties of the natural and cultural transactional forces that a good many of its teachers manage to tap into, but without being able to name and understand them. Our hope is that this naming and understanding will eventually serve to transform the profession as a whole, bringing it into full alignment with what its best practitioners—like Jeff's teachers—have always intuitively done.

In the second part, we will start to apply this broad vision of a transformed discipline of "English" to classroom practice. We will revisit and extend the understanding of the evocative, connective, and reflective dimensions of transactional responsiveness to literature that Jeff originally laid out in *"You Gotta BE the Book."* And we will illustrate these new understandings with examples of how we can teach literature to vivify life at all levels of learning, helping our students tap into and traverse these dimensions of their experience through their reading.

In the third part we will show—again illustrated by numerous classroom examples—how these dimensions of responsive reading also operate in generating responsiveness to life in general, "reading beyond the book," and how learning that responsiveness *to* life, at larger and larger levels of it, leads us in a natural way to take larger and larger responsibility *for* it. Here we will first show how the educative transactions between teachers and students parallel those between authors and readers in seeking to generate free, loving, and wise responsiveness. We will then show how educative democratic communities are formed, in classrooms and beyond, as people learn to share their lives with one another, and to persist in seeking mutual recognition even amidst trying differences. Finally, we will show how we can resee the story of humanity itself as the story of our slow and irregular progress as a species in learning to transact lovingly and wisely both with one another and with the world we mutually inhabit.

Through this we hope you will come to clearly see how it is not just accidental that the words *response* and *responsibility* have a common root: how it is the feeling for the life inside ourselves and one another that draws us to care feelingly for the world around us, and thus to act to responsibly take care of the world in which we have become feelingly involved. This, we think, is the basic lesson Dan Feight learned from Jeff's teaching so long ago, and what Bruce's student who wrote that anonymous evaluation was able to articulate.

But this is also a book that asks teachers to take the full responsibility that is theirs. And that will be the focus of our conclusion: "What Can 'English' Become?"

To be fully responsible citizens of the world at this point in time, we believe it is necessary for us to act in many ways, large and small, to remake what we now call "English" into a discipline that is centrally and explicitly focused on "being the change," on the spread of the transactional mentality that Dewey said was the only thing that could save the modern world from chaos.

Strange as it may now seem, "English," we believe, can become the central social and political locus for what physicist Peter Russell in his *Waking Up in Time* (1998) has called the "Wisdom Revolution" that now needs to succeed the Agricultural, Industrial, and Information revolutions if we and our planet are to survive and prosper, given the perilous social, political, and ecological conditions under which we now live. But this will only be possible if teachers like Rachel, Andrew, Debra, Sharon, Sarah, *and you*, better understand, better explain, and better practice just what it is that lies at the heart of what we now do under the banner of "English."

In the following pages, we seek to take you on a historical, philosophical, and pedagogical journey, exploring the roots of our profession in ways we believe can bring us to make it flower anew, so that we can come to do openly and publicly, in the name of "the human spirit," what many of us have long been doing under various names derived from "the letter": "language arts," "literacy," and the like. We believe, and hope you will come to believe, that if we can just bring people to understand both the need to teach fundamentally for life, for love, and for wisdom, and some of the rudiments of just how we can do so through what has long been called "English," we may just be able to bring this Wisdom Revolution about before it is too late.

Since the stakes are as important as that, we very much hope you will take the chance both of accompanying us on this journey, and then extending it on your own terms, in the particular existential situations of your classroom, school, and community.

Since you're most likely already at least thinking of becoming an English teacher, or a teacher in some other field in the humanities, you're already very good at "being the book." You're already halfway there. We invite you to seek with us how to parlay that skill more consistently into the attendant skill of "being the change."

This is something that is almost never easy, as Bruce's anonymous student and Dan Feight learned, but when it happens, it, as an old prayer goes, "inscribes us for blessing in the book of life." And our world needs many, many more such blessings these days!

Part I

WHAT *IS* "ENGLISH"?

Democracy, obviously, can't be forced on people; nor can it be marketed like televisions or refrigerators. It can only be arrived at through processes that lead to its internalization.

—Václav Havel, "Democracy's Forgotten Dimension"

There are acres of Edens inside ourselves.

—Toni Morrison, "The Future of Time"

CHAPTER 1

A Brief History
of a Nebulous Subject

"I teach English." "Guess I better watch my grammar then, huh?"
"I teach English." "Don't you ever get tired of looking for hidden
   meanings?"
"I teach English." "How will this poetry stuff ever help get me a
   job?"
"I teach English." "Why do you always want to know what I'm feeling?"

What *is* "English"? No one knows, at least in any way that has proved
generally convincing, in the way that teachers of every other subject
taught in schools and universities can, with relative unanimity, explain
to the general public what their subject is about.[1] And, considering the
standard responses we English teachers get when we tell people what we
do, not many beyond our profession seem to care a whole lot what the
answer to the question of what "English" is either.

For well over a century now the central curricular discipline of K–12
education has gone by this name. And in the humanities divisions of most
colleges and universities, English departments still tend to be the largest
and most influential ones, and the introductory composition and literature courses they offer are still the ones most commonly required of all
students in higher education. But few now teaching in the field of English
find that this word offers anything close to an adequate description of
what it is they teach.

Most of the leaders of the profession at the K–12 level prefer the term
literacy. The National Council of Teachers of English a few years ago even
debated changing their name to the National Council of Teachers of Literacy, but in the end decided against it. Many leaders of the profession at
the university level now tend to prefer the term *cultural studies.* But "English" remains the coin of the realm, the official denomination, despite the
fact that the meaning behind it—and thus a good deal of its recognizable
value to the public—has been largely effaced. And this lack of an appropriate, meaningful designation for what we do as teachers and scholars is
a particularly egregious one for a profession among whose core concerns,

at all levels, are the finding and making of meaning. We are the Cinder-
ellas of the curriculum, sensing our vital inner gifts, but knowing that
those gifts are hidden by the menial tasks we are assigned, the outworn
garments we are made to wear, and the outworn name we now go by—a
name that doesn't begin to describe to the world the great human importance most of us privately, or in our own circles, ascribe to what we do.

IN THE BEGINNING

There was a time when that name made a clarion call, a clear rallying cry
for purposes of the highest importance to democratic peoples. In America
at the turn of the last century, English was the central curricular crucible
of the national melting pot, seeking to provide a standard grammar and a
common literary tradition to the most polyglot people the world had ever
known. And in England itself, English was once conceived of as the state's
central bearer of spiritual blessings and spiritual unity to the people. In
what may well be the strongest statement ever made on the part of a
national government for the noble aims of public education, *The Teaching
of English in England*, the Board of Education's Newbolt Report of 1921
named for the poet who was its chair, stated that the goal of English was
no less than to provide "a liberal education for all English children, whatever their position or occupation in life," that this should be understood
by the people as "the greatest benefit which could ever be conferred upon
any citizen of a great state, and that the common right to it, the common
discipline and enjoyment of it, the common possession of the tastes and
associations connected with it, would form a new element of national
unity, linking together the mental life of all classes by experiences which
have hitherto been the privilege of a limited section" (Bacon, 1998, pp.
302–303).

The name of the language, in other words, once served as an extremely powerful public metonym for the curricular pursuit of "national
unity," "national spirit," and "the common good" within democratic nations characterized on the one hand by great ethnic diversity and, on the
other, by great differences of economic and social class inherited from
predemocratic times. A national language and a national literature, uni-
versally transmitted through the educational discipline called "English,"
would constitute a democratic nation in higher, deeper, and more thor-
oughgoing ways than democratic laws alone could do.

Perhaps the profession's holding on to this name for itself is a tacit
recognition that much of the remaining, dwindling hold it has on the
public imagination comes from its tacit invocation of these old nationalistic goals. Most professionals believe that such goals are outdated in these

times of globalism, multiculturalism, and increasingly complex systems of communication, but the public they serve does not necessarily feel the same way. Any successful attempt to change the name of the field of English to better fit the needs of our times will probably have to have an inspiring public appeal at least the equivalent to that so clearly addressed to and so clearly accepted by the public of a century ago, of achieving a more perfect cultural union. And this is probably why "literacy" and "cultural studies," though they have become the favored designations of the field by professionals in K–12 and university education, respectively, have not yet been put forward as legitimate replacements for "English" to the general public on a broad scale.

In what follows, we will recommend a replacement for "English" that we indeed think will make an even more inspiring appeal to the general public than the earlier nationalistic ones upon which it was founded: an appeal that meets the deepest educational needs of the present time, that can be equally embraced at all educational levels, and that also fully answers to and accounts for the deep human call that has summoned so many of us to do what we do in this strangely named and strangely misunderstood profession of ours.

We will try to show you how the discipline we now call "English" is, at its base, an evolved and evolving way that the human species has found of bringing vivifying, humanizing, and regenerative meaning to the lives that we lead; that it is a discipline, not just of language, or of culture, or of critical thinking, but through these things—as we say in our title—a discipline for human love and for human wisdom, a discipline whose origins were key to our prior evolution as a species and whose further development may be key to our survival.

Once we understand the deep human origins of our subject we may finally be able to fully justify to the public we serve the importance of what we do, and be more able to summon forth with the students in our classrooms the human power that originally called so many of us into this profession. The long story behind what is now called "English," once it is generally understood, can justify placing our discipline at the curricular center of democratic education—not just as it is now, in terms of numbers of required classes, but in terms of actual centrality to the democratic worldview that a system of democratic education should facilitate in democratic society.

That new curricular center will be a humanistic rather than a scientific one—though derived from and in full alignment with the findings of science. And it will help us tell a new story about the power of education to advance human life that might be more successful in actually advancing it than the story many of us were told in our youth about how the development of science and technology alone—coupled with the spread, through education, of the ability to reason "objectively"—would bring us infinite benefit.

To recenter human education on the disciplined cultivation of love and wisdom—and to recenter our understanding of the story of humanity on our ability to do this, which has grown and waned over time—may actually turn out to be the most decisive factor in our ability, under current global conditions, both to survive and to further thrive as a species on this planet. Should this surprise us, in the second decade of the twenty-first century? On the very day the first atomic bomb was dropped on Hiroshima well over half a century ago, Albert Einstein, the man then esteemed both as the world's greatest scientist and as one of its great humanists, had this to say: "Everything has changed—except the way we think" (cited in Isaacson, 2007, p. 408). Since that time, the destructive capacities of the technologies that scientific understanding enabled our species to invent have increased manyfold. Even if we don't destroy ourselves with the bang of nuclear devastation, it is not unlikely that we will go out with the whimper of the gradual warming and species extinction that will eventually drastically alter the global ecosystem—unless, as Einstein said, we are somehow able to change the way that the masses of our fellow human beings think, to help our species live move lovingly and with more wisdom on this planet than has hitherto been our lot.

How can English do this? Clearly, it can't—if we insist on calling it "English." And "literacy" and "cultural studies" hardly do much more: these words are patch jobs on a discipline that needs a complete overhaul. "Literacy" expands the range of skills and topics from the standardized grammar and literature of the old "English" but doesn't distinguish moral skills from merely technical ones: It may make our thinking more versatile, but it doesn't clearly represent in any way a call to fundamentally change it. "Cultural studies" admits the need for fundamental criticism, but its orientation is fundamentally toward critical rather than constructive thought: It shows us where we have the need to change the way we think, but doesn't in itself accomplish the change it sees we need. "Literacy," it can be said, simply provides us a broader, less chauvinistic view of a discipline centered on "the letter," when what we need is to recenter that discipline on "the spirit" that lies behind "the letter" and gives it life. "Cultural studies" satisfies itself with the mere criticism of previously unexamined life, but that satisfaction with criticism appears in many ways as simply a new form of dogmatism at a time when it is more and more transparent that mere criticism is woefully inadequate for the *renewal* of life that we sorely need.

Before we can begin to lay our cards on the table about what *we* propose should be the future of our subject, though, we first need to take you —in the balance of this first chapter— through the two largest, broadest, and most important efforts over the past half century to redefine, and further deepen and illuminate, the meaning and purpose of "English."[2] Though neither succeeded in the end in capturing the public imagination, they did capture the imagination of large swaths of teachers, significantly deepening and expanding their understanding of what they do in their classrooms from the nationalistic agendas of language and culture to which "English" had been superficially tied. It is in part by finding the hidden complementarity of these two efforts—separated from one another by 2 decades and from the present day by another 2—that we can begin to find what the discipline that has, since about the late nineteenth century, been called "English" may have been meant to be all along, in a way that can finally make a broad new appeal to the general public.

DARTMOUTH, 1966: "GROWTH THROUGH ENGLISH"

The Dartmouth Seminar of 1966 was undertaken in the midst of the cultural upheavals of the 1960s—and the challenges to democratic systems of education raised by the success of Sputnik—seeking both to respond to grassroots movements for social and cultural change and to capitalize on the state-sponsored movement for educational reform that had already brought forth strong, widely influential "new math" and "new science" curricula. It brought together 50 eminent scholars from Great Britain and North America for an entire month to discuss how to update the teaching of English. And according to Arthur N. Applebee (1974), these conversations "sharply altered the emphases of [the profession's] leaders" (p. 229).

"Growth Through English" became its motto. This was the title of Yorkshireman John Dixon's official report to the profession summing up the results of the various conversations held that summer, published the following year on behalf of the National Association for the Teaching of English in the United Kingdom and both the National Council of Teachers of English and the Modern Language Association of the United States. The "language skills" and "cultural heritage" models of "English" were to be superseded by a discipline connecting "language and personal growth." What was to be cultivated, in other words, was no longer simply *national* unity, through the media of national language and national literature, but the *personal* unity of each member of a democratic people, through language as the symbolic medium through which "each individual takes what he can from the shared store of experience and builds it into a world of his own" (Dixon, 1967, pp. 4–7). The discipline once seen as serving primarily to constitute a *people* as a group was now seen as helping to constitute *persons* as individuals.

This approach had both a tremendous advantage and a great drawback compared to the previous ones. The advantage was the new focus on present experience rather than on past inheritances, on what *we* can make of language and literature rather than on what *it* can make of us. The importance of this new emphasis cannot be underestimated. For the first time, it gave firm professional credence to the belief that a democratic society had to have one curricular discipline that was primarily student- and experience-centered rather than subject-matter-centered, a discipline whose central purpose was to inspire and guide the cultivation of personal freedom. In very important ways it represented an advance upon and expansion of even the very high aspirations for "English" of the Newbolt Report of 1921: More than a vehicle for unity of national sentiment, for cultural nation building, it became the vehicle for free individual *world* building, laying the inner foundation for a democracy of free beings.

Yet it had its limitations. The "personal growth" agenda as formulated in the 1960s could be summed up by the well-known line from Fritz Perls's (1969) "Gestalt Prayer": "You are you, and I am I, and if by chance we find each other, it's beautiful." Quite unlike the versions of English of previous eras, our coming together no longer seemed either urgent or necessary in comparison with the fostering of individual life. At the end of *Growth Through English*, Dixon even inveighed against "discussion culture," because of the way it obscured "the profounder possibilities of a considered and extended exploration of experience, permitting slower realizations and more individual, personal growth" (pp. 111–112).

The central goal of English now seemed something like creating a curricular cocoon—a snug, warm "room of one's own," as Virginia Woolf (1929) put it—for the free development of individuals. But there was no clear understanding yet of what those individuals would do with that freedom when they emerged from those cocoons, if and when they ever chose to do so. Or even of how to convince a sufficient number among the democratic masses that they needed these cocoons in the first place.

The irony of this as a serious proposal for the redesign of national programs of education was not lost on Herbert Muller, who was given the unenviable assignment of preparing a report on the conference, not for the professional community but for the general public: *The Uses of English* (1967). At both the beginning and the end of Muller's report, probing questions were raised about the public viability of the curriculum for "personal growth" that so powerfully ignited the hearts and minds of so many who attended the Dartmouth Seminar. How was this vision of creating a democracy of freely developing individuals ever to move from their tiny professional choir loft of 50 into democratic congregations numbering in the hundreds of millions?:

Supposedly the most fundamental subject, English is in fact commonly regarded as about the least practical one . . . ; congressmen do not consider it
really vital to the "national interest." And what popular concern there is over
it brings up deeper social problems. . . .

The ordinary teacher . . . is always under pressure to conform to the
conventional beliefs of the community. . . . Certainly most parents, as well as
most personnel directors in business, want young people first of all to become
well adjusted. A serious consideration of the role of English in education
ultimately forces the fundamental issue of the relations of the individual and
society, actual and ideal. (pp. 16–17)

The Dartmouth Seminar, it is worth repeating, was an immensely
important event, in that it helped the profession of English for the first
time to articulate and publicly declare clear ends for itself that were more
than nationalistic. But it ended up placing the leadership of the profession more firmly within the counterculture than within the mainstream
culture of democratic society. And with the fall of the hopes of that counterculture for imminent social transformation—with the deaths of Martin
Luther King and Robert Kennedy and the ascent to the presidency of
Richard Nixon in 1968, the year after the two reports on Dartmouth were
published—Muller's skepticism certainly seemed to have been borne out
over Dixon's optimism.

In the ensuing years the many critiques and revolts staged against
curricula designed for "personal growth" put the installation of such curricula into severe public question (see, particularly, Moffett, 1988). And
over the course of decades in which they were generally out of fashion,
it may have been only the powerful convictions that had been fostered
among many in the profession around the ideas that coalesced at Dartmouth—enforced by the power that they could see the "personal growth"
agenda had to dramatically affect the lives of many, if not all or even most
of their students—that kept those ideas alive and kept many in the profession thinking about how to better justify their broad adoption.

WYE PLANTATION, 1987: "DEMOCRACY THROUGH LANGUAGE"

In 1987 another major conference was held, called the English Coalition Conference, which gathered representatives of eight major American
professional organizations for 3 weeks of discussions at the pastoral setting of the Wye Plantation in Maryland, lent by the Aspen Institute. As
opposed to Dartmouth, whose invitees were almost exclusively university
professors, over a third of the sixty in attendance were K–12 classroom
teachers.

   This time, one of the central reasons for convening the meeting was to help the various professional organizations within the profession of English coalesce *against* the policies and public rhetoric of the Reagan administration and its intellectual allies, unlike the Dartmouth conference, which in large part sought to catch the waves of positive educational change. Four years earlier, the National Commission on Excellence in Education (1983) had released the report *A Nation at Risk.* In a time in which the American economy was losing ground internationally, this report sought to put a large share of the blame for that upon the laxity of the education system, which it found to be more concerned with social issues and "feelings" than with training workers. "History is not kind to idlers," it began, as it claimed that we could retain our great Nation's global "preeminence" only by assiduously putting every last one of our children's noses constantly to the grindstone.

   Though the participants at Wye knew they were swimming against a powerful political stream, there seems to have been an even more positive spirit at this conference, and even more powerful feelings generated by it than at Dartmouth. This was in part because the conference was organized to allow for plentiful and multifarious sorts of interaction among its greatly varied participants. And probably also in part because the ferment within the profession that the Dartmouth Conference catalyzed had in the intervening years begun to give a new tenor to the best teaching and thinking in the field, which the open-ended format developed by the organizers both exemplified and unleashed.

   No fewer than three official accounts of the conference were published as books: (1) *Democracy Through Language,* the report sponsored by the Coalition as a whole and edited by two university professors, Richard Lloyd-Jones and Andrea Lunsford (1989); (2) *Stories to Grow On: Demonstrations of Language Learning in K–8 Classrooms,* sponsored and written by the 14 members of the elementary section of the conference and edited by Julie Jensen (1989); and (3) *What Is English?* sponsored by the Modern Language Association (the largest professional group of university educators in the humanities) and written mostly by Peter Elbow (1990), though short pieces by a large number of the participants were interspersed throughout.

   Despite the agreement on the slogan "Democracy Through Language," these three accounts still are enormously different from one another, in ways that are quite illuminating both about lingering tensions within the profession and about the lingering issue of how to explain and justify itself to the democratic public. This can be seen simply by comparing their titles.

   Lloyd-Jones and Lunsford, speaking for the conference as a whole, articulated a new, specifically political agenda for English to compete with and counter the narrowing of national educational vision that began soon after the publication of *A Nation at Risk*. While not exactly dissenting from this new political theme, the elementary teachers, by and large, held on to the inspiring but politically troublesome "personal growth" agenda from Dartmouth. Elbow, interestingly, decided that what the actual results of the conference most called for was "a picture of a profession . . . percolating at various levels . . . that cannot define what it is" (p. v).

All report that the group achieved an "astonishing consensus" early on in uniting *against* the ideas presented in the first few days by Chester Finn and E. D. Hirsch, representing the government. Hirsch at the time had just started to propound his "schema theory" of "cultural literacy," claiming that a culture needed, above all, a shared knowledge base to unify itself and that it was the paramount duty of the schools to impart the "solid content" of this shared knowledge base. This harkened back to the original rallying call of cultural unity that lay behind the institutionalization of English a century before, though Finn and Hirsch's version of this call was certainly an extremely dessicated one compared with the Newbolt Report's claim that English could offer the people not just shared bits of information but the highest form of emotional and spiritual welfare.

Elbow (1990) quotes a telling exchange that occurred between Hirsch and Marie Bunscombe, an African American teacher at Brooklyn College, who asked this question in the question and answer session following his talk:

> "But can't I be literate and *different* from you?" I [Elbow] expected to hear Hirsch argue that a common core of shared information and shared culture would of course permit enormous cultural diversity. But in fact he replied by talking about the loss of cultural diversity as a "downside" (his word) . . . that we must choose between cultural pluralism and cultural literacy. (p. 31)

Not long after this pointed exchange, the 60 professors and teachers arrived at their "astonishing consensus" that the central theme of the conference—and thus, in important ways, of the immediate future of the discipline of English—would be "Democracy Through Language." Rather than the mere absorption of knowledge, the heart of the discipline would be seen as the "language arts" (used interchangeably with "English studies") required "to assimilate, evaluate, and control the immense amount of knowledge and the large number of messages produced every day." And this understanding of the synthesizing value of the "language arts" led to an understanding of a new political purpose for English: the acknowledgement and appreciation of "diversity." Lloyd-Jones and Lunsford (1989) report the official position about "Democracy Through Language" that the entire group adopted:

Citizens of a democracy must be able to appreciate diversity even as they advocate their own beliefs about what is good and true. Teaching students how and why different ways of reading can find different meanings in the same text can provide important experience in understanding and appreciating opposing perspectives. Learning about the many different kinds of writing and ways of thinking which are the subject matter of the language arts curriculum can expand the capacity of students to imagine and value worlds other than their own. The ability to communicate their views in written form and to listen with comprehension to the views of others is also indispensable to citizens in a democratic society, and enhancing this ability is a major aim of language arts education. (p. xx)

This was a coherent new direction for the profession, seeming to reinvent English for a new age of democracy, an age of radical diversity and difference and truly universal enfranchisement. English so defined had a clear public agenda again, as opposed to the more private one of "personal growth" from Dartmouth. It was still "student-centered," but in a more complex way, interested more in interactions than in internal growth. It recaptured the focus on rhetoric that long had been the center and summit of liberal education before the study of literature gradually took its place with the rise of English. And this was a more democratic version of rhetoric that saw close listening as at least as important as powerful speech. As such, "English Language Arts" appeared ready to become the central curricular vehicle for a truly vibrant democracy, in which each and every citizen could be both personally empowered through the acquisition of the varied skills of the "language arts" and, in addition, could appreciate and acknowledge the diversity of identities and points of view within democratic life, benefiting from literate exchanges among people coming from differing perspectives. "Democracy Through Language"—or, perhaps more accurately, "Diverse Democracy Through Diversity of Language Use"—certainly did seem as if it would make a more powerful public appeal than the implicit "Unity Through Facts" approach offering nothing more than a determined single-mindedness. Finally, in the face of deep political adversity, English seemed to have found its true political calling: as the curricular guarantor, not of unity, but of diversity.

And yet, and yet, and yet. . . . Though Elbow was deeply impressed at how rapidly and solidly the consensus on "Democracy Through Language" was formed, this was hardly what impressed him most about the conference. Before coming to this nominally central consensus in the third chapter of *What Is English?* titled "Democracy Through Language," he presented what to him was a more important, actually central, and more remarkable one in the second chapter, *titled* "A Remarkable Consensus About a Main Theme": that English now seemed to be centrally about the twofold process of (1) the making of new meaning in experiences of immediate engagement with texts, other people, and oneself, and then (2) reflecting on the process of how that new meaning got made.

For Elbow, at least (and, it seems, for many others at the conference as well), the making and understanding of meaning was even more fundamental to the profession than reconstituting democracy, perhaps was even a prerequisite for democracy, even if it was not suitable at the time as a public slogan to oppose the authoritarian understandings of education being fed down the political pipeline. Still, we know now who won that battle for the public imagination. And perhaps the major reason why the political Right did win the battle for education, why our current national program of education is much closer to one of "Unity Through Facts (and, now, Skills)" than of "Diverse Democracy Through Diverse Use of Language," was because the latter agenda was not, in the end, fully satisfying to anyone—the professionals, the policy makers, or the public—while at least the policy makers and the public could both easily rally behind the simple agenda of "Unity." In this light, we might well expect that until English finds an agenda that is broader, deeper, and more publicly appealing than *both* "Democracy Through Language" *and* "Unity Through Facts (and Skills)," the latter may well continue to prevail as our central educational agenda, even when the forces of the political Right are out of power.

As we've said, "Making and Understanding Meaning" would at this point probably have an even less powerful hold on the democratic public imagination (despite how central it is to the *existence* of such an imagination) than "Democracy Through Language" did. We need to look elsewhere—beyond the "astonishing, remarkable consensus" that was achieved and toward the areas in which there was strong dissensus—to begin to understand and conceptualize just how English was, in Elbow's term, "percolating." And what it might percolate *into*, should the subterranean flavors and juices that some at the conference were able to summon up more fully than others be brought to prevail, to permeate what is now called "English" with those natural substances so that it finally becomes a satisfying brew that we can give another, truer name to. A name with powerful and enduring appeal to the democratic public. A name that will encompass, all together, the goals of democratic unity, democratic diversity, personal growth, and the making and understanding of meaning. A name that will clearly convey its capacity to help us summon the creativity and courage to live together with one another in new ways.

INKLINGS OF SYNTHESIS

The last main chapter of *What Is English?*—"The Danger of Softness," the most emotionally powerful part of the book— is about the dissensus of two subgroups, a dissensus not mentioned in Lloyd-Jones and Lunsford's official report, which ironically did not quite manage to adequately acknowledge and appreciate the diversity of its own constituents. First, it tells of how three women from the College Section left the main group and formed their own, calling themselves "the wholistic subgroup," while others called them the "Joy group." [3] Then it spoke, in a deeply admiring way, about the entire Elementary Section, who seemed, more simply, to be able to exemplify holism and joy and to tell stories about how it was exemplified in their classrooms, without having to advocate "needlingly" for it as the subgroup of the College Section said they needed to do.

In the next chapter we turn our attention more extensively to these two groups and to other teachers who exemplify these same holistic concerns. Before that though, in order to see more clearly just what it was they needed to dissent or part ways from, we consider some of the inherent limitations of understanding "English" as "democracy through language."

First, there are certainly ways in which the opposition of this new version of new English to the old, original English of a century earlier can be seen as being far too pat to have achieved in any way a stable resolution of what English is. The old English was for democratic unity, the new for democratic diversity. The old English centered on the passive absorption of language and literature, the new on the active construction of meaning. Most important, the old English was, in a way, a condescending "gift" from "cultured" to "uncultured" classes to "uplift" them, while the new English, in a way, was a conscious leveling of culture, in that its stated goals involved no more than the acknowledgement and appreciation of differing, supposedly inherently equal points of view. In short, Hirsch and Finn represented a particularly moribund form of the nationalistic goals of the old English. And from the action they proposed, on behalf of the government—the equivalent, even though they probably didn't know it, of recuperating the old rationale for English—a pretty much equal and opposite reaction was formed by the members of the conference. This brought them to coalesce strongly against the old English, by positing "diversity" against sheer "unity." But the new English for diverse democracy has not to date gained the powerful grip on democratic society that the old English immediately gained, and in many ways still has. This may only arrive once, not just the acknowledgement of diversity, but a regular process for resolving or transcending it is brought to light.

Diversity in itself is not enough, not humanly satisfying, unless through it we are able to attain new unity. Without that means of attaining new, regenerative, re-creative unity, people will often prefer—sadly, we feel—a tyrannical unity to a condition they perceive as dangerously anarchic. Insofar as we are not alike, there is always the potential—even, realistically speaking, the likelihood—that we will be engaged, not in the nice acknowledgement of and appreciation for diversity, but in a struggle for power. Where is the line between "democracy through language" and identity politics? How do we govern ourselves, how do we become a people positively connected to one another, if the acknowledgement and appreciation of diversity is our *best* means of being connected? The shadow side of *pure* diversity is anarchy

The danger of the "personal growth" agenda from Dartmouth was that it made English too private a thing to be of clear public use. The danger of the "democracy through language" agenda was that it didn't yet give us a clear way to talk *to* one another, which the goal of acknowledging and appreciating diversity and the new rhetoric of listening it introduced tacitly acknowledged. If the limitations of Dartmouth could be summed up by Perls's "Gestalt Prayer," the limitations of Wye—the public face of it at least—could be summed up by a negative variation of it: "I am not you, you are not me, and we can only come together under false ideological and nationalistic pretenses" (i.e., acknowledging and appreciating our diversity is the only clear way we have of getting along).

The pointed exchange between Marie Bunscombe, the Black woman, and E. D. Hirsch, the White man—"Why can't I be literate and *different* from you?"—pointed the way to the "astonishing consensus" on the general theme "Democracy Through Language" among the Wye participants, by opposing a variety of authentic subjectivities to a single inauthentic objectivity. But it did not point the way to any kind of democratic understanding beyond the acknowledgement and appreciation of diversity and difference.

The second major shortcoming of the "democracy through language" agenda was that it did not begin to account for the very powerful legacy that the Dartmouth conference had had on the teaching of English in the intervening years. This can be seen in the above description by Lloyd-Jones and Lunsford, which emphasizes taking others' views into consideration, but generally assumes that otherwise our opinions are as fixed as our social identities, that they are things we "advocate" for, rather than think and feel our way through, growing and changing and transforming and being transformed as we do so. The public face of the profession suddenly altered itself from being about growth, which was under political attack, to being about democracy, which was seen as less susceptible to attack. The elementary teachers showed that their division of the profession of English had taken the "personal growth" agenda from Dartmouth and run with it, helped it grow and flourish in powerful ways. But it was necessary also to *tell* just how and why it had grown to make effective arguments for "softness" in the hard realm of public policy where it was perceived, in the language of *A Nation at Risk,* as "idleness."

The elementary teachers showed the power of kinds of teaching that many of the others perceived as dangerously "soft." This spoke to the three women members of the College Section and led them to boldly separate themselves from their colleagues committed to the "democracy through language" agenda, to pursue what they (and Elbow) found to be the higher calling of "soft" "wholism" and "Joy." Though these things were not yet articulated in such a way that they could form a clear basis for national educational policy, they were already able to be exemplified in ways that boded well for the future, as gestures toward a unity that lay beyond diversity rather than being imposed upon it. That power also needed to be effectively explained, and much of the work we do in this book is to try to explain it more or less definitively by searching for its deep sources in human history and human evolution. But seeing, first, the powerful call that these two groups of teachers felt—the call that drove them to separate and demark themselves from their more powerful colleagues—will ground us in that search. And that is what we will show you in the following chapter, "The Power of Softness."

The third major shortcoming of "democracy through language" was that in its pure opposition to the old English, it didn't look beyond the relatively brief history and relatively narrow concerns of "English" itself to consider what might replace it. It didn't consider the prehistory of English, as the Newbolt report did, by grounding itself in the tradition of liberal education. It assumed that our helping one another use the tools of language artfully and well (fully equating "language arts" and "English studies") would in itself be sufficient to reconstitute democracy—not considering that the human and natural basis for democracy might, in fact, be at least somewhat extralinguistic. It failed to consider either any extralinguistic sources of the emotional satisfactions English tends to bring when taught well—which, of course, predate in their origin the nineteenth-century naming of the discipline centered on the teaching of vernacular language and literature—or the general human needs that it and its predecessors were shaped to further, needs that "percolate" deeper even than language and the arts of language do.

In the chapters that follow, we seek to expand and deepen the "personal growth" agenda from Dartmouth and do so by investigating the long prehistory of English as a way, not of overcoming, but of deepening the "democracy through language" agenda. If "English" is not fundamentally about language, but about both the role of meaning in human life (the *main* "consensus" at Wye, according to Elbow) and how that can be furthered through a certain kind of democratic educational policy, we might take as an intermediate and synthesizing catchword for both Dartmouth and Wye—eliminating "English" and "Language" from their two slogans—the slogan "Growth Through and for Meaning-Making Democracy" or, perhaps better, "Democracy Through Growing Together." The psychological and the political agendas alone, in other words, were inadequate to compete with the old nationalistic agenda for English. And they were each partially covered up by the attention that the name "English" called to national language and culture, rather than to general psychological or political phenomena. But convincingly brought together they might amount to something that will finally definitively transform "English" into something else, into something that will be fully answerable to the deep sense of vocation that has belonged to English *teachers* all along. If we can understand why the very ideas of "democracy" and "personal growth" are inherently linked to and inherently enrich one another—in ways that have hitherto been little understood and little appreciated by those concerned more with either the public or the private sides of these linked phenomena—we might be able to finally begin to understand what "English" *actually* is!

CHAPTER 2

The Power of Softness

Intimations of Deepened Humanity from Stories of Classroom Life

In Peter Elbow's account of the Wye conference, *What Is English?* (1990), his most powerful chapter, "The Danger of Softness," discussed the "wholistic/Joy" group of the College Section before it did the Elementary Section, moving from the politics of theorizing holism and joy to the seemingly apolitical practice of them. We will do the reverse here: first showing the full power "pedagogical softness" can have when it can be practiced in a safe environment, then starting to make our way, as the three college teachers did at Wye, to justify to the broader world why it is so vitally important to create such spaces of softness, not just for children, but for the world as a whole. We are going to take you, in other words, from a moving picture of this softness in a simple state to an initial understanding of how the deliberate creation of such spaces of personal and interpersonal openness can become the pivotal political act for the growing together of humanity we need to accomplish. Through this, we hope you will come to see a certain kind of softness less as a "dangerous" lack of intellectual rigor than as an attitude of openness to what is alive both within and beyond ourselves—an openness from which all intellectual life must begin if it is in fact to exist and be grounded in the real world rather than in one that is abstract and unreal.

A STORY OF GROWING TOGETHER

Stories to Grow On, the 1989 publication of the Elementary Section of the Wye Plantation conference, including contributions of the majority of its members, opened with an account by its editor, Julie Jensen that described the key role the spirit of their relatively small group played in shaping the overwhelmingly positive spirit of the conference as a whole: "Time and again they helped others understand why and how to put students first—before a textbook, a favored literary work, a trusted teaching method" (p. xvi). Testimony from seven of the most prominent figures attending the conference—all teaching at the university level—affirmed this. The strongest testimony, though, came not from the authorities, but from the stories the teachers told about their teaching. What follows is what most would find by far the most powerful of the many vignettes of teaching the three volumes offered.

LAURA
BY CAROL AVERY
NATHAN C. SCHAEFFER ELEMENTARY SCHOOL, LANCASTER, PA

May 8, 1987

We celebrate Mother's Day in our first-grade classroom this Friday afternoon. The children perform a play for their mothers entitled "The Big Race"—the story of the tortoise and the hare. Laura is the "turtle" who wins the race.

A few minutes later, Laura reads aloud the book she has authored about her mother. The group laughs as she reads about learning to count with her cousins when she was 3 years old. Laura writes: "I was learning 6. Then my Mom came in and asked what we were doing. I said, 'I'm learning sex!'" Laura's mother is delighted. The reading continues with a hilarious account of a family squabble between mom and dad about a broken plate. Laura concludes the anecdote, "So then I just went in and watched TV." Laura looks at me and smiles as she pauses, waiting for her audience to quiet before she goes on. I wink at her; I know she is thinking, "Wait till they hear the next part. It's the funniest of all." She reads about a llama spitting in mom's eye on a visit to the zoo. Laura's way with words has brought delight to everyone. I remember a week earlier when Laura and I sat to type her draft and she said, "This is the best part. I put it last so that everyone will feel happy at the end."

May 9, 1987

Saturday night, around 11:45 p.m., a light bulb ignites fabric in a closet outside Laura's bedroom. Laura wakes. She cannot get through the flames, and by the time firefighters reach her it is too late. Laura dies. No one else is injured.

May 11, 1987

The children and I gather on our Sharing Rug in the classroom. I have no plans. We start to talk. There are endless interruptions

until Michael says, "Mrs. Avery, can we shut the door so people
stop bothering us?" So Michael shuts the door. "Are you going to
read us the newspaper?" they ask. "Is that what you'd like?" "Yes,"
comes the unanimous response. The children huddle close; a dozen
knees nuzzle against me. I read aloud the four-paragraph story
on the front page of the *Sunday News* that accompanies a picture
of our Laura sprawled on the lawn of her home with firefighters
working over her. I read the longer story in Monday morning's
paper that carries Laura's school picture. We cry. We talk and
cry some more. And then we read Laura's books—writing that
Laura determined was her best throughout the year and that was
"published" to become part of our classroom library. These books
are stories of Laura and her family, stories with titles such as *My Dad
Had a Birthday* and *When My Grandmother Came to My House*. Laura's
voice comes through loud and clear with its sense of humor and
enthusiasm. We laugh and enjoy her words. "Laura was a good
writer," they say. "She always makes us laugh when we hear her
stories." Then Dustin says, "You know, it feels like Laura is right
here with us, right now. We just can't see her."

A short time later we begin our writing workshop. Every child
chooses to write about Laura this day. Some write about the fire,
some [share] memories of Laura as a friend. I write with them.
After 45 minutes it is time to go to art, and there are cries of
disappointment at having to stop. We will come back to the writing.
There will be plenty of time. The last 5 weeks of school will be filled
with memories of Laura as we work through our loss together.
The children will decide to leave her desk in its place in the room
because "It's not in our way and anyway, this is still Laura's room
even if she's not really here anymore." Laura's mother and little
brother will come in to see us. On the last day, they will bring us
garden roses that Laura would have brought. Laura will always be a
part of us and none of us will ever be the same.

In the days immediately following Laura's death and in the weeks
since then, certain thoughts have been rattling around in my head:
I'm so glad that I teach the way I do. I'm so glad I really knew Laura.
I know that I can never again teach in a way that is not focused on
children. I can never again put a textbook or a "program" between
me and the children. I'm glad I knew Laura so well. I'm glad all of
us knew her so well. I'm glad the classroom context allowed her
to read real books, to write about real events and experiences in
her life, to share herself with us and to become part of us and we
of her. I'm grateful for a classroom community that nurtured us all

throughout the year and especially when Laura was gone. Laura left a legacy. Part of that legacy is the six little published books and the 5-inch-thick stack of paper that is her writing from our daily writing workshops. When we read her words, we hear again her voice and her laughter. (quoted in Elbow, 1989, pp. 193–194)

"When we read her words, we hear again her voice. . . ." There is an echo here of an old philosophical idea. At the end of Plato's *Phaedrus*—a dialogue about Socrates's playing midwife to the birth of the love of wisdom in a shallow but passionate young man who later, at the end of the *Symposium*, acts as a noble teacher—there is a famous passage about the importance of "voice," "living speech," as opposed to "dead discourse" (275a). According to this passage, the inventions of mathematics and writing, useful as these were to human economic life, came with the hidden propensity to deaden human intercourse, insofar as we came to rely *exclusively* on "external marks" (276a), and thus to forget what we know from within. A similar distinction formed the core idea of the main and best work of theory to emerge from the Dartmouth Conference, about how to give life to the curriculum of English, which to that point had been falsely centered on the "external marks" of language, hence largely ignoring the spirit that gave life to those marks. Lying at the center of the living universe of discourse, said James Moffett in his *Teaching the Universe of Discourse* (1968), is the "I-You" relationship:

> There is one thing no grammar book will ever tell us about the trinity of discourse: first and second persons are of a different order of reality than third person. Whereas *I* and *you* are existential, unabstracted persons, *he, [she]*, or *it* has merely referential or symbolic reality. (p. 11)

Grammar—the teaching of "the letter" (*gramma*, in Greek) in itself—when we see it as self-sufficient, kills the life we find in the "I-You" relationship of discourse. It literally removes us from reality, asks us to enslave ourselves to an abstracted force, rather than helping us draw on the life force we each carry within, which—when embodied in discourse that recognizes our own and others' reality—can become personally and mutually enlivening, "giving life," as Paul said when he distinguished "the spirit" from "the letter."

It's easy to see how the literacy methods of Carol Avery's classroom proceeded from Moffett's recommendations of best practice. Following shortly upon the previous passage was another for what a good English classroom should look like:

Somehow we must create more realistic communication "dramas" in which the student can practice being a first and second person with better motivation and in a way more resembling how he will have to read, write, speak, and listen in the "afterlife". . . . It is amazing how much so-called writing problems clear up when the student really cares, when he is realistically put into the drama of somebody with something to say to somebody else. (Moffett, 1968, p. 12)

The near effect of these methods, the clearing up of what have been labeled "writing problems"— which may in reality be nothing more than the reflection of the reluctance of students to have their spirits killed by the deadness of words detached from voices—can readily be seen from the joy of Laura's writing, shown in the first part of this passage, and the joy with which it is received. But the rest of what Avery wrote about Laura—about how her words take on new life after her death—shows something more far-reaching, highlighted by Plato, who, like Moffett, sees that certain uses of language have both an immediate life and an "afterlife" that stems from it:

The serious treatment of words employs the art of dialogue: Words founded on inner knowledge contain a seed whence new words can grow up in new persons, through which the seed proliferates, and is granted a kind of immortality, its giver and receiver attaining the fullest measure of blessedness that is granted to humanity. [1] (Plato, *Phaedrus*, (276e–277a)

"When we read [Laura's] words, we hear again her voice," and insofar as that voice speaks to those who hear it—in this case, "those" being both Laura's classmates and all those reading this passage—Laura has become both alive before us and also, in a way, immortalized, through the children's experience of her after her passing, and our experience of these children's experience. What we have experienced of Laura's life becomes part of our own. Her and her teacher's artistry has somehow converted the matter of "external marks" into energetic life force. Her words are alive in her absence when readers take them in and give new life to them.

There are educational implications here that extend far beyond the first grade. Teaching the arts of discourse—Plato, Moffett, and Avery all aver—is central to the art of humane living, in which we see ourselves and one another as real and alive, instead of simply as better or worse competitors or cooperators with regard to the manipulation of "external marks." When we learn these arts well, we all become teachers and students of one another, learning to draw on our own and one another's voice. Our words become embodiments of our voices, given and received as life rather than as external tokens. We learn to live for people rather than just for things. And learning this is to learn *real* democracy—government not just "of" and "by," but above all "for" people who dedicate their lives to one another and through this are mutually enriched.

A STORY OF JOY DISCOVERED AND SUPPRESSED

Ralph Waldo Emerson's "The American Scholar" (1837/1983)—often called "the American Declaration of Intellectual Independence"—ends with the following claim: should humanistic study become truly democratic, "a nation of [human beings] will for the first time exist because each believes him [or her]self inspired by the . . . Soul which . . . inspires all. . . ." We have just seen a story of a joyful, innocent girl (though she does know the difference between "six" and "sex") become an inspiration for the members of a first-grade classroom and, indirectly, for the readers of the volumes documenting the Wye Conference, and us. Yet how do we turn that story, and others like it, into an inspiration for democracy as a whole? How do we found what Moffett would call "a democracy of alive interpersonal discourse," recognizing the reality and life force of real persons, not just the force of abstract laws, and the grammar of the language, to which they agree to submit?

The story of the "wholistic/Joy" group of the College Section shows us some of the obstacles to that, not just outside but also within the very profession of "English." Following is the group's story of how it originated and evolved (edited from Elbow's somewhat longer version of it), its three members, Marie Bunscombe, Betsy Hilbert, and Eleanor Tignor, given a single collective voice:

> We just happened to catch each other's glance, and the glance said, . . . "Let's form our own group and get down in very direct and simple terms what we think . . . the goals should be". . . . Together, in the quiet of one of the lounges, we decided to write a brief, simple statement about the teaching of English, a "wholistic statement". . . . We did not see anything startling or revolutionary about [it]. We started by asking ourselves such questions as, What made us become English majors in college? Why did we become English teachers? What is it about literature and language that turns us on? How can we best communicate this enthusiasm we have for our subject to our students? How can we get them to recognize the power and experience the joy of well-expressed language in both oral and written form? (from Elbow, 1990, pp. 200–203)

The three central planks of the statement the group submitted treated the interrelated nature of literature, writing, and teaching from a holistic perspective:

1. Literature is the honest and eloquent re-creation of experience through language.
2. When we teach students to write, that which they write is itself a literary text and an introduction to the literary community.
3. Whatever the text being studied, the teacher's communication of the joy of literature, of a sense of discovery and freedom in approaching the material, is crucial. (Elbow, 1990, p. 201)

Given much of what we have heard about the conference so far, we might think these claims would have been perceived as noncontroversial, and embraced. But that would be only partly right. Here is the story of what happened when this statement was submitted to the larger group:

> I have a clear memory of general surprise that what we had said wasn't all that radical! People had apparently been expecting fists shaken in the air but discovered that we were saying some eminently rational things. A couple of people commented on how close our position was to theirs, and the college strand decided to endorse the statement.
>
> Then something very interesting happened. Twenty people began to hack away at a position paper that three of us had written. They wanted one thing changed, then another. Somebody objected to the word *joy* as being too pollyanna; red pencillers began to play with our wording. [We] took the statement back and rewrote it according to others' suggestions, then went back to the college section again, where again they tried to revise it by consensus. The three of us met again after that to look at our poor, pitiful little statement, which by that time had a couple of points flattened and the word *joy* excised, and a quiet thunder of NO! rose in our tiny committee. If it was radical and uncooperative to stand up for saying simply what we wanted to say . . . then radical we would have to be. We went back to our original statement, took it to the college section, and submitted it as a minority report. (Elbow, 1990, p. 201)

The final report of the College Section, though it made some mention of the importance of "integration," made no mention whatsoever of the minority report submitted to it by the "wholistic/Joy" group. In fact, it emphasized an "issue-centered" rather than either a "joy-centered" or "student-centered" curriculum, ignoring the very issue of whether there were "simple" and humane truths that could guide teaching, as the "wholistic/Joy" group and the entire Elementary Section apparently believed there were: Moffett's simple truths of personhood, where the first and second persons, the "I-You," are involved in a real relationship, the first and third persons, the "I-It," only in an abstract one.

The report emphasized the teaching of "hows," in effect renouncing any of the shared understanding of important "whys" that the small group believed they had arrived at. And, though one member of the "wholistic/Joy" group said she "had no trouble endorsing the final document," neither the word "Joy" nor any feeling of it, can be found in that text. Elbow later reported, "We were good boys and girls, doing the work we had come there to do" (personal communication, 2009). Questioning was dutifully stressed, but no human reason for it was given—no sense of the discovery and freedom it could unleash in both individuals and groups. Above all, there was no sense of the special role of something the "wholistic/Joy" group called "literature": a certain kind of extraordinary, humanizing use of language allowing us to uncover our "honesty" and "eloquence" for one another in an experience of "community"—that "turns us on" to language, to ourselves, to one another, and to life, whether written by Shakespeare or a first-grade girl. We have seen that Plato, James Moffett, Carol Avery, and the "wholistic/Joy" group share an understanding that literature is comprised by any instance of living discourse that manages to be conveyed from one person to another by means either of letters or other kinds of external marks—"letters" we imbue, as writers and readers, with life-giving spirit that enables us to share life with one another and live on after we are gone, as Laura did for her classmates. The "issue-centered" curriculum recommended in the end by the College Section (which ironically chose to suppress the issue raised within itself of why being "issue-centered" was more central than being "wholistically" "student/voice/literature-centered") focused on divisions—paralleling the emphasis of "democracy through diversity of language use" chosen to represent the center of the conference as a whole, rather than "the creation of and reflection on the making of meaning" by discrete but growing and communicating persons that Elbow and others saw as its true center.

The powers-that-be in the critical-issue-driven profession of English turned out to be, for all their emphasis on diversity, about as suppressive as the powers-that-be in the monolithic political world represented by Finn and Hirsch of the spirit that can bring us to grow poetically together. They made room for that actively unifying spirit within their midst, but, in the end, gave it no political voice. *We* need somehow to give that voice the political power—the vital power to poetically unite the democratic many—that has to this point been denied it, by both the political and the professional powers-that-be. We need to provide the rationale for something like a political party within the profession of English that would be a permanent, growing, life-affirming Joy group, warranting permanent validation and embrace by our profession as a whole, so that it can in turn be embraced by the world—in which the various "critical issues" we each care *about* would be dealt with within an attitude of solicitous caring *for* one another.[2]

JOY AND GROWING TOGETHER IN THE PREHISTORY OF "ENGLISH": WE *AREN'T* FAMILY NORMALLY, BUT CAN BE SOMETIMES

Let's begin by looking at the word *joy*—both the central emotion that young Laura sought to evoke when she was alive and the central end sought by the holistic splinter group of the College Section. This word has a key, yet largely forgotten history within the modern humanities before they became "English." And that history may well have been unconsciously echoed in the designation of the Joy group. In any case, it is a history of clear and deep thinking about how joy can be turned into a vital political force.

We have already seen it projected as the greatest result of the democratic humanism forecast by Emerson's "The American Scholar" (1837/1983): "The dread of [humanity] and the love of [humanity] shall be a wall of defence and a wreath of joy around all" (p. 71). Before that, it was the centerpiece of one of the greatest poems of English Romanticism, Wordsworth's 1807 ode "Intimations of Immortality from Recollections of Early Childhood," where it is called "the fountain-light of all our day/ . . . a master-light of all our seeing." But 2 decades before Wordsworth wrote this ode, joy was, of course, the subject of another even more famous one—perhaps the single best known piece of literature in any language because it came to crown the last movement of Beethoven's Ninth Symphony—Schiller's 1785 "Ode to Joy." Here is the first stanza (in Bruce's translation):

> Joy, radiant spark of divinity—
> Child sent to us from paradise—
> Made drunk by your fire, heavenly power,
> We step out of ourselves into your holy sanctuary.
> Your magic charms bind together again
> What our customs strictly divide;
> All human beings become family
> Wherever the gentle wings of your spirit hover.
> Let yourselves be embraced, millions of you!
> In this kiss of the whole world!

Brothers and sisters, underlying all we see,
There is an abiding life force that brought us into being,
And will surely care for us, if we only hold it dear,
Letting ourselves be embraced by the joy it lends our lives.

In this poem we find an early, deeply influential expression of what the nineteenth-century sage Thomas Carlyle (1834) and, later, the twentieth-century literary critic M. H. Abrams (1971) called "natural supernaturalism": the modern attempt to recapture and respark for humanity as a whole those powerfully uplifting life forces previously expressed principally through sectarian religions. (The fifth line even incorporates the Latin root of *religio*—"to rebind"). Carlyle, in the same work in which this phrase was coined, *Sartor Resartus* went so far as to name "Literature" as *the* "Religion" of modern life.

Both Emerson—Carlyle's first publisher, who became his best friend—and Matthew Arnold—whom major scholars agree was the principal intellectual figure behind the founding of "English" (Applebee, 1974; Bacon, 1998; Graff 1987; Scholes, 1998) and whose spirit and ideas pervade the Newbolt Report we examined in Chapter 1—clearly took this idea to heart. They believed that if everyone could be helped to feel the joy of literature so conceived, "letting ourselves be embraced" in the life force of "the universe of discourse," as Schiller and Moffett would have put it, we could all become brothers and sisters, bringing joy to the human world and making it its predominant spirit through our "growing together."

It's pretty clear that Jeff's teachers—Rachel, Sarah, Andrew, Sharon, and Debra—the two of us, and many of you reading this, are direct heirs of these ideas. But it's difficult to convey their importance nowadays because both literature and education have gradually been detached from the deeply, humanly democratizing political agenda that they were once more clearly an integral part of—and that the name "English" has helped to obscure, very much as Plato found the invented artifices of mathematics and writing obscured the power of the human voice.

Ten years after he wrote the "Ode to Joy" Schiller himself was the first to put this humanizing agenda in explicitly educational—and explicitly political—terms, in his *On the Aesthetic Education of Man in a Series of Letters* (1795/1967). Writing at that point, just after the French Terror, he saw at first hand the dangers of newly "free" human beings being collectively carried away by the "goodness" of abstract principles before they had first learned to freely cultivate their individual humanity—what Arnold later came to call "the best self" (1869/1993, p. 99). The only *permanent* antidote he saw to this new Terror—as more and more peoples freed themselves from political authoritarianism only to plunge themselves into various forms of mass hysteria, then back into authoritarian-ism (a pattern we can easily recognize in the electoral swings of our own times)—was an educational program that would teach each human being "to idealize their own concrete existence" (p. 14): "To achieve a solution to the political problem, the road of aesthetics must be pursued, for it is through the awareness of feeling that we first achieve our freedom" (Schiller, 1795/1967, p. 8). Free willing and free thinking alone, Schiller saw, result only in what Arnold later, in his great poem "Dover Beach," called "ignorant armies clash[ing] by night," unless we first manage to induce the preponderance of individuals composing democratic societies to compose *themselves*. Finding meaning in the individual felt experiences we have each been given, we also each find our own source of personal authority and personal truth through the thoughtful honing of the oth-erwise arbitrary and vacillating individual will. This personal authority can then become a new anchor for common life, as we give of ourselves to one another. As Arnold memorably put it, the "sweetness" of Joy can be transformed into common "light" through which "the ignorant armies clashing by night" (or in an "issue-centered curriculum") can come to see one another.

THE RECOVERY OF JOY IN OUR NEW TIMES OF TRAUMA: GETTING BEYOND "ISSUES," TOWARD A DISCIPLINE OF CREATIVE LISTENING

Perhaps not so accidentally, something very like these founding concerns of English were again brought to life in another, more recent time of trau-ma and terror—the time just after September 11, 2001. Lisa Ruddick, of the University of Chicago, published an article in the November 23, 2001, issue of *The Chronicle of Higher Education* that provoked a torrent of positive response from teachers in the humanities. Titled "The Near Enemy of the Humanities is Professionalism," it began:

> Since September 11, many scholars have discovered that the challenges of meeting their traumatized students on some shared human ground has evoked some of the most meaningful encounters of their teaching lives. . . . [T]he conversation often turns on how to bridge the chasm between the syllabus—whatever it contains—and the students who are looking for help in figuring out how to sustain a human connection to a world that is overwhelming them. (p. B7)

Later she contrasted two forms of *"ascesis"* or "self-discipline": one a "self-transformation that is . . . a loss of self" in submission to the "rigors" of professional discipline (as Elbow's "good boys and girls" of the College Section did); another "self-transformation that produces integrity, flexibility, and moral independence." She portrayed the latter through a chant of a group of contemporary American nuns, found through an internet search of "*ascesis*":

> Monastic tradition
> immersing itself in the mind and heart of Jesus
> urges us to purity of heart
> and invites us to take up
> in personal freedom and joy
> those tools of *ascesis* which shape us
> to inner stillness, fullness of love.

Once again we find the idea that "personal freedom" and "joy" are to be found by receiving "tradition" with a creative life force that will "shape us" both within and without, will religiously rebind us through the "purity of heart" it brings forth. Ruddick concluded:

> Most people who decide to become teachers in the humanities . . . do this kind of work because we had an experience early in our lives of being taught how to let go of whatever we thought was the whole of reality and to take the measure of a larger moral and human universe. A first step in rethinking what we care about as a profession may be ways . . . to foster the more intuitive and receptive dimensions of our communal and intellectual lives. . . . Our profession may in time develop a culture that somehow uses literature as the basis for a complex exploration of the art of listening that is one of the creative forces of the world. (p. B9)

Our task from this point onward will be to investigate just how "external marks" somehow, sometimes get transformed into aesthetic experience, in which we learn, as Ruddick says, "to take the measure of a larger moral and human universe." Our times demand that all of us learn to operate with such a compass. The "ignorant armies clashing by night" are far, far deadlier now than when Schiller, Carlyle, Emerson, and Arnold wrote in the late eighteenth and nineteenth centuries.

THE HARD SCIENTIFIC AND PHILOSOPHICAL WARRANTS FOR THE POWER OF SOFTNESS

As we shall discuss in the next chapter, contemporary evolutionary psychology has shown the development over time of nuanced feeling and aesthetic experience to be critical to human evolution (e.g., Dissanayake, 1992); and contemporary neuroscience has shown them to be critical to the development of individual moral life (e.g., Damasio, 1999). The moral compass Lisa Ruddick called for to assure our future survival as a species, in other words, actually seems to have been a central force in our survival to this point in time! As Plato and James Moffett said before her, we have forsaken, but can recover, the moral compass of living discourse. But to recover it, we need to see clearly how this discourse is more fundamental to life than either standard grammars or competitive rhetorics. In Chapter 3 we will show how we can use "hard" science to justify "the power of softness," to literally overrule both the political and the professional forces that now tend to suppress joy in our classrooms. And that hard science of softness can be linked to philosophical conceptions of the value of our "growing together."

If standardization seeks to produce mental sameness among the individual atoms of democratic life, and issue-centered curriculum seeks interaction within an understanding of basic, irresolvable, unbridgeable difference,[3] the broadest aim of holistic curriculum is to chemically unite us: to transform us, insofar as possible, from separate atoms into compounds, diverse *wholes*, both as individual persons undergoing discrete stages of growth and as ever larger groups of persons seeking to grow together into complex self-governing organisms. In 1817 Coleridge, borrowing conceptually from the philosopher Immanuel Kant (1790/1952), coined a simple phrase for this: "multeity in unity," a formula altogether for the composition and appreciation of a work of art, for the living of an integrated and personally meaningful life, and for the coming together of a diverse but unified democratic people. The scientific investigation of the evolutionary development of aesthetic experience can thus serve to ground an aesthetic, holistic philosophical worldview of evolving "multeity in unity," that can, in turn, serve to ground a new, thoroughly thought-through program for holistic education in democratic life.

Together, these scientific and philosophical findings should be tremendously reassuring to us. To a significant extent, all that is needed to transform our profession is

1. to let teachers know they already, to a very large extent, have the moral compass they need;
2. to help them understand where they got it from and how better to follow its guidance; and
3. to help them communicate to others why we all so need to take direction from this moral compass, rather than either merely passively complying with static standardization or going actively for each other's throats.

Most of this book will be occupied with the more practical aspects of teaching and communicating out of this reassuring worldview regarding the power of softness. But it first needs to be laid out as a coherent worldview before it can be thoroughly and convincingly taught out of and advocated for within a broader culture that is in many ways deeply averse to the human power of "softness" for which it speaks. And that is what we shall seek to do next.

CHAPTER 3

Understanding the Power of Softness Through the Deep Prehistory of English

By the time you get to the end of this chapter, we hope you will have an initial grasp of a new, larger, far more complete, far more encompassing view of the meaning behind the educational practices of what has been long called "English"—largely for lack of a better name. To accomplish this, we are going to try to connect the following aspects of science, philosophy, and pedagogy in a way no one has done before us:

- The findings of contemporary science regarding the critical role of art and feeling aesthetic experience in the processes of human evolution and the workings of the human brain
- The findings of contemporary philosophers and psychologists about how human beings find and share meaning, how they create shared mental, emotional, and moral life out of "external marks"
- An initial vision of a pedagogy consciously devised to tap into and further these processes through a revised English curriculum, and an initial rationale for justifying this reframing of "English" to the public.

We are well aware that this is quite a lot to cover in a single chapter, but we believe it is actually more effective to present this vision all at once and together in a single giant leap or paradigm shift than to try to arrive at it by small steps. We will later retrace large parts of the leap we take here—particularly the parts of its trajectory that cover classroom life and life-centered educational policy—as we explore the practical application of these ideas later in the book.

But this is not a leap into the blue. There is almost nothing original to be found in this chapter other than the fact that we are tying these things together as no one has done before. We are drawing on congenial strains of mainstream science, mainstream philosophy, and mainstream educational theory to make revolutionary recommendations for main-

50

stream educational policy, in light of the fact that we now live in a world in which we clearly need to dramatically change the way we teach.

CONSILIENCE: LINKING SCIENTIFIC KNOWLEDGE TO PHILOSOPHICAL THOUGHT AND THE EDUCATION OF FREE HUMAN BEINGS

Not even the idea of definitively uniting science, philosophy, and pedagogy is original to us. In some ways, it is an idea as old as Plato and Aristotle. But we have taken our idea of this directly from Harvard biologist E. O. Wilson, coming first in his Pulitzer Prize–winning *On Human Nature* in 1978 and further developed in his *Consilience*, published 20 years later, in 1998. *Consilience* is the belief in the desirability and possibility for all fields of human knowledge and endeavor to be linked together in a coherent, hierarchical series ("con-sil" = "linked by a series of jumps") rather than being allowed to exist in essentially separate fields.

It's not just that all scientific knowledge should be hierarchically linked together but that this knowledge of the underlying basis of life should form the basis of philosophical thought about the meaning and value of life, an endeavor the scientist Wilson avers to be higher than scientific knowledge of any kind. And, finally, philosophy should pave the way for "liberal education," for the broad institution of the free, conscious evolution of life among multitudes of free, conscious human beings: work that is higher and more important than isolated philosophical thought. Our work here is an effort to carry out Wilson's vision—the first such effort, we believe, to be undertaken by those who see themselves principally as teachers.

GRAMMAR, "GRAMMATOLOGY," OR CONSILIENCE?

We saw in the last chapter how in the wake of the trauma of 9/11, Lisa Ruddick, and the hundreds of humanities teachers at the university level who responded to her article in *The Chronicle of Higher Education*, began to seek a new moral compass beyond currently confining "professional rigors." At this point we need to say a little something about the specific professional rigors she was referring to, namely, the extreme version of the "issue-centered" curriculum that has dominated humanities teaching and scholarship at the university level for the past several decades, called variously *grammatology, deconstruction,*[1] *postmodernism, cultural studies, critical theory,* or simply *theory*. Like Ruddick, we see that we are going to need eventually to definitively supplant or supersede the professional authority of this understanding of "theory" if we truly want to center professional authority in the humanities on a culture that uses literature as the basis for creative listening. This is why we think it is important to acquaint even those who teach far away from this "theory" with some of the rudiments of it. We need to rigorously criticize "rigorous critical theory" through rigorous hard science in order to lay firm ground for the establishment of this new life-centered professional culture that we hope will stretch all the way from the earliest schooling to the most advanced research.

A now-old joke goes: "After the horrible cultural battles of the 1960s, the Right and the Left got tired of fighting. The Left decided that they would take over the English Departments of all the Ivy League universities. And they did so with some dispatch, achieving their goal nearly completely by the end of the 1970s. At the same time, the Right decided they would take over the Presidency, the Congress, and the Supreme Court. And one reason they were able to do so relatively completely, just after the 1970s ended, is that so many of the best and the brightest among the Left no longer thought that politics outside the academy was worthy of their intelligence." This *is* a joke, and presents a grossly exaggerated version of reality. But it is not divorced from it. For example, a distinguished international symposium at the 2010 meeting of the American Educational Research Association, entitled "Curriculum Theory: Dead Man Walking?" (Westbury et al.) pointed out that there are now basically only two schools of thinking about the nature of what is taught in schools: a radically conservative one coming from government, concerned almost totally with the implementation of mindless standardization and accountability; and a radically subversive one coming from universities, concerned almost totally with the sophisticated critical theory undermining the same standardization and accountability, but having negligible impact on actual schools. Blind power exerted by truly powerful forces on the one hand; trenchant but powerless criticism, emptily endorsed by the highest intellectual powers-that-be on the other.

In the previous chapter, we saw how James Moffett differentiated living discourse among people from abstract "grammar," the preset rules of language that, when dissociated from real communicative life, are the source of so much that is deadening in education. "Theory" seeks to critically subvert fixed "grammars" of all kinds—most importantly, the psychologically entrenched grammars of social and political domination. But it replaces the tyranny of those "grammars" only with highly intelligent forms of anarchy.

No one put this more succinctly than Paul de Man (1979), Derrida's first American apostle, who claimed "the impossibility of reading," contending that meaningful communication—whether through speech, writing, or literature—is an illusion; we can only "deconstruct" our fantasies of the existence of meaning that support our illusions of personal and cultural power. Robert Scholes (1998), a member of the College Section of the Wye Conference, gave "deconstruction" a positive pedagogical spin, by calling it "textual power," the important ability to critically see through cultural illusions, including those conveyed through literature. And our friend Deborah Appleman, whose life has centered on educating secondary English teachers, has continued in this vein with her *Critical Encounters in High School English* (2009), which advocates teaching students, beginning in high school, to read through a wide variety of "critical lenses."

As one of Deborah's high school students trenchantly pointed out, though—in a way only high school students can do—deconstructive textual power can be abused as readily as any other form of power: "Deconstruction is dumb. It's people who want to feel important trying to destroy meaning." And that's just where *we* want to begin to criticize "critical theory." It has, by and large, thrown out the baby of meaning with the dirty bathwater of both knowing and unknowing exploitative power. Though deconstruction has performed, and can continue to perform, a great service—helping many people see through the many ways in which their life force has been subtly suppressed—few would deny that it has also bred a false sense of sophistication among academic elites, itself a form of exploitative power.

As Deborah's student indicates, deconstructive reports of the death of meaning may well be premature, which might turn out to be a very good thing. "I'm sick of the pseudo-empathy of theory!" a grad student in English, a member of a minority, confided to Bruce one day during a conference. For Moffett, life was beyond grammar; what we will soon see is how it may also be beyond grammatology, deconstruction, and critical theory—or, perhaps more precisely, that there is more *to* life than can be found in our current, purely critical theory. There may well be a science of life, consiliently tied to a philosophy of the making of meaning within life, that helps us see the making of meaning as also the making of new life, and will provide us a basis for pedagogically bringing forth more meaning and more life. And because few critical theorists would dispute that life came into existence before either grammatical language or Derridean grammatological "arché-writing," it might be a good idea to try to tie the making of meaning to the processes of life before we give up on it altogether to be able to devote ourselves fully to deconstructing ourselves and one another, as Derrida (2001) claimed should now be the goal of all of the humanities. Just as there was life before it, there may be life after deconstruction: Existing in natural and cultural processes, we can first explicate and then replicate, through which in themselves dead letters can be converted into the energy of living human speech and living human spirit.

RECONCILING HUMANISTIC AND SCIENTIFIC CULTURE: ART AND THE ASCENT OF HUMANITY

What most of us learn about the process of the evolution of life in school can be summed up in a single phrase: the survival of the fittest. Life, in this view, is the competitive struggle for existence in which only the strongest survive and propagate. And because our own culture happens to be set up in many ways to foster just such a brutal competitive struggle, this view of life as a whole seems to many of us to make eminent sense.

Darwin himself, though, adamantly and repeatedly insisted that *human* evolution does not take place primarily through the process of the brutal struggle for existence: that the evolution of our own species is, in fact, fundamentally moral and integrative in nature, working in ways that could eventually lead us to a condition of relatively universal peace; and that when we find ourselves enmeshed in brutal competition of one kind or another we are in fact *de*volving, not evolving, making ourselves, others, and the world less rather than more fit for survival than we otherwise could.

In *The Descent of Man* (1871) Darwin traced four primary stages of human evolution that enabled us, more and more, to consciously evolve, to integrate our own development with others' and with the development of life in general: These were "care," "language," "reflection," and "habit" (Darwin, 1871; Loye, 2004). How interesting that Darwin saw "care" as the foundation of "language"! That he saw "reflection"—remember, the last of Jeff's three dimensions of aesthetic responsiveness—as a further stage of evolution from language! And that he saw the reflective, educative formation of cultural and personal "habit" as the summit so far of human evolution!

Darwin's hierarchy of dispositions and skills was purely speculative, but it has been reinforced by many of the findings of contemporary evolutionary psychology and neuroscience. We will proceed momentarily to those findings, but before we do, we need to first consider how, in these biological, evolutionary terms, both linguistic grammars and deconstructive grammatology, considered and taught in isolation, lead us into setting up a kind of Ptolemaic astronomical system—requiring all sorts of complex, maneuvering explanations—because they present improperly centered pictures of what Moffett called "the universe of discourse."

Besides Darwin, all our figures from the last chapter found the fully human use of language to occur only when communication is governed by care, by what Moffett called the "I-You" relationship lying at the true center of the universe of discourse—and at the center of what we shall see in the following pages is an understanding of how art and literature are distilled forms of care that evolved precisely as ways of infusing new life into the persons *using* language and culture, at the same time keeping language and culture themselves flexible and alive. That is why seeing the dynamic workings of "care" and "reflection" (the "love" and "wisdom" of the title of this book) through art and aesthetic experience is fundamental to the revival of educational systems that have become deadeningly engrossed, on the one hand, with the inculcation of standardized cultural "grammars" and, on the other, with the mere critical subversion of those same grammars, detached from the processes of life through which they can be thoughtfully renewed. Subversive rhetorics could be said to chip away at these large, frozen blocks of ice, where living discourse seeks to melt them, to get them to flow in streams of life.

In his famous essay "The Two Cultures" (1959) C. P. Snow bemoaned the fact that the "humanistic" and "scientific" cultures no longer spoke to each other and lived in two separate worlds, one "hard" and the other "soft," with the hard tending to count as far more serious and important than the soft in the broader culture. We believe we now have the "consilient" scientific, philosophical, and pedagogical means to begin to reconcile and harmonize these two cultures, to scientifically and philosophically ground humanism and to pedagogically advance it from the secure base of this solid grounding of what we are fairly sure we know about how our species has evolved. In the remainder of this chapter, we are going to *cover* this ground fairly quickly. Then in the rest of the book we will, at a bit more leisurely pace, see how we can envision and communicate our teaching so that it can be more clearly depicted as the awakening and renewal of life so many of us already sense it to be.

HOMO AESTHETICUS:
ART AND AESTHETIC EXPERIENCE AS *HUMAN* LIFE

Darwin's speculations on the evolution of human moral development in *The Descent of Man* were forerunners of the important and flourishing field in contemporary science called *evolutionary psychology*, the study of how the various complex characteristics of the human mind evolved through the attempt to understand their survival value.

On the surface, of course, art seems to have little survival value—a big reason why teaching it has so little credence in schools, and why our education systems tend neither to take the teaching of art or the funding of that teaching terribly seriously. By contrast, the survival value of language is immediately evident, so we teach language, and even the artistic use of it, mainly as possessions that can help us jockey for advantage in a brutally competitive world. We dismiss the "sweetness" of art as mere dessert, without stopping to examine how it might, in fact, be not only deeply nourishing to us, but key to our survival and flourishing as a species.

Just as all extant human cultures have language, all have and highly value some form of art, even if they don't stress it in the processes of formal education. However diverse we are, we are similar in this respect. What are the reasons for this? How has art served us as a species? And how might the de-emphasis or removal of art and literature from our schools be serving to devolve rather than evolve us?

For the past several decades, these questions have guided the thought and research of Ellen Dissanayake. Over the course of 3 decades, and the publication of three books—*What Is Art For?* (1988), *Homo Aestheticus: Where Art Comes From and Why* (1992), and *Art and Intimacy: How the Arts Began* (2000), she has pursued a Darwinian, evolutionary, "species-centric" view both of the origin of art and of its enduring meaning in human life. Others have followed in her wake: "The Next New Thing in English" was the title of the most highly e-mailed article in the *New York Times* in early April 2010, and was about other neo-Darwinian theories of art. But we are going to stick with Dissanayake here, both because she is the pioneer in the field and because we find the presentation of her findings to be singularly empathic: Among the evolutionary psychologists concerning themselves with art and literature she is particularly concerned with the elemental experience of art in "primitive" cultures, similar to those in which art originated, in large part because she has lived a good deal of her life amidst such cultures in Sri Lanka, Nigeria, and Papua New Guinea.

For Dissanayake (1988), art is characterized as "the evolved behavior of *making special*":

> In whatever we are accustomed to call art, a *specialness* is tacitly or overtly acknowledged. Reality, or what is considered to be reality, is elaborated, re-formed, given not only particularity (emphasis on uniqueness or "specialness") but import (value, or "specialness")—what may be called such things as magic or beauty or spiritual power or significance. (p. 92)

This behavior of "making special" evolved in the human species as a way of "making socially important activities gratifying, physically and emotionally," attaching individuals to their cultures, as young children grow attached to their parents, "learning to respond and to cause response in another."

This last fact is key. As we have already noted, because art takes time away from activities that sustain human physical survival, we tend not to see it as having survival value. Certainly, the notion of evolution as "the survival of the fittest" would predicate that the time we spend making and experiencing art is biologically anomalous, as Stephen J. Gould found the panda's thumb to be (1980), and as Steven Pinker (1997) claims most art to be in his *How the Mind Works,* famously calling it "mental cheesecake" for the way it pleases without providing vital nourishment. However, as mental and emotional attachment of individuals to their societies is key to the survival of those societies as enduring collectivities, providing not just physical but psychological and emotional prosperity to its members becomes critical—as critical as children's emotional attachment to their parent(s) is to their survival, psychic health, and potential. This is where art comes into play, as cultural parenting and responsive reciprocation.

"To respond and to cause response in another" through experiencing and creating art—and, by extension, living in artful, feeling discourse with one another—are as fundamental to cultural life as the cultivation of relationships between parents and children is to family life. Aesthetic experience *literally* "fraternizes" us, as Schiller put it in the "Ode to Joy," by inducing us to respond to one another culturally as loving families do. This is the justification for the title of Dissanayake's second book, *Homo Aestheticus,* and its claim that we are fundamentally not "knowing" or "making" but "feeling" beings. And it is the justification of her severe criticism of contemporary society for failing to provide the cultural sustenance that is not just one aspect of our makeup, but central to our existence and evolution as a species: "The myths that for millennia have explained the world and themselves to humankind are evaporating, one by one, as societies undergo the civilizing process and acquire a rootless, unsettled sameness. Yet roots are there" (1988, p. 193). It is Dissanayake's and our view that it is only by collectively reconnecting with our roots through the educative cultivation of aesthetic experience that we will ever learn to "grow together." Yet how do we now tap into those roots, in our present condition of "rootless, unsettled sameness"?

Readers of Jeff's earlier work will have noticed Dissanayake's use of the word "response." *"You Gotta BE the Book"* centered around his finding that there were three central dimensions to the "transactional aesthetic response" identified by Louise Rosenblatt as central to the experience of literature. What we are now going to set forth is a "consilient" understanding of how these dimensions of responsiveness came into being through the processes of evolution. Once we have done this, we will be in a position to reexamine the dimensions of response and how they can be enlivened through our teaching in a way that serves the goals of creating transformative and democratic spaces in our classrooms.

THE GREAT CHAIN OF RESPONSE

First, we are mammals. As such, we are biologically characterized by the various kinds of sustained sustenance we provide for our young, sustenance that comes from within us and is given through physical contact. Art is a form of such sustenance in cultural terms: a means of nourishment imbibed through holistically embodied experience, drawing also on the evolved mammalian behavior of play (which we'll say much more about in Chapter 4, on the evocative dimension of response).

Second, we are primates. Many primates provide nurturance through what biologist Sarah Blaffer Hrdy, in *Mother Nature* (1999), calls *alloparenting*, parenting by those "other than" biological parents (*allo* is Latin for "other"). The major evolutionary benefit of this alloparenting is the increase of the *meme pool*—the range of cultural practices, character traits, and patterns of interpersonal responsiveness that children can choose to appropriate to themselves and pass on to the next generation. When Bruce asks his teacher education students who the wisest person in their lives has been, the most frequent response by far is "my grandmother." Hrdy writes of how the development of menopause in human females dramatically enhanced the evolutionary and educative potential of our species: A generation of women, freed from childbearing and, for the most part, physical labor, could, with the benefit also of the experience of age, devote themselves exclusively to the provision of care. Grandmothers, in other words, were the first professional teachers and still are some of our best. As cultural parenting and reciprocation, art and the response to it are an important form of cultural "alloparenting." The next link in "the great chain of response" shows us just how important and transformative they can be.

This third link is that we are symbolizers: in multifarious ways, we use "things" to stand for "beings," and this is far from limited to the symbols of language. Dissanayake draws heavily from the "attachment theory" developed by John Bowlby (e.g., 1969); popularized in the United States through the parenting books of T. Barry Brazelton, (e.g., 1983), and from much of the "object relations" theory of psychoanalyst Melanie Klein, who was Bowlby's teacher. She could have perhaps even more pertinently drawn from the work of Klein's most famous student, Donald Winnicott, known as the "Dr. Spock" of Britain, whose work centered on the developmental role of art and play in human life. One of Winnicott's (1953) best known ideas is the "transitional object"—things like teddy bears that parents give to children, both as symbols of themselves, and as playmates with which to make free meaning of their own. Transitional objects are a way of promoting what Bowlby called "secure attachment," attachment that is neither fearfully avoidant of nor fearfully, ambivalently "clinging" to the parent, but secure enough in the parent's love to explore the surrounding world. Cristina Bruns, in her brilliant *Why Literature?* (2011), has shown how the patterns of "aesthetic response" set forth by Rosenblatt, Jeff, and others derive from the nature of art as such transitional objects given by their creators to their audiences to promote the making of free meaning through the processes of aesthetic response. Just as alloparenting itself enriches the meme pool, art does so in an exponentially richer way: first, through physical objects that are transportable across vast distances of space and time; second, through holistic experiences, specifically geared to be readily appropriated by those receiving them, providing a kind of rich cultural "milk" not even mothers or grandparents have; third, through the promotion of not just connection and pleasure, but freedom—not just the "engagement" emphasized by Dissanayake, but also the personal meaning making and reflection that Elbow emphasized, and that Jeff emphasized equally, along with engagement, in *"You Gotta BE the Book."*

We are now in a position to understand why those three propositions about literature, writing, and teaching advanced by the three women in the "wholistic/Joy" group at the Wye Conference in 1987 (see Chapter 2) were deeply biologically conditioned in ways the "issue-centered" curriculum recommended by the College Section simply were not, why "the power of softness" is also the power of life itself making its way through us, not just the stimulation of arguers jockeying for the power of their side of any given question, with resolution rarely if ever in sight. These three propositions provide an elementary theory of the promotion of democratic attachment through the cultivation of the attachment to literature and other forms of art, a theory, not just of "diverse democracy through language," as the Wye Conference as a whole put it, but of democracy that facilitates the free complementary unification of diverse people through the careful cultivation of transactional aesthetic experience.

First, if "literature is the honest and eloquent re-creation of experience through language," then it exists to promote cultural renewal through the renewal of personal experience. Second, if "when we teach students to write, that which they write is itself a literary text and an introduction to the literary community," then writing—insofar as it is aesthetic and transactional—becomes an act both of the reciprocation and of the further generation of care among the human community. Third, if "whatever the text being studied, the teacher's communication of the joy of literature, of a sense of discovery and freedom in approaching the material, is crucial," then teaching, too, becomes fundamentally an aesthetic, transactional, literary act, a conduit to broad, cultural renewal through personal and community renewal.

How, though, do we transfer these understandings of the power of art and literature into concrete teaching practices? If art is cultural milk, how, precisely, do we learn to access and extract nourishment from it, and how do we teach it in a way that will maximize its potential to freely nourish our students? How do we learn to tap into the processes of aesthetic experience, developed through the ages, to methodically maximize their beneficent potential?

Here it is time to take a break from the chain of consilient leaps this chapter mostly consists of, to give you a pedagogical image of how free life can be generated through art and artful teaching, when art is considered as a Winnicottian "transitional object," a free gift of life from one being to others.

RE-CREATION AS MAKING *TIME* SPECIAL: FROM MEMES TO MIMEMES

Gabriele Rico, Professor Emerita of English at San Jose State University and bestselling author of *Writing the Natural Way* (2000b/1985) and many other books, draws on neuroscience to understand how to help people write from a fullness of being. Many teachers now use the technique of "clustering" she invented to help writers draw on their intuitive/visual right brains without initial interference from their logical/grammatical left brains—often without knowing it was Rico who developed this freeing technique. More recently, Rico (2000a) has developed a technique called "re-creations" for helping students of all ages to become fine poets—quite often with no prior experience—in a very short span of time. We find her method brilliantly illuminates not just "what art is for" but how it *works*.

Students are first read a short poem; then, as it is read again, they circle the words that resonated with them; finally, they write their own poems, in 2 1/2 minutes, the time Rico has found optimal for creativity. The products are usually stunning. A friend of Bruce's tried it at a workshop the week after he attended a conference Bruce put on with Rico as a featured speaker. One after another, people came up to him telling him how grateful they were, how they'd never written anything like that before in their lives.

We encourage you to do your own "re-creation" from Denise Levertov's (1987) poem "Writing in the Dark" (see Figure 3.1) and then compare what you've written with what six of Rico's students and the two of us wrote (see Figure 3.2). We are going to be building quite a bit on this exercise through the next section of the book, as a common literary experience we can draw on as a community of readers. Taking the time to do this short exercise now will enable you to participate fully in

FIGURE 3.1. Re-creation Exercise Using "Writing in the Dark" by Denise Levertov

It's not difficult,
Anyway, it's necessary.

Wait till morning, and you'll forget.
And who knows if morning will come.

Tumble for the light, and you'll be
stark awake, but the vision
will be fading, slipping
out of reach.

You must have paper at hand,
a felt tip pen, ballpoints don't always flow,
pencil points tend to break. There's nothing
shameful in that much prudence: those are our tools.

Never mind about crossing your t's, dotting your i's—
but take care not to cover
one word with the next. Practice will reveal
how one hand instinctively comes to the aid of the other
to keep each line
clear of the next

Keep writing in the dark;
a record of the night, or
words that pulled you from the depths of unknowing,
words that flew through your mind, strange birds
crying their urgency with human voices,

or opened
as flowers of a tree that blooms
only once in a lifetime:

words that may have power
to make the sun rise again.

Before you continue to the next page, try to do a "re-creation" of your own. Make sure to have a timing device with an indicator for seconds on hand. First, read the poem slowly to yourself, out loud if you can. Next, read it once again. Circle each word or phrase that particularly resonated with you when you're done reading, or write the words on a separate sheet of paper, with lots of space between them. If you didn't write your words and phrases on a separate sheet of paper, do so now. Circle them. Then write other words or phrases around them, just free associating with whatever ideas or memories come up for you. This is Rico's "clustering" technique that draws on the image-rich right brain with as little interference as possible from the linear left brain.

Finally, with your timing device handy, give yourself exactly 2 1/2 minutes to write either a verse or prose poem of your own. (You can even try actually doing this in the dark!)

FIGURE 3.2. Eight "Re-Creations" of Levertov's Poem (by six of Gabriele Rico's students, Bruce, and Jeff)

Tools

Paper
Pencil
      pen
These are our tools
Don't be ashamed of such prudence.
Language has the power
   to pull ideas from their depths
   to let our thoughts bloom
   if only once in a lifetime
   to make the sun rise again.

Writing a Vision

Darkness and light
primal, instinctive motions of the hands
   keep a record of the night
a record of the light blooming in the free
   of forgetting and remembering.
Tools of writing won't tear up the world,
rather shape it to your vision,
vision of the word,
vision of the sun rising again.
Bloom, unknowing forms,
write into the night.
Freedom,
freedom,
freedom in the dark.

Idea

These shapes I have made
   are almost letters.
I can almost read them. And now
I am sure there was vision there
that was so clear, so pure
that its urgency was like the blooming
of a flower, the flight of a bird.
now the sun has risen with its own
urgency,
and I can see now that there must have been something more,
but I cannot remember exactly
   what it was.

FIGURE 3.2. Continued.

Courage

Keep courage through your darkest moments.
It's necessary when you're slipping, sloping.
Don't cover your heart—it's not shameful.
The power of the word,
the flow of the voice,
the bloom of the feeling,
makes clear hearts rejoice and fly
　　　like startled birds.
Hearts open and bloom not once
　　　but many times, life times.
Pain is a prudent necessity.
The sun will rise after the night.

Do It Now

Write now,
right now,
chasing the ephemeral
chattering birds of midnight.
Help yourself to see the
fading visions of a once-blooming tree.
Trust your trails along the
grainy paper.
They will lead you
out of the darkness into the light,
right now, if you write now.

Playing in the Dark

Hear that tune
singing to itself in your head.
It may not stay like the fading memory
　　　of a seventies hit . . .but there is nothing shameful
　　　in forgetting.
Feel how one hand presses the strings,
　　　the other plucks,
　　　aiding each other, working together,
　　　pulling a song from the depths
　　　of uncertainty.
It may be a strangely-marked bird,
　　　or an exotic flower that only lasts
　　　one evening
　　　but causes the sun to rise again.

FIGURE 3.2. Continued.

Words Before Morning, *by Bruce Novak*

Morning has not come
But I keep writing.
And writing.
"Words, words, words"
And more words—
Crying their urgency
And mine.
Hoping someone,
Some where will hear.
But will they?
Who knows?

But I keep writing.
And writing.
And—some days—
Like, maybe, today,
Waking before the sun
And writing—urgently—
I pull the words
And they pull me
And something opens.
May be a door!
With some one on the other side!
And *without* these words,
Coming in the dark,
Who knows?

Notes:
Who knows if morning will come?
the vision
take care not to cover
practice will reveal
words that pulled you
crying their urgency
opened
to make the sun rise again

Process: The poem was written in under two minutes, before sunrise, after a short night's sleep. On looking at my notes, I see I obscured "the vision" and "will reveal" and "the sun" in the poem itself—something untypical for me. I wanted to hold on to the tentativeness and let go of seeing and knowing for sure for the richness of imagining that possible person on the other side of the door. *Editing:* I put the italics on "maybe" and divided the word, as I also did for "some one." I then separated "somewhere" in the first stanza, added "maybe" in the second, and italicized "without" near the end. I considered adding "(u)" within "morning" in the title, but decided against it. Everything else is just as it came to me.

Thoughts: I like the ending. The way it captures the tentativeness, the hope, and the irreducibility of how we take chances to find friends, and can't find them otherwise. And I also like how I skirt my usual "confident" visionariness throughout—showing a bit of how we use the creative process for reflective growth.

FIGURE 3.2. Continued.

And She, Sleeping in a hospital bed, *by Jeff Wilhelm*

Now—
There is urgency—
A pressure on the heart—
To be done with it:
To heal and be healed.
In the night,
You are afraid,
yet all is uncovered
And you would not cover it again
Although who knows
If the morning will come.
From the depths of unknowing
you suddenly know—
falcons cry
and take flight,
Their talons
unleash your heart
And beat the wind
And suddenly your heart
is released—
And breaks into blossom—
And wills the sun
to rise again.

---

this conversation and become a full member of this community. Even if it doesn't fully work for you—it can't always work for everyone—you'll at least gain some direct experience of the kind of aesthetic meaning-making processes we'll be discussing. And if it does work for you, you'll have all the more reason to read on.

This process encapsulates the "transubstantiation" process we've been referring to in a fairly pure way: how literature is a gift of life from one person to another, and how that life can give birth to even more life as we see how others have re-created it. Putting your poem against the eight others, you can see them as sisters and brothers, living with no sibling rivalry; each takes the genetic material in the original poem and brings a different form of new life to that material, which in turn helps illuminate what the others brought forth. They can be set together in a gallery to make a single exhibit, or into a chapbook as variations on a theme, and they are turns in a human conversation. All "are alive in each other" (Pradl, 1996) and create a sense of "multeity in unity"; both the poems and the people who wrote them "grow together."

A century ago, the realm of aesthetics was held to be the realm of "art for art's sake." (The dissertation that Louise Rosenblatt wrote at the Sorbonne, *L'art pour l'art* (1931), was, in fact, a refutation of this very doctrine.) What Dissanayake brought us to see in biological terms, and Rico, here, brings us to see pedagogically, is that art actually is *"life for life's sake"*: One person's embodiment of meaning that can be "transubstantiated" into another's, under the right circumstances. The process is not magical or mysterious here. We can understand it. It requires three elements: a creator, a transitional object, and a re-creator or responder. The creator pours something of herself into the object; the re-creator or responder imbibes it; then pours something new out of himself in response. And the fact that this intercourse occurs at a temporal and spatial distance makes it potentially more, not less meaningful. Just as Laura's writing gained power after her death, so does any artistic creation, when it is received by others in a different time and made into new meaning by them. This process literally transports the experience of meaningful life across time and space in a way that creates mutual understanding across personal and cultural differences—quite an important development in evolutionary history!

Art is a cultural practice, a *meme* (pronounced mem), but a very special kind of meme that we think deserves a special name—and this name will be the one original contribution of this chapter. The "transubstantiation" that Rosenblatt and her teacher, the philosopher John Dewey, called "transaction" might in biological terms be called a *mimeme* (pronounced me´mem), playing on the Greek term *mimesis*, or "creative imitation," which since ancient times has been central to the discussion of art in the West. Rosenblatt's "efferent/aesthetic" distinction might well be termed a "meme/mimeme" distinction. Many, many cultural practices—memes pure and simple—require an exact knowledge of "how" they are to be performed: recipes, surgeries, and the like. George Hillocks (1996) calls this "procedural knowledge." Other, particularly special, practices—which Rosenblatt and Dewey called "transactions" and that *we* are now calling "mimemes"—evolved to be re-created, reinterpreted, effecting not just translation, pure and simple, but renewal, a re-creation that occurs through the passing on of life—powerful insights, inspirations, ideas, feelings and the like—*over time*. "Mimemes," in other words, are memes with an evolutionary life process built into them. Through them, habits of self- and cultural transformation are naturally acquired. Here we have the *evolutionary* source of our "being the change!"

Dissanayake spoke of art in general as "the behavior of making special"; but considered in this transactional, "mimeme"-centered way, art—and, more broadly considered, the aesthetic feeling that can be experienced apart from particular art works when life itself is artfully experienced—is behavior that makes not just "things," but "times" special. This is why the awareness of making meaning was so precious to Elbow and so many others at the Wye conference—the process of meaning making is the process of finding and becoming wide awake to life in *moments* of life.

This is the point where we need to tie the biological processes we've been describing into philosophical understandings of the meaning and value of those processes. If "reading is seeing," as another of Jeff's titles (Wilhelm, 2004/2011c) has it, it is seeing *in moments*, and not just about how those moments are immediately felt, but how they are tied meaningfully to other moments and modes of time.

REGAINED HORIZONS: SEEING HUMAN TIME *AS* NARRATIVE

Howard Gardner's seven "multiple intelligences" from his 1983 work *Frames of Mind* are well known to many teachers. Far fewer know that he has since added two more to his list: "naturalist" intelligence, which appreciates the diversity and interconnectedness of life (owing much to E. O. Wilson); and "existential" intelligence, which he defines as "spiritual concerns . . . approached in a . . . personal, . . . creative manner" (Gardner, 1999). Actually, Gardner was quite tentative about this last form of intelligence. He didn't want to include "spirituality" in general as a form of intelligence, as many had urged him to do, because he didn't believe it to be assessable. He thought existential intelligence was *potentially* assessable, but didn't know how to assess it—hence its tentative status.

We think that this form of spiritual intelligence can be readily assessed—as it is in fact assessed all the time in ordinary human life, whenever we assess the personal meaning of any given moment in time—once we understand the way "mimemes" work. For this we are going to call on the existential philosopher Paul Ricoeur,[3] whose three-volume *Time and Narrative* (1984–88) sets forth how time itself, conceived in human rather than mechanical terms, is narrative *in nature*, perceived as stories and interpretable as stories are. *Human* time does not consist of a simple, linear past, present, and future of discrete moments connected by purely mechanical, interactive cause and effect. Human time—or what we could call "transactional time"—is, literally, "story time." It consists of a "present-present" experienced as *alively* present, not just as a mere chronological "now"; "a present-past," a historical horizon experienced as feeding *givingly* into the aliveness of the present moment; and a "present-future," a temporal horizon into which we see the present feeding, which it is our moral task to act to feed and *give of ourselves* as responsibly as we can. Ricoeur calls these three dimensions of human time "mimeses"—mimesis$_1$ being the present-past; mimesis$_2$, the present-present; and mimesis$_3$, the present-future. We propose, and will work to clearly establish through the rest of this book, that what Dewey and Rosenblatt called a "transaction" and we are calling a "mimeme," is experience in which all three dimensions of human story time are implied: an alive present moment of experience that both evokes a meaningful inheritance from the past and invokes a meaningful legacy for the future of the person experiencing it.

When you wrote your "re-creation," you most likely felt each of these three dimensions of time. Something in the poem first awoke you to the "present-present" of story time, just as something actually awoke Levertov from a condition of literal sleep. Then, as you responded to the various words and phrases that struck you, you came to see the poem as a gift, a creation of the author, coming from the past, that had *somehow* been meant for you. You yourself were "writing in the dark," finding composed meaning in what was written without yet, most likely, being able to see its precise meaning *for you* at this moment. Finally, as you wrote your "re-creation," you were able to see that new existential meaning, its meaning for you—again, echoing what happens in the poem itself, your poem being both a kind of flower "that blooms / only once in a lifetime" and a new source of light for your own life "that may have the power / to make the sun rise again" for you through its insight, qualitatively affecting your future from this present moment.

This was the "magical" power that Bruce's friend found when he did this activity for the first time with a group of total strangers. This "copoiesis" or co-creation draws directly on the power of story time that evolved over time in the human species. And once we understand its elements, we have gone quite some way in understanding "the power of softness" we saw draw out the humanity, first of Laura, then of so many others in the last chapter. But it's not quite so mystical anymore. It comes right out of life itself and how it has evolved to help us appreciate and extend its specialness.

Once we see the elements of story time, it's fairly easy to see how we assess existential intelligence within it. We do so precisely in the terms that make stories "good" ones: Does it immerse us somehow in immediately experienced life (mimesis$_2$)? Does it make our previous individual and/or collective experience of life more understandable and meaningful (mimesis$_1$)? Does it open for us new horizons of possible life (mimesis$_3$)? Most important, does it do all these together?

What makes existential intelligence intelligible in the first place is our willingness to center our lives in aesthetic, transactional, existential story time. Once we see the memic laws of efferent knowledge as set within the broader "mimemic" aesthetic horizons of story time, life as a whole becomes meaning-centered rather than rule-centered.[4] It becomes a storied path we make by walking not just a race course already laid out for us ("race course" being the meaning of the Latin word *curriculum*).

Seeing our lives as stories leads us, first, to see others' lives in the same way, as intertwined, for better or worse, with our own—as Jeff, in *You Gotta BE the Book,* observed how important it was for him to see that he would always, for better or worse, play the role "seventh-grade teacher" within the drama of every single one of his students' lives. This is the relationship we'll examine later when we discuss the transactional elements of teaching in Chapter 7. Second, it leads us to see the collective life we lead with others—in communities, societies, and historic peoples, and also as a species—in story form, in which the past and future, the history we inherit and the history we make, come greatly into play. Finally, we come to see life itself as an evolved and evolving story in which each of us plays an important and essential role. How we can teach to these deepest dimensions of story time will occupy the last two chapters of this book: on aesthetic democracy and aesthetic humanity.

ADDING UP RICOEUR AND ROSENBLATT: THE THREE DIMENSIONS OF MIMESIS AND THE THREE DIMENSIONS OF THE READER'S RESPONSE

When Dewey spoke of the central importance to modern life of understanding and cultivating "transactional mentality" in his late work *Knowing and the Known*, it was in terms of understanding and activating "the right, namely, to open our eyes to see . . . the right to see together, extensionally and durationally, much that is talked of conventionally as if it were composed of irreconcilable separates" (Dewey & Bentley, 1949, p. 69). Transactional mentality is inherently aesthetic in nature: It brings seemingly separate strands of experience together into a new whole with new possibilities; it "lives *into*" life (a direction Cristy Bruns gives her students when they read literature); it feels it so it can see it and live it anew. In his earlier work *Art As Experience* (1934), Dewey spoke of the nature of aesthetic experience in terms of the "flow" it evokes:

> Every successive part flows freely, without seam and without unfilled blanks, into what ensues. At the same time, there is no sacrifice of the self-identity of the parts. A river, as distinct from a pond, flows. But its flow gives a definiteness and interest to its successive portions greater than exist in the homogeneous portions of a pond. In an experience, flow is from something to something. As one part leads into another and as one part carries on what went before, each gains distinctness in itself. The enduring whole is diversified by successive phases that are emphases of its various colors. (p. 43)

Ricoeur's matrix for understanding the narrative flow of human time helps us see the process of aesthetic flow as longer and deeper than that of a single experience of a single individual. And Jeff's laying out of the three dimensions of transactional responsiveness taps into that same depth.

What Ricoeur calls mimesis$_2$, the present-present, is what Jeff calls the *evocative dimension* of response: the immediate imaginative call of the story world to the reader's mind that Dewey refers to, on the surface, in the passage above.

What Ricoeur calls mimesis$_1$ the present-past, is what Jeff calls *the connective dimension*, the understanding that authorial and cultural meanings have been embedded in aesthetic texts and that, as we connectively infer these meanings, we connect the flow of our own lives to the deep flow of the historical and cultural past. We recognize that the play of our imagination has been intentionally rendered through a gift, the Winnicottian "transitional object" that connects us—insofar as we are able to summon up a positive, "transactional" response to it—to the mental life of its creator who gave that gift to us in the hope that we would both enjoy it on its own terms and, in addition, bond personally in subtle ways through this gift, just as children playing with their teddy bears bond with their parents.

The connective dimension is the dimension through which art is "cultural parenting." Wayne C. Booth, in *The Rhetoric of Fiction* (1961), coined what has become a well-known literary term for this: the *implied author*. When we read transactionally, we don't connect with the historical author, the flesh-and-blood person who wrote. But we do connect with an imagined beneficent person who created something for us, not just to give us immediate, playful pleasure, but to find meaning that can seriously enrich our lives. (In Chapter 5 we'll reconstruct how each of the eight readers of "Writing in the Dark" did this with Denise Levertov.)

If, as Dewey says in the above passage "in an experience, flow is from something to something," if aesthetic experiences in general have beginnings, middles, and ends—*artistically created* aesthetic experiences seek also to flow from someone to someone, from one human source into another, through the care that is evoked for the presented life world. Implied authors evoke, not just pleasure, but a new capacity for beneficence, for care and doing good, in those who feelingly receive their feelingly embodied gifts.

This is where the third and most important dimension of narratively conceived human time and transactional aesthetic experience enters in: what Ricoeur called mimesis$_3$, the present-future, and what Jeff calls the *reflective dimension* of the reader's response. This is the dimension where Gardner's "existential intelligence" comes fully to bear, and where narrative time becomes consciously evolutionary. The reflective dimension involves the finding of meaning illuminating how we might rethink and relive our own lives. The connections we make to authorial and cultural meanings help us find new insights into our own past, present, and future lives—help us, not just to experience life more feelingly and fully, but to decide to live better lives than we might otherwise have done.

Another passage in Dewey's *Art As Experience* (1934) directly depicts this process of *transpersonal* transactional "flow":

> No [person] is eloquent save when someone is moved as [they] listen. Those who are moved feel . . . that what the work expresses is as if it were something one had oneself been longing to express. . . . In the end, works of art are the only media of complete and unhindered communication between [persons] that can occur in a world full of gulfs and walls that limit community of experience. (p. 110)

Art provides "unhindered communication," not because there is perfect understanding of authorial intent, but because the flow of life that it connects people's lives and life experiences one to another. This transpersonal flow of experience—when our reading, writing, and teaching are able to fully evoke it—forms quite a large part of art's educative power. And if we are aware that this flow did not originate entirely in the self-contained mind of the implied author, but that that mind and creative capacity were themselves formed by the gifts of others ad infinitum, then the experience of the flow of art connects us, and the flow of our lives, into the flow of life itself. As we respond to art, we understand that we, too, have the capacity to aesthetically evoke beneficence in others around us. This is the dynamic connection between the evocation of aesthetic response and the evocation of moral responsibility for others and the world: *It creates the desire to keep the flow of life going.* Insofar as the mentality of transaction is, as Dewey said, the recognition of the human "right to see" beyond both conventional standards and divisive issues, it is also the recognition of our ability to feel, to see, and to actively facilitate the flow of life.

INTRODUCING THE FIELD OF PERSONAL STUDIES

Here at last we get to tell you how we think "English" should be renamed. But first, a little background.

In the 1930s, the subject of social studies became an integral part of the American K–12 curriculum, decentering and to some extent replacing history. This was not just a junior version of the academic "social sciences," as you can easily see from the decade in which this subject suddenly became popularly received. From very near the onset of the Great

Depression, people were *ready* for a new understanding of the various ways that people were connected to one another. [See Dickstein's *Dancing in the Dark* (2009) for a moving depiction of how this was manifested in the cultural life of that time—which, in a way, was a massive, collective "writing in the dark."] One of Dewey's students, Harold Rugg, had a curriculum ready for that, and the textbooks that proceeded from it sold like hotcakes in the early part of the decade, even before the election and then the stirring oratory of Franklin Roosevelt that helped the people as a whole actually connect with one another (Kliebard, 1995). In Dewey's later adopted terms, though, "social studies" is fundamentally about how people *inter*act. It is not centrally about how people transact *feelingly* with one another—how they form meaningful relationships and communities, rather than just cooperating more effectively through the recognition of their likenesses and differences. More than that, social studies, though it can be recast in suprahuman, ecological terms, is not fundamentally about how humans connect existentially as individual beings, either to others or to life.

For that we need a new discipline, a discipline both complementary to social studies and intentionally and explicitly making deeper and more human connections to the flow of life itself. "Personal studies" does these things, though we, of course, need to make clear somehow—perhaps without using Dewey's terms with our students—that we mean "personal" in a "transactional" rather than merely "self-actional" way. We originally wanted to name this book "Personal Studies: Literacy for Love and Wisdom," but soon realized with others' help that the shift was too radical at this point to be put in a title, or even the table of contents. So we put our original subtitle up front and added another one: "'Being the Book' and 'Being the Change'." This, we felt, in a time in which the American people clearly, at least for an interval, responded to a call for transformative change, said the same thing in clearer and more immediate language.

We all know change is coming, one way or another; and a good many of us sense that we are all responsible for whether that change is beneficent or destructive, evolutionary or devolutionary. We are becoming convinced of many inconvenient truths that most or all of us—not just a few leaders—will have to take responsibility for addressing to avoid consequences that will be absolutely devastating.

"Personal Studies" would be a discipline explicitly intended to elicit the change we truly need: the natural cultivation of beneficent responsibility among democratic citizens, precisely through the deliberate cultivation of the "transactional mentality" of aesthetic responsiveness that Dewey thought was the sole force that in the end could save the human world from the "chaos" into which it had been plunged by modern life. This move will get us to the heart of the matter of teaching "English," both as it was laid out by visionaries like Schiller, Emerson, and Arnold before it became "English," and as it is actually seen and taught by the majority of its practitioners in Britain and the United States, as shown, respectively, by Goodwyn (2005) and Grossman and Stodolsky (1996). But it will also take us to the heart of the matter of teaching and education more generally, in all subject matters, insofar as they seek to educationally draw out the feeling humanity of students engaged in the world, not *just* instruct them in efferent facts and procedures.

The time to institute Personal Studies is now, at the same time as we seek to *inter*actively solve our social, political, and ecological problems. In the meantime, each of us can integrate transactional elements into our teaching and classroom projects, no matter the subject or conditions under which we teach. The deliberate cultivation of life, love, and wisdom would hardly be a bad thing under any conditions; in the conditions under which we now live, our very survival is in peril unless we collectively decide to cultivate these things, to "change the way we think," as Einstein said, from self-actional and interactional toward transactional mentality. We need, now, to collectively choose life. And we need to help "English/ language arts/literacy" teachers, of all people, to help us do so!

So, let's start to explore the dynamics of how we can help this happen: first, as we revisit Jeff's three dimensions of responsiveness to literature in the next three chapters; then, as we explore, in the third part of the book, how those same dynamics can be brought to bear on the basic understandings of education, of democracy, and of the development and potential of our species, that we convey through our teaching.

Part II

THE WAY LIFE TEACHES
Revisiting the Three Dimensions of Aesthetic, Transactional Responsiveness

Everyone is a story. . . . It is the way that wisdom gets passed along. The stuff that helps us to live a life worth remembering . . . and to remember that the real world is made up of just such stories. . . . It's the way life teaches us how to live. . . . Hidden in all stories is the One story. The more we listen, the clearer that Story becomes. Our true identity, who we are, why we are here, what sustains us, is in this story. . . . Stories that touch us in this place of common humanness awaken us and weave us together as a family once again.

—Rachel Remen, *Kitchen Table Wisdom*

CHAPTER 4

The Evocative Dimension
Story Time and Human Life

The first question we need to ask about how we are to teach the complex three-dimensional matrix of story time to our students is simply, How do we get them out of chronological time and into story time? Without this, there is only the Scylla of standards-centered grammar on the one hand and the Charbydis of issue-centered grammatology on the other. Their reading will be either merely mechanical and structural or merely critical and deconstructive. Certainly, valid understandings and life skills can be taken from either of these kinds of reading. But the life of literature—and the value for life itself that it evokes in us—will either be totally lost on such readers or, at best, will be found only in the private space of their reading but not in the more public space of the classroom.

George Hillocks's students know how vitally important the construction of "gateway activities" is in the teaching of units of literature. This is what Jeff calls "frontloading" in his book *Strategic Reading* (Wilhelm, Baker, & Dube, 2001), which followed from Hillocks's work. These activities activate what students already care about and know, so these prior interests and knowledge can be used as resources for learning something new and also put students in situations that open them to personal and social points of contact in what they will read. What we explore in this chapter is how literature itself works in its fundamental nature as frontloading for and a gateway to life. It evokes life in us, immerses us in immediate feeling—in what Ricoeur called the "present-present," the "there-ness" of palpable aesthetic experience aware of itself as experience—and helps teach us to live life fundamentally for life's sake, for a deepened sense of life rather than merely for outward, efferent ends. This is important in and of itself, but it is also the prerequisite to entering the deeper dimensions of literary reading.

There are three stages of pedagogically evoking the evocative dimension of literature. Before reading, we first evoke students' lives in ways that will help make their reading come alive for them and prepare them for success in negotiating whatever challenges a particular reading might make for them. While reading, we evoke students' sense of life, engaging them in creative activities that plunge them into immediate story worlds and immerse them in characters' lives and situations. Surrounding reading, we evoke life itself, imagining and constructing, as carefully and artfully as we can, curriculum we believe will help students develop not only an understanding of the world they live in as capable of supporting their own flourishing, if they attend closely to it, but also an understanding of how the world needs our help if it is itself to continue to flourish. This is the essence of inquiry: The intensely personal is connected intimately to the material at hand, and this is connected back to the world. The interconnectedness and interdependence of the self, text, and world is explored and highlighted.

We're going to focus on frontloading activities here, which are the most fundamental and mirror the frontloading of literature itself—stressing the two other forms of evoking story worlds as we discuss teaching the connective and reflective dimensions of literature in the next two chapters and, as we discuss, teaching itself in Chapter 7.

FRONTLOADING: EVOKING LIFE TO EVOKE ART

It's the first day of the fourth quarter of the school year. Jeff spends the first two periods of the day in Rachel's Senior AP English classes. They are beginning a new unit on satire, parody, and absurdism framed with the essential question: "What work does humor do?" The first subquestion of the unit is: "What is funny?" Over the spring break the students have been asked to post something that they think is tremendously funny on the class wiki. The only rule is that what they post must not offend their parents nor the principal.

Astonishingly, although students are only required to do a single posting, every single student has posted at least three items. Many have posted six or more items. The students have all been reading each other's posts and doing preliminary rankings of the various postings on a scale of "funniness." Most of them continue posting and reading each other's posts well into the unit, as indicated by their comments on the wiki but also how they enter the classroom and comment to each other, "That YouTube video you posted was *so* NOT funny." or "I showed my family your cartoon and we laughed our heads off."

This first day is devoted to starting off with frontloading the unit, the last unit of the year before the class begins specific preparations for the AP test. Rachel projects the wiki onto the screen at the front of the room. The class views the different postings and the students rate the funniness of the different examples, identify the kind of funny (slapstick, misdirection joke, parody, irony, satire, pastische, and so on) exhibited, and describe what moves contribute to the funniness. The students are seated in groups of four and after each example they think-pair-share with an elbow buddy, face buddy, or crisscross buddy to share individual thinking and to identify the kind of work that this particular example and kind of funny might do. The students leave class enthusiastically talking about the uses and power of different kinds of humor. Using the students' own texts and thinking, the class is well on the way of undertaking the substantive work of their unit.

Jeff next walks over to North Junior High School where he works in Andrew Porter's ninth-grade classroom. It is the first day of the *Romeo and Juliet* unit, framed by the essential/existential question: What makes and breaks relationships? Their first subquestion is, What should we look for and try to avoid in relationships? Andrew has asked the students to bring in MP3 files of favorite songs that deal with love and relationships, and he plays these over the class computer. As they listen, students are completing an opinionnaire about romantic relationships and writing about the statements that they most agree or disagree with. In their writing they answer the question, What makes you say so? and provide evidence from their lives about why they agree or disagree with the statements so strongly. It's a little bit chaotic, but the average-level freshmen are all highly engaged. After each song the person who brought it in must "testify" about why she likes the song, how the song makes her feel, and what it makes her think about love. Twice during the class Andrew insists to the class that they must now listen to one of his songs. They groan, but he insists and emotes about how "This is the greatest love song ever."

In both classes prodigious kinds of work are being done. First and foremost, the students are engaging with texts. The texts they engage with are their own choice of popular culture texts that already resonate with most of the students. They share their own favorite texts in ways that stake their identity. They are relating to texts and to each other, sometimes learning surprising things about one another. For example, in Andrew's class one Sudanese girl sings a bit of a tribal "promise" song and translates it for the class. She reveals that in her refugee camp she was promised to a future husband when she was only 12 years of age. The students are experiencing intense pleasure and even a measure of what we might call joy, even when they are resisting the funniness of a YouTube video or the quality of a love song. This is valuable work in and of itself.

But the work also helps them prepare for the future work of reading more complex texts and eventually canonical literature. Rachel continues next with studying jokes and two episodes of *The Simpsons* episodes featuring literary works, then ironic monologues from contemporary comedians, then Browning's "My Last Duchess," and then moves on to Swift's "A Modest Proposal," Voltaire's *Candide*, and Beckett's *Waiting for Godot*.

Andrew continues his unit with a study of dating surveys, love poems, and fables about love before moving on to *Romeo and Juliet*. As students read, they are connecting personally and intensely to the social meanings and purposes of the unit. They are evoking textual worlds and intense sensory experiences. These experiences allow them, in many ways, to evoke the life of language itself, their own and each other's lives, and their collective life together in this classroom and out in the world, both present and possible. These evocations make connections possible inside the texts they are sharing, across other texts, to the self, to each other, and to the world. This kind of evoking of the self and current identity, and the sharing and comparing of these with others, besides being pleasurable, is essential to democratic thinking and living.

THE PRACTICALITIES OF FRONTLOADING

Have you ever been told a joke that you didn't get? If you didn't give a fake laugh, you might have asked to have the joke explained, perhaps complaining that you "didn't get it." Once the joke was explained, you might have given a deadpan "ha-ha-ha". Why? Because you can't re-habilitate a joke. If you don't get it on its first telling, then it's just not going to be funny. Likewise, it is very difficult to rehabilitate a reading or composing assignment that has left the student struggling or failing. It is not motivating to feel incompetent. It *is* incredibly motivating to see your developing competence and this leads to a "continuing impulse to learn" (Smith & Wilhelm, 2002). We have both learned from the example and research of George Hillocks that teachers contribute much more to student learning by spending their time planning supportive instruction delivered before and during reading and writing than they do by respond-ing to student work after it is done. In sum, teachers are much better off proactively frontloading instruction and preparing students for success then reactively trying to correct and save a failed attempt.

Frontloading accesses the prior experience, values, and feelings of the reader so that these resources can be used to evoke the textual world and then converse with and learn from it. Without accessing students' preex-isting knowledge, these readers will have no resources to face the new challenge and create new meanings. If there is no resonance nor correla-tion between the world of the reader and the world of the text, there can be no meaning for the reader: The reader can make nothing of the text; no secondary world can be evoked and enjoyed. When some correlation does exist, the reader must first allow the text to continue triggering or enlivening his own memories, thoughts, and feelings, and then he must allow the text to shape that which it has drawn forth into a new experience and an ensuing conversation. This is much more likely to happen if the students' prior knowledge has been activated. Increasing interest, engaged and intense relating to characters, and imaginative visualization of the secondary story world can now proceed to fully evoke the experience of living.

To frontload her unit on "What work can humor do?" Rachel provided the following directions:

> Post at least one item (video, cartoon, joke, and so on) on your wiki page that you think is funny. Before we all return from spring break, view as many funny postings from your classmates as you can and rank the top five with an explanation of why you think each of these postings is funny and what makes it funny. On our first day of class we will view your favorites and classify them according to the genre of humor (irony, pastiche, misdirection joke, slapstick, satire, and so on) and the kind of work each kind of humor can do. The only rule is that anything you post should not offend your parents or the principal!

The postings on the wiki provided direct and immediate experience of humor that activated what the kids already knew and built upon this, since they read and enjoyed each other's postings, which often challenged or extended their own thinking about funniness.

The frontloading also provided assistance before any reading of assigned texts. After viewing two episodes of *The Simpsons* and naming the moves that made them laugh (which corresponded closely to the conventions of satire), the class began to read "A Modest Proposal" by Jonathan Swift. Rachel and Jeff provided assistance to help the students evoke that text through guided reading and thinking aloud, naming the same satiric conventions used in *The Simpsons,* as well as new ones. The frontloading with the wiki and *The Simpsons* episodes helped the students access their resources and get into the game, and allowed Rachel and Jeff to demonstrate enthusiasm and high expectations—to model the evocative reading and the moves that they later mentored the students to use, and then monitored how the students independently used these moves.

Throughout the unit, the class returned to the wiki, the classification of genres of "funny," and continued to flesh out their theory of different ways of being funny and the work that each can do.

Interestingly, students began to internalize very different reasons for being funny and even monitored each other's humorous remarks in class. For instance, they identified "silencing" as a reason to humorously speak

FIGURE 4.1. Frontloading Criteria Sheet

Please check your frontloading activity's quality by responding to the following questions prior to discussion of your frontloading in our seminar.

1. How does your activity/ies activate and build the students' prior knowledge or background experiences regarding your unit's essential question/inquiry theme?

2. How does the frontloading activity/ies work to motivate students for reading and the inquiry, forging interest, personal connections, and high expectations?

3. How might the frontloading activity/ies work to organize inquiry, setting purposes and consolidating learning about the inquiry throughout the unit, that is, how will it help students (1) set purposes for their reading, (2) focus their learning, (3) clarify what they are coming to understand, (4) help them to monitor their own growth, and (5) help them see how others see life in ways that both contrast with and add to the way they see it? How can the frontloading be returned to in various ways throughout the unit and also be used as a template for considering how personal understandings of life are changing?

what is unspeakable—either because it cannot be directly said, will be punished by repressive authority, or is politically incorrect or too painful to address directly. Such insights were recorded on the class anchor charts. The class was creating meaning that was applicable to their lives, instead of receiving from outside themselves what an authority thought they should know.

Jeff used a checksheet with the mentor and student teachers in his VPDS project to create discussion regarding their frontloading efforts (see Figure 4.1).

WHY DO WE READ LITERATURE?

Before continuing, we turn now to some frontloading "essential/existential questions" of our own: Why do we teach literature? Why do people read literature outside of school? Only by addressing these questions can we proceed in a conscious fashion to consider how best to help students evoke the richest experience of reading, and then how to reflect on this and use the experience.

To explore this, we invite you to take the survey shown in Figure 4.2.

We have found this activity a powerful one to do with teachers, with English departments, and with National Writing Project groups precisely because it makes us consider why we do what we do and brings our thinking and justifications about teaching literature to the conscious level. In some ways, it doesn't matter what people come up with or the nature of

FIGURE 4.2. Why Teach Literature?

Please rank the following statements in order from most (1) to least (16) important. Try to avoid ties. Expect frustration. Be prepared to justify your choices.

___ 1. To help young people explore their own feelings about literature
___ 2. To help young people explore their own feelings about their personal experience
___ 3. To introduce students to great literary treasures
___ 4. To introduce students to other cultures, especially those distant from their own experience
___ 5. To provide a meaningful context for learning to read and developing reading strategies
___ 6. To develop students' aesthetic sensibilities
___ 7. To develop critical thinking
___ 8. To provide a context for developing writing and writing skills
___ 9. To learn to "read the world" from a critical perspective
___ 10. To discuss timeless themes such as love, loss, identity
___ 11. To create an opportunity to discuss contemporary issues
___ 12. To help students think for themselves and create their own philosophies of life and living
___ 13. To help students live through experiences that are distant from them in time, place, and experience.
___ 14. To experience pleasure
___ 15. To educate the imagination and promote creativity
___ Other? _____

Talking points: How do these purposes relate to each other—which are prerequisite to others? What is in service of what? How can any of these purposes be related to personal or social transformation?

Source. Adapted from a workshop presentation by Deborah Appleman, based on her fabulous book *Critical Encounters in High School English*, 2009.

---

disagreements. What matters is that we articulate why we do what we do, so we can monitor how happy we are with our reasoning and how well we act out our beliefs. When we do this activity, we end up arguing that all of the purposes we value are tied first and foremost to the prerequisite of pleasure, and to the specific pleasure of evoking and living through a secondary world. Therefore, no matter what we want to achieve through the teaching and reading of literature, we must first evoke the text itself in ways that are pleasurable and can become meaningful to us. By pleasure we don't mean "fun" per se as much as we mean "resonant"—like a pebble hitting the pond of the self and sending waves through it from the point of immersion that is the pleasure of the text.

THE POWER OF PLEASURE AND
THE POWERLESSNESS OF PLEASURELESSNESS

In *"You Gotta BE the Book"* Jeff names the first of ten interdependent dimensions of literary response as "High expectation of the text to be read." All other forms of response followed from this prerequisite condition.

Yet in this and two other of Jeff's studies (Smith & Wilhelm, 2002; Wilhelm & Smith, in press) the engaged readers bifurcated reading into "home reading" (good—because it is pleasurable) and "school reading" (bad—because it is boring, disconnected, too hard, insipid, not useful, and so on). Ron, an informant for *"You Gotta BE the Book,"* had this to say: "Don't confuse school reading with my real reading."

Jeff's daughter Jasmine is a case in point. Jeff well remembers how she repeatedly refused to come to dinner or go to bed as a second grader because she was reading Lemony Snicket's *Series of Unfortunate Events.* She would lie on the couch and yell "Noooooo!" and "I can't believe it!" as she read. This state of affairs has persisted through her graduation from high school (with different books, of course) as she reads several books a week with the proverbial flashlight under the covers. But when she went abroad to be an exchange student in Tasmania, she left a pile of her schoolbooks, including *To Kill A Mockingbird* and *The Scarlet Letter*, on the woodpile next to the woodstove. When Jeff skyped her after her arrival in Hobart and asked her about this, she said, "It's my editorial comment on school reading" later adding, "at least those books would be good for starting a fire."

Kelly Gallagher (2009) has argued that the ways schools present and teach reading has led to what he calls "Readicide." J. Hillis Miller proclaims "the death of literature" (2002). How is it that reading and literature have "died"? We would argue that it is due to a focus on skills and strategies and away from the pleasures of reading, from a primary focus on critical reading and analysis instead of first emphasizing the evoking of the secondary worlds available to us from reading. The way we teach reading and literary texts takes us away from the enrapturing and immersive experiences that are prerequisite to all other powers that follow from the act of reading. Given that a high expectation of enjoyment is prerequisite to reading, creating this expectation and fulfilling it must be a first order of business for teachers.

Anyone who has consciously labored to teach reading and/or literature at the upper elementary to high school level knows the many ways in which school works against engagement and ignores the evocation of textual experience. Instead of seeing reading as skills or a form of scholarship, we need to first and foremost promote reading as good fun—perhaps good hard fun, but fun nonetheless. We need to foreground reading as an intensely satisfying transformational pleasure. We need to help students first read "with" a text, giving themselves over to it and stepping willingly inside it, before we ask them to read "against" it by stepping outside the text, considering and analyzing it.

Walter Slatoff (1970) observed that essential differences exist between the stance taken by a good reader and that taken by a good scholar, producing conflicts in reading education and literary study that are often unrecognized and at least unacknowledged: "differences between the kinds of detachment, objectivity, narrowing of interest and focus required in scholarship and the kinds of sympathy, engagement, general responsiveness and openness, and emotional susceptibility involved in good reading" (p. 25). The very skills and stances called for by reading educators and literature teachers are in many ways antithetical to the qualities necessary for a reader to completely evoke and engage with a literary work—for a reader to become and to be a reader.

Ironically, Jeff found that strategies and critical analysis can be learned with great engagement and joy after the fact of the evocative experience. But teachers often ask students to reflect on and analyze an experience that they never had, and were never assisted to have. One of the great tragedies of schooling is that we could so easily meet *all* of our purposes simply by widening our vision and reframing what is prerequisite and thus most important.

Jeff was recently asked by an interviewer about the ways in which school undermines reading. His answers are shown in Figure 4.3.

When the focus of instruction is solely on the *method* of reading—on definable skills that can be named, circumscribed and put into a curricular script that is easily taught or purveyed (in this case phonics drills and literal comprehension questions presented typically through worksheets), rather than on the *nonmethodical*—the deep, transformative and intensely personal, and situated kinds of understanding which give reading itself and any method for teaching it all of its ultimate meaning—is going to be lost through misdirection and a focus on the wrong prize, and reading will become nothing more than a "schoolish" and ultimately meaningless exercise. This is why "transaction" and the transformations in the self and the world that it can engender must be our focus. This is why skills, strategies, and concepts must be taught in the context of existential inquiry and in service of deepened personal understandings, not as an end in themselves but as a means to deepening understanding and new use.

Reading a text that is resonant with one's own concerns and experience, immersing oneself in a state of "flow experience" (Csikszentmihalyi, 1990; Smith & Wilhelm, 2002; 2006), developing visible signs of competence and control—these are all intense pleasures and sources of great empowerment and joy. If we wish to promote reading and teach for

FIGURE 4.3. Ten Easy Ways to Ruin Reading

- We teach texts that are too hard for our students, and that are too distant from their experiences and concerns. Instead of focusing on specific human beings (our students) and promoting the human activity of reading, we focus on texts. And we choose texts that are highly nuanced and written for expert adult readers, instead of from the rich sources of literature written particularly for students in their current state of being and stages of literacy development— children's and young adult literature. A related problem is that we define reading and "text" too narrowly and put students in a double bind: We marginalize the literacies that they do possess and are passionate about (e.g., gaming, teen zines, blogs, fan fiction, and so on) and therefore refuse to validate their current literacies, thereby denying them access to the only resources that would help them develop new kinds of literacies. Embracing the reading of popular culture would endorse our students as literate beings and provide us with the resources and a bridge to reach other kinds of literate development.
- We do not provide, negotiate, or explore the personally compelling purposes and social reasons to read, neither in general nor with particular texts.
- We assign texts but do not prepare students for success; we do not assist students to enter into and evoke textual worlds, expecting them to do this on their own though many readers and most struggling readers don't know how to enter into and evoke text.
- We assign texts but do not provide adequate time to read them.
- We often read excerpts instead of complete texts and therefore lose any sense of coherence, satisfaction, or closure. Instead of sitting back and savoring the experience of reading, reflecting on what has been experienced, students are taught that the end of reading is answering questions and doing activities at the end of a selection. What could be a bigger drag than that? We could do better by reading more shorter and complete texts and by working to experience these texts fully.
- We present texts as something to study instead of enjoy. We focus on social competence instead of what Patrick Shannon (2005) calls "the sociological imagination"— the capacity to read the story behind the story, to see what is unsaid and implied, to think about the consequences of particular stories or ways of thinking and being.
- We read to analyze instead of to experience. And we analyze to answer someone else's questions or to prove that we have read instead of to extend, deepen, and elaborate on our experience.
- We focus on what we want kids to know and how we want them to read and who we want them to be in some distant future instead of on engaging them as who they actually are today.
- Teachers play the judge before playing the advocate, the referee before they are the coach. We need to approach literacy the other way around—modeling and mentoring, coaching and facilitating, doing literacy for and with students before we monitor and evaluate, asking them to do it by themselves. We need to provide "grace" to students in terms of providing time and assistance and support and encouragement— and allow them to make mistakes and misfires so necessary to growth—so that they can develop the self-generosity that is necessary to take risks and grow as literate beings (see Newkirk, 2009).
- We neglect to emphasize and celebrate the considerable pleasures of reading. Who would ever want to read if it was not a pleasure to do so? After ruining reading for the whole school year, many schools require summer reading of the same kinds of texts and with the same tasks, thereby ruining reading for the remaining three months of the year. As Tom Newkirk expresses: Put more axiomatically, *unless we can persuade students that reading is a form of deep sustained pleasure, they will not choose to read; and because they will not choose to read, they will not develop the skills to make them good readers* (p. 117; emphasis in original).

transformation, then we must attend to these possibilities of reading. Everything else that is taught in the name of reading must be done in service of these energizing higher purposes.

Jeff is currently completing a study of students who love to read texts that are marginalized by school, such as fantasies, video game novels and video game texts, shock literature like Chuck Pahluniak, and graphic novels and manga. One thing that has struck him about the initial domain analysis is the intense psychic pleasures that his students get from their reading, the archetypal energies they face and fully embrace, the shadow elements of themselves that are brought to bear whether in fully conscious or somewhat unconscious ways. In other words, what they love to read is personally compelling and pleasurable at the same time that it challenges who the reader is and how she thinks (Wilhelm & Smith, in press).

Ron, a student profiled in *"You Gotta BE the Book,"* offers this description of the process of immersing oneself in the world of the text.

> When you're not into a book yet, it's really obvious [laughs]. It's like you're standing in line for the diving board on a windy day and you're freezing your nuts off, if you'll excuse the expression [laughs]. Where was I? Oh yeah. It's like you're in pain and you have your arms wrapped around you and the concrete is scratching your feet. The first part of the story is the line and the ladder and the board. When everything comes together and you jump, it's like you're in this underwater world like INSTANTLY and then you just stay down there and never come up until someone makes you. (p. 77)

For Ron, engaging with a work of fiction feels so much like immersing himself it is like diving and staying underwater, reluctant to come up. Arriving and dwelling in that secondary world is as all-consuming as the experience of total submersion. He is so utterly eager to enter this alternative world that he physically experiences his anticipation.

Cora, another informant from *"You Gotta BE the Book,"* interrupts a think aloud to observe: "It's almost like I've stopped reading and I'm dreaming, I guess."

This is the foundational experience we want for readers that makes all else possible. This is the prerequisite to learning and transformation through literature. Concentrating on evoking textual experience and preparing students attitudinally, conceptually, and procedurally for success seems to us to be the best use of our time in the classroom.

Jeff's work with the evocative dimension makes these two essential points: first, that the ability to re-create the secondary world of the text within oneself and to enter into that world is not natural or universal but for many students must be explicitly highlighted, actively supported, and cultivated over time; second, that the capacity to evoke text is the basis of all reading, all enjoyment in reading, and the prerequisite to all the lofty goals we have for readers and human beings through the teaching and reading of literature. Evoking secondary worlds makes possible the transitional and transformational use of literature—the connecting and reflecting that involves the consideration of one's experience with a text and can lead to reconsidering one's self and relationships to the world. Evoking the text is a kind of "world making" that makes all other forms of world making possible.

PLAY'S THE THING

On the basis of playing is built the whole of [humanity]'s experiential existence.

—D. W. Winnicott, *Playing and Reality*

Why are "text" and "world" necessary to one another? And if playful or imaginative world making is fundamental to all other forms of world making, where does reality lie? Here we would like to tie Jeff's prior work with the evocative dimension of response back to the evolutionary development of our species. For once we see how it was that the flowing "dream" state that Cora and others have learned to access in their reading evolved for reasons that have been key to our survival as a species, it will be much easier to justify evocative teaching as a central means to our continued surviving—and, perhaps, thriving—by tapping into those "acres of Edens" Toni Morrison (2008/1996) has said lie "inside ourselves" and can lead to a newly "unfettered" future for our species.

In *Play: How It Shapes the Brain, Opens the Imagination, and Invigorates the Soul* (2009), Stuart Brown documents the neurological and ethological research showing how play is the central complex of behaviors evolutionarily developed to facilitate learning and social bonding among mammals. Social imagination is facilitated through members' sportive, artful, innovative participation within loosely rule-governed frameworks lying comfortably between the extremes of total anarchy and total standardization. There is actual evolutionary truth to the saying "All work and no play makes Jack a dull boy."

Much of the controversy we have seen between the standards-driven and the issue-driven curriculum might be resolved by our seeing how the most important learning of all may occur in our coming into play with one another. Of course, in some ways Rachel's and Andrew's frontloading were both issue driven: They engaged students in inquiry about what "funny" and "love" were, and no full agreement was possible (except for the fact that all his students completely agreed that Andrew's choice of love songs was totally stupid!). But the point was not really to come to agreement, or for these understandings to compete with one another, but for the various understandings and the people holding them to come into play. In fact, we'd interpret the success of Rachel's and Andrew's frontloading—and of their teaching moves in general—as largely due to how they open up a space of imaginative play for their students. Accompanying their having a high expectation of what is being read, written, and learned, they have a playful attitude toward learning and accept risk taking and mistakes with grace, accepted as a natural part of learning and often as something to laugh about. They see reading and writing as "play that does work" and "work that helps us play." They are able to joke and have fun with their students. Most of all, they enjoy reading and writing, and they enjoy their students and the process of learning together in a classroom.

Humor, of course, immediately turns life into play. Highlighting the absurdity of what we ordinarily take seriously, for instance, serves to put a temporary stay to the efferent task-drivenness of so much of teaching and learning. And, as all good teachers know, humor also serves to lighten heavy tasks. Though humor can serve very serious purposes—think of the satire of comedians Jon Stewart and Stephen Colbert, which has come to serve as the main source of news for American college students in this early part of the century—it serves, first, to shake us out of our ordinary efferent "reality" by creating an alternate space of possibility for aesthetic play. Behind the irony and fun, this creative space always offers a promise that things could be different.

Humor and courtship (topics of Rachel's and Andrew's featured units here) are two longstanding cultural practices in which we learn and show how we have learned to "play well with others." What we want to show next, though, is more precisely why and how the space of play is also the space where we appear humanly to one another, and how the evocative dimension of response works by opening this space of personal and social play within the mind. This is where we will come to understand the relationship between playing, our sense of reality, and human possibility.

THE POEM AND THE WORLD:
INDUCING FLOW THROUGH IMMERSION IN THIRD SPACE

The psychological process through which evocative play occurs in literary reading is depicted with great care, thoroughness, and sophistication by Cristina Bruns in *Why Literature?* (2011). Before we begin to speak in more depth about how we as teachers can help our students leave chronological time and enter story time, we need to bring in one more idea—an idea Bruns actually arrived at through reading Jeff's *"You Gotta*

BE the Book," but took one step further. This idea is that in the process of imagining story worlds we need somehow to lose our selves in those worlds, allowing ourselves to become "immersed" in them (echoing Ron's diving metaphor above), in order for them to become aesthetically evocative for us:

> The literary transaction . . . is largely an immersive mode of engagement, as Rosenblatt urges the reader to become fully absorbed in the experience of the "poem" as he evokes it from the text, attending to the experience itself just as one might attend to an experience of a symphony or a rock concert. Central to such absorption or immersion in an experience is a loss or diminishment of self-consciousness as the self becomes preoccupied with the unfolding experience of the object, in this case, the literary work . . . as we allow it to take us to unknown places within ourselves. (pp. 54, 56)

In Chapter 6, we will see how this "losing" of ourselves is critical in enabling us to reflectively "refind" ourselves. What we want to emphasize here is that along with the active process of imagining story worlds is also a process of acquiesence, *loosening* of our selves, "letting our selves go" in the flow of these imagined worlds. Rosenblatt's "transactional poem" is evoked, in part, by our giving the texts we encounter permission, as Bruns says, "to take us to unknown places within ourselves." By temporarily relinquishing our selves, we are able to better immerse ourselves in the flow of life.

What Bruns emphasizes most of all is that without the understanding of the primacy of this immersive, evocative process in the teaching of literature—by students and teachers alike—Scholes's (1998) "textual power" and Appleman's (2000) "critical lenses," can only use literature to criticize life from outside it, not renew it from within. The other side of this is that learning to become immersed in aesthetic texts can become instrumental in students' learning to become immersed in learning itself, and—no less important—to become immersed in and with one another.[1] This is why the opening of the evocative dimension of aesthetic experience may be fundamental to the creation of the full-fledged democracy of people seeking to "grow together," as we shall explore later in Chapter 8. We don't grow together through an issue-centered curriculum debating the essential meaning of common concepts; we may grow more reasonable and like-*minded,* but even then it is only abstract concepts that we share, not how ideas are played out in life. We grow together as human beings only through becoming mutually immersed in the flow of one another's life processes—as we saw happening so vividly in Gabriele Rico's "re-creation" exercise in the last chapter.

It is what Rosenblatt called "the poem" that makes the world our shared home. By temporarily suspending the boundaries that normally exist between "self" and "other" and "self" and "world," the fantasy world of "the poem" opens transitional space in the world, what Winnicott calls a "third space" *between* the "subjective" and the "objective," in which we learn to travel in one another's worlds. We freely create a common reality through our being mutually—even though differently—immersed in the flow of experience. The shared immersion helps us accommodate our differences, makes those differences literally "inter-est"-ing, as shared, related *being*—as we saw in comparing the fraternally related poetic "re-creations" of "Writing in the Dark."

Immersion in the evocative dimension of the text is how we start the journey, how we *enter* the flow. In the next chapter we explore how through the connective dimension we acquire traveling *companions*. And in the following one we will explore how through the reflective dimension we acquire new *destinies*, new bents, and new vistas for our individual and collective journeys, how "being the book" frees us to "be the change." But this new connection and transformation both depend on the initial, freeing experience of aesthetic immersion. We don't get to "being the change" without first in some way "being the book."

To conclude, we believe that reading must first and foremost be about building an expectation of pleasure and then evoking the pleasures of the text, which means evoking the pleasures of the possible, the pleasures of imagination, the vividness of language, of metaphor, beauty, and personal truth. It is about evoking the students' actual lives and their possible lives, and the actual and possible lives of cultures and the planet. In this evoked vividness of experience lies tacit understanding of what life is and could be: awareness both of actual experience, values, and feelings, and of new possibilities of what we can experience, value, and feel.

Given all the life that we can evoke through our teaching, it is extremely troubling that teaching seems less fun to most teachers than it has at any time during our thirty-plus-year teaching careers. We think that this is because teaching is being put under ever more mechanized pressure to achieve constrained skills and information rather than higher unconstrained functions. The notion of teaching as an artistic, creative, and imaginative endeavor is being lost in favor of information and skills delivery and test preparation. In turn, the idea of reading, writing, *and living* as creative and imaginative pursuits is also, sadly, lost on students. And when imagination and creativity are lost in the educative socialization process, then so is the possibility of personal and cultural transformation lost to society as a whole. These are the ultimate stakes of a curriculum that centers itself on the static organization of efferent information and skills rather than on evoking the flow of aesthetic immersion in life! So let us continue seeing what can happen once that flow gets going.

CHAPTER 5

The Connective Dimension

Finding Love by Sharing Insight with Implied Authors

Reading is an intimate act, perhaps more intimate than any other human act. I say this because of the prolonged (or intense) exposure of one mind to another.

—Harold Brodkey

I will call them my people, which were not my people; and her beloved, which was not beloved.

—Romans 9:25, the epigraph to Toni Morrison's *Beloved*

When Jeff wrote "*You Gotta BE the Book*," he was astonished by how intensely "relationships" played out in the engaged informants' reading and thinking about their reading: "Ron, reading a story about a boy whose dog was killed, told me that he felt so strongly that he was the boy in the story 'that I couldn't stand how sad I felt about it'" (p. 46). He then repositioned himself as the boys' grandfather and "it still hurt, but not as bad." Cora constantly referred to literary characters as "a friend I know," "someone I care about," "I know a person who. . . ." She thought of characters in a very caring and loving way. "I realized I really loved Gilly (from *The Great Gilly Hopkins*)." "[W]hen the author is good at writing then I get to know the people in the book and I carry them and their ideas around with me just like we were best of friends. And in a sense, we are, we really know each other, better than you almost always know people in real life" (p. 46).

Moving beyond relationships with characters, the four reflective dimensions of literary response Jeff describes all involve a consideration and relationship with an author. The first two reflective dimensions (considering significance, recognizing the use of literary/textual conventions) often do so somewhat implicitly: recognizing that there is an author—an intelligence behind the text—who is making particular communicative moves for the purpose of relating to the reader. The final two reflective dimensions consider the author explicitly (recognizing reading as a transaction; evaluating the author and the self as a reader). Cora was one reader who almost always considered herself in conversation or communion with an author. In regard to several Katherine Paterson novels: "When I read her books I feel like I'm getting to know a very kind and sensitive person who has a powerful heart and . . . an ability to understand people." She regarded Paterson as "a great-hearted person" and looked forward to her new books as a "chance to talk to her again. To renew our friendship, and get to know her a little better, what she's been thinking about and that kind of thing" (p. 103). Jeff had the chance to relay this personally to Paterson, and the author was deeply moved, commenting: "Cora is precisely the person who I write to when I am writing. Please tell her that."

In both of Jeff's studies focusing on boys (Smith & Wilhelm, 2002, 2006) and in his forthcoming "trash" studies about students who engage intensely with texts that tend to be marginalized by school (shock literature, horror, fantasy, manga/graphic novels, video games and video game novels, and so on), he found that consciously considered relationships with characters and authors were of central importance to engaged readers. He also found that these "reading" relationships promoted "real" relationships with others: family members, friends, other readers, and teachers in ways where the reading played out directly as a way of relating (e.g., as a basis of conversation) and indirectly (e.g., as an imaginative rehearsal for understanding or relating to that person).

We too have experienced these kinds of intense and often loving relationships with characters, and with authors, which is the relationship we will explore here. As a high school and college student Jeff read every poem, short story, and novel ever written by the prolific German author Hermann Hesse. He remembers thinking of Hesse the author while he read, considering him a mentor, and imagining what life experiences informed his writing. He was convinced that Hesse himself communicated directly through certain characters (like Goldmund or Klingsor) and through several of his favorite poems. In many ways Hesse has been Jeff's close authorial friend and confidante over the course of decades. Jeff's reading of *The Glass Bead Game* gave him the first intimation that he should become a teacher. (And, strangely enough, the same goes for Bruce.) He still rereads Hesse, and has reread *Narcissus and Goldmund* at times in his life when he is seeking balance between his various drives and personae. Reading *Steppenwolf*, he was inspired to enter into Jungian dream analysis, seeking to converse with his unconscious, an endeavor that he continues to this day just as Hesse did throughout his life. He read a new translation of *Siddhartha* by a Buddhist monk within the last year, which he found hugely comforting while his wife Peggy struggled with a life-threatening vascular disorder. He proceeded to read several books by the Dalai Lama and Thich Nhat Hanh, which he put into mental conversation with *Siddhartha*. He found himself practicing deep breathing, praying in a profoundly different way, and reminding himself to walk with compassion and kindness upon the earth. He monitors his changes in response to Hesse's works as a measure of his growth as a human being. He thinks of Hesse's life journey and his writings as an archetypal guide to his own life and writing. He appreciates the embracing of the psychic and spiritual struggles shared by Hesse through his characters.

For Bruce, the key relationship over time has been with Shakespeare. He can still hear the voice of Richard Burton's Hamlet that his sophomore English teacher played complete over a week of class—he'd never heard such a deeply human voice before, so awake to so many of both the joys and the sorrows of life. In college, he decided to become an English major—switching over from philosophy after his second year—because a paper he wrote on *Othello*, "The Poisoning of Love," helped him understand *life* philosophically in ways no philosophy paper he'd written had ever done. Since he wrote that paper, he's made many pilgrimages to the Shakespeare Festival in Stratford, Ontario, where he found a joyous and thoughtful theater community devoted to deeply felt and deeply thoughtful performances. As a high school teacher, he took many of his classes to see local productions at the terrific Chicago Shakespeare Theater—once getting as many as 80 sophomores to attend a production of *As You Like It* on their own time (with short stops beforehand at Niketown and McDonalds). And recently he has come to understand that there are certain ways that the ideas of this very book about democratic "growing together"—particularly those of this particular chapter—originate in what could be taken as the central ides in all of Shakespeare's work, "the marriage of true minds" of Sonnet 116.

Still on a personal level, but also at an age level closer to that of the students most of us teach, Jeff has seen these relationships to authors in his own daughters' reading. During a sabbatical to Australia in 2000–01, Jeff was invited to speak at the Australian Association of Teachers of English and while there to bring his daughters to a breakfast reading and conversation with Daniel Handler, a.k.a. "Lemony Snicket," the author of *The Series of Unfortunate Events* books beloved by Fiona and Jasmine. When Jeff got word of this invitation, his girls were already in bed, but he went in to wake them up to give them the news. They jumped out of their bunks, hugging each other and dancing. Jazzy, then 7, proclaimed: "You are the best dad EVER!" They then engaged in a discussion whether they would meet the real Lemony Snicket or his "legal guy." (Daniel Handler, the author, posed as the reluctant front man for a "reclusive" Lemony Snicket.) At the breakfast itself, the girls asked Handler directly if he was really the author, which he vehemently denied, saying he hated the books and that he warned them against reading them as "things are only going to get worse! There is not going to be a happy ending!" Afterwards, they agreed that even if Handler was the real author, that they preferred their notion of Lemony Snicket and were going to stick with thinking about Lemony as the author. When asked why, Fiona said: "[Lemony] is nicer. He cares more about the characters. He wants to tell their story to us. That other guy [Handler] doesn't even want us to read their story and that is just wrong!"

The girls, now college students, have persisted in speaking this way about favorite authors, such as J. K. Rowling, often wondering "How is she going to finish the story [in the final book]?" "How is she going to deal with Snape?" "She isn't going to disappoint us, is she?" Before the release of *The Deathly Hallows*, they decided that there was no way that Rowling would disappoint them—for example, by killing Harry (although they were greatly distressed by Dumbledore's death and later by that of Harry's owl) or coming up with a facile ending. "I trust her more than that," Jazzy opined. "She's earned that from us. We can trust her. I'm sure of it. She'll take care of things." Jeff got the sense that Jazzy didn't just mean that Rowling would take care of the plot and characters, but that she would take care of her readers, and of Jazzy and Fiona in particular.

This relationship with authors involves loyalty, trust, friendship, and something that we have to call mutual care and love. It can be as intriguing and mysterious as the myriad forms of love we experience for those who are our closest friends and family. There is a great mystery at the heart of our most enduring relationships—whether with a lover, with a child or student, or with a notion of God—a desire to know a person fully, always at least partially denied us, yet very real and resonant in the mystery of personhood. That mystery forms a good part of the enchantment and enrichment in our relationships, and part of how deep relationships help us to relate more deeply to ourselves, to know ourselves more fully than we can on our own.

This chapter is about how understanding the formation of relationships with authors can help us understand something of this mystery, and help us learn to form better relationships, not just with authors, but in general. As Bruce mentioned above, in a book about the importance of our learning to "grow together," this is the central, and in many ways the key chapter. The subtitle of Jeff's *"You Gotta BE the Book"* stressed teaching "engaged" and "reflective" reading. Here we are going to stress that between engaged and reflective reading is something we might call "caring" reading—reading in which we learn to care about others different from ourselves by sharing life with them for a time. The activity of imagining life together with authors is both what gives our relationships with the authors we deeply love such intensity, and also what makes our relationships with those authors a model for understanding the mysterious nature of other forms of love and relationship, to those with whom we are more present in chronological time but less directly present in story time.

THE GIVER BEHIND THE GIFT:
THE CONNECTIVE DIMENSION OF THE TRANSITIONAL OBJECT

In *"You Gotta BE the Book"* (2008/1997) Jeff wrote about the "connective dimension" of response lying between the "evocative" and "reflective" dimensions. In *Why Literature?* (2011) Cristy Bruns questioned whether such a dimension in fact exists, seeing the experience of reading as a dialectic between "losing oneself" in the experience of immersion and "refinding" oneself in the new reflection that this enables (pp. 45–46). In this chapter, we are going to lay out a new layer of understanding regarding the connective dimension of aesthetic response, as the mysterious love we come to experience for the authors of literary texts through the experience of reading—an understanding developed from Bruns's and others' conception of the literary work as a transitional object. In fact, after Cristy's manuscript had been submitted, she and Bruce did an NCTE talk on this very idea (Novak & Bruns, 2010). If we see literary texts as transitional objects, the meaning we create through them is not just subjectively personal. It is *transpersonal,* experienced as personally shared.[1] Just as much of the emotional power that teddy bears and security blankets have comes from their tacitly evoking the caring presence of those who have given them to us, so likewise much of the emotional power of works of art comes from their tacitly evoking the caring presence of authors. It is not just the flow of life evoked by immersion *in* the story world, but also the flow of life from one person to others *through* the story world that art evokes.

This is the connective bond we are going to explore in this book, and we will show how the transactional bonding process enables deep connections to be drawn not only between authors and readers, but between two or more readers, between teachers and students, among democratic communities, even toward the social and natural world as a whole. Art, and aesthetic experiences generally, are not just "the way life teaches us how to *live,"* as Rachel Remen says. They are also the way life teaches us how to love, to connect with others in a way that nourishes our own life, and helps us similarly nourish the lives of others. Love, for most of us, is the most important of all aesthetic experiences. So it is very important for us to understand just how the connective dimension of responsiveness works, and how to help students make deep connections with authors. It is only once we better understand the *transpersonal* dimensions of transaction that we can fully tap into the power Dewey saw it could have: the power, eventually, to definitively end the chaos of modern life, through the power to both respectfully and feelingly connect people in their diversity.

LOUISE M. ROSENBLATT AND WAYNE C. BOOTH, A LOVE STORY: THE IMPLIED AUTHOR WITHIN THE TRANSACTIONAL RESPONSE

In 1995, in his last year of high school teaching before he entered a doctoral program in English Education with George Hillocks, Bruce happened to run into his old teacher Wayne Booth, the famous author of *The Rhetoric of Fiction*, at a summer weekend of amateur chamber music on the eastern shore of Lake Michigan. Though they lived in the same neighborhood, they hadn't had a chance to interact in the fifteen years since Bruce had taken courses with him.

Naturally, when they saw each other again, Wayne asked Bruce, "What have you been doing?"

Bruce answered, "I've been teaching high school English, and have become a disciple of a 90-year old student of John Dewey's named Louise Rosenblatt."

"Well, isn't that interesting!" said Wayne. "Louise and I have been friends since the Dartmouth Conference in the 60s. And I've just finished writing the Foreword to the Fifth Edition of *Literature as Exploration!*"

This took Bruce very much aback. On the surface, Wayne and Louise Rosenblatt had very different concerns with literature—his focused on the "implied author" we infer in works of fiction, hers with the reader's transactional response to texts. But, Bruce started to think, "Maybe together their ideas make even more sense than they do separately!"

Transactional responsiveness, after all, occurs between *beings*. We can isolate our own pleasure and thought in considering it, but to do so actually seems narcissistic, when that pleasure is coming from a person who is giving of themselves to us, and can evoke from us, not just personal enjoyment and thought but love and personal *connection*.

Booth's 1995 foreword to the fifth edition of Rosenblatt's *Literature as Exploration* (originally published in 1938) began with a lament about how much richer his own thought on the experience of literature could have been if he had thoroughly integrated that thought with hers: "I could have done a better job of celebrating not just how authors 'make their readers' but how good readers construct and then revise the constructions of the authors they meet." On the other hand, there is also no mention of Booth in Rosenblatt, other than her saying in a footnote to *The Reader, the Text, and the Poem* (1978) that "it would be possible to rephrase many of Booth's points in transactional terms."

How, then, do we tie these two together, who both so wanted to be connected to one another, without managing ever to explicitly do so? Booth didn't mention in his foreword that he had also cited Rosenblatt at the beginning of *The Company We Keep: An Ethics of Fiction* (1988). But it is not the citation at the beginning of the work that provides us with the clearest connection between Booth's notion of "the implied author" and Rosenblatt's notion of "transactional responsiveness." That connection comes, implicitly, in the central chapter of Booth's book, Chapter 6, "Implied Authors as Friends and Pretenders." This chapter builds on a distinction Aristotle made among kinds of friendship: those that exist primarily for pleasure, those that exist primarily for usefulness, and those that exist primarily for their own sake. As Booth mentions, almost the entire history of literary criticism has treated literature as either *dulce* or *utile*: existing primarily for the pleasure it gives us or primarily for its usefulness in helping us lead better, wiser lives—the best usually combining the two in one way or another. But seeing authors as friends, as travelling companions, may just be the missing link that teaches us how to definitively connect pleasure and usefulness in the experience of art.

The connective dimension of aesthetic experience is what connects the pleasure of the text in the evocative dimension to the new wisdom acquired by the reader in the reflective dimension. If immersion in the text is the essential first step for aesthetic flow to take place, the tacit awareness of the mind of the implied author accompanying us through the experience we are having is the psychic energy that turns the flow of pleasurable experience into the flow of meaningful insight. In Paul Ricoeur's philosophical terms, the evoked presence of the present (mimesis$_2$) is accompanied by a connected presence toward the past (mimesis$_1$), to the giver of the transitional object, whose creative presence of mind at some point in the past when the text was fashioned has brought us to present life.

"By their fruits you shall know them," Jesus said. If we emphasize the "them" in that sentence, we have as distilled a statement of the connective dimension of aesthetic experience as we can get: evocative sweetness casts loving light back on the planters and tenders of the seeds whose fruits have nourished us. We recognize tacitly and implicitly that art is an educative gift bestowed by some person or creative force—some combination of author/culture/muse.

We perceive the meaning we find in that gift as at the same time both our own and the author's—as indeed it *is*, because we needed to undergo a process of reconstructing the meaning that we infer the giver of the experience intended for us to find.[2] And through the experience of this shared insight, we become attached, often extraordinarily deeply, to the authors who half-gave them to us, hoping in doing so to enrich our lives with meaning. As surely any English teacher can attest, we come to love those authors as deeply as anyone we love in our "actual" lives—sometimes even more so. The names Shakespeare, Hesse, Toni Morrison, Harper Lee, Robert Cormier conjure a welling up of love in many of us by just thinking of them—even if we know nary a drop about their actual lives.

IMPLIED AUTHORS AND TRANSACTIONAL AUTHORITY

This love, we believe, is absolutely integral to the full experience of art and literature, for reasons that will occupy us through the remainder of this chapter. Because we live in antiauthoritarian times—or, to be more precise, in times in which many political and religious forces have strong authoritarian tendencies—education in the humanities tends to take anti-authoritarian tones and approaches as a way of combating those tendencies in the broader society. Many of us tend to be reluctant to ascribe authority to literary authors in our teaching of them. Robert Probst, one of Rosenblatt's most prominent students, for instance, has said that we need to discourage *all* "reverence" in reading (2010).[3]

What we are going to try to show you here, though, is that there is something we might call "aesthetic, transactional authority" or "aesthetic, transactional power" that constitutes a form of nonauthoritarian personal authority. This is personal authority in the sense of adding to or augmenting our ability to experience life, as the etymology of the Latin *auctoritas* implies. It is authority that must be evoked, and cannot be commanded or enjoined. And it is authority that, as we shall see in the next chapter, asks for personal reflection to become fully accepted. When someone has added to our experience of life, it is only natural to feel reverent toward them. This reverence for authors, in fact, is a form of the virtue that Albert Schweitzer (1965) called "reverence for life" (Novak, in press; Rud, 2010; Rud & Garrison, in press; Woodruff, 2001).

As we showed in Chapter 3, the belief in the power of irreverent criticism can itself become dogmatically reverenced—as was pointed out by Deborah Appleman's high-school student, who saw deconstruction as an effort by some people to make themselves important by killing off others' experience of meaning. The dogmatic belief that "seeing through" others is always more powerful than "seeing with" them has been trenchantly criticized by both Wayne Booth in his book *Modern Dogma and the Rhetoric of Assent* (1974) and Peter Elbow in his extensive work to articulate how we must learn to play a "believing game" alongside a "doubting game" in the life we lead with other people (e.g., Elbow, 1973; 2009a; 2009b). But transactional responsiveness, understood in all three of its dimensions, gives us a way of seeing how sometimes it is not just a matter of alternating between believing and doubting, but of first seeing with others we "connect" with in order then to see anew and "reflect" for ourselves.

Understanding this indirect form of personal authority may actually be the key for contemporary societies to reconcile themselves with the notion of authority in general, rather than slipping into either authoritarianism or antiauthoritarian anarchy—another way of putting Dewey's vaunting of the saving power of the spread of transactional mentality. The authority of imaginatively shared insight is authority gained through the experience of life and the experience of love, and it leads to the authority of wisdom. Properly understood, we think, it introduces a new principle of authority into human life—properly democratic authority, constituting a reasonable middle ground of human relationship, a conjoint understanding of self and other, a way of freely moving from "me" and "you" to "we." It introduces "government of people, by people, for people" not merely through mutually agreed-upon laws or intelligent use of language to negotiate differences, but by educing the search for shared and mutually fulfilling meaning. We move from immersion in life itself, through the finding of love in shared meaning, to the finding of wisdom in the reflective application of that meaning to the personal situations and paths of our own lives.

This is how aesthetic, transactional literacy is literacy for humane, democratic "growing together," for what Lincoln called the search for "charity for all" that would bring about "a new birth of freedom." As Rosenblatt's student and NYU colleague Gordon Pradl (1996) puts it in his *Literature for Democracy* (citing a poem by his friend Peter Stillman), "we [grow] alive in one another." We don't just share ideas, trading them, as we do material commodities, for pleasure and mutual benefit. We share life and being; we become true friends, who value one another for their own sake, not just for pleasure and/or use. We become existentially tied to other beings who have fed our lives with meaning. Our understanding of who and what we are and can become expands as we take others' lives into our own. And as we have been fed, we become capable of feeding in turn, as we saw so vividly in Gabriele Rico's "re-creation" exercise.

In the last chapters of this book we will show how we can reenvision education, democracy, and even the whole movement of human history to center our understandings of them on aesthetic, transactional authority and aesthetic, transactional power. The connective dimension of responsiveness provides the human ground for that authority, which is why it is indispensable and central to the responsive process, even if its workings are necessarily more hidden than those of the other two dimensions. Transactional connection makes powerful and practical compounds of democratic atoms. Through it, deep human time and deep political space open to us, becoming *peopled*. This is why it is so important for us to see how it works.

MAKING LOVE VISIBLE

Why is it so much harder to see the connective dimension of the reading process than the evocative and reflective dimensions? We know when we feel pleasure and what we see when story worlds are evoked for us. And we know when we reflect and our minds have been challenged or changed by an experience. "Being the book" and "being the change" are both immediately palpable, though in different ways. But, as intense as our feelings for authors sometimes are, it's hard to see just how we get those feelings, how we manage to fall engage and even in love with people not directly visible to us.

So let's first try to do this in the most elementary way we can, by looking again at the eight "re-creations" of Levertov's "Writing in the Dark" in Chapter 3 (see Figure 3.2). Let us just ask the simple question, What was it, centrally, that each re-creative poet found to love—to deeply and passionately consider —in Levertov's character, as implied by the poem she wrote? For the author of "Tools," it seems to be something as simple as having "prudence" in when and how to use writing "tools" to elicit ideas. For the author of "Writing a Vision," it seems to be the wisdom of finding "freedom in the dark" (*freedom* was not a word used in the original poem, but is clearly a value expressed by it). The composers of "Courage" and "Do It Now" admire the virtues stated directly in their titles. The authors of "Idea" and "Playing in the Dark" are similar in their admiration for Levertov's appreciation of the value of ephemeral but intense meanings, of more human worth than clear and distinct Cartesian ideas. And Bruce, similarly, loved her devotion to the possibility of experiencing enlightenment and personal revelation through trusting in the meaning of one's nebulous instincts—which, of course, is why he chose this particular poem from all the dozens in Rico's book for our book. Most movingly, Jeff took Levertov's experience of writing in physical darkness as an authoritative metaphor for dealing emotionally with his wife Peggy's suffering from her mysterious illness: the metaphors of words emerging urgently but dimly onto a page turning into metaphors of the grimmest and holiest knowledge of matters of life, love, and death.

Since we don't know the other re-creators, we are only hazarding a guess on this, but we believe each of us saw something both like and unlike ourselves in Levertov, and saw certain ways it would be good for us—and for others—to become more like her. We saw both what was real and what was possible in ourselves; we found pleasure in her words and images, and food for thought in the ideas conveyed by those words and images. But we also each constructed an image of a person who was somehow wiser and better than we were, someone we wanted to become more like, someone who in important ways was a teacher to us, and who illuminated and extended our own perspectives in healthy, life-giving ways. Note that the images we each constructed were different from the others—though some were *quite* different and others quite similar—but none could be called "better" or "worse." Each is an instance of the expression of one person's personal existential truth existing in relation to another's. And those truths easily "fraternize" with one another, as Schiller's "Ode to Joy" promised. There's enough love and meaning to go around for all. And there are complex and fascinating harmonies created when the "re-creations" are set beside both the original poem and one another. Differing meanings amiably coexist and draw more meaning from one another—a weblike pattern of connection. A community of free existential inquiry has been created. And this can serve for us as a microcosmic image for all larger forms of such community.

How, then, does art teach? Bruce's favorite definition of a *teacher* is Robert Inchausti's, from his *Spitwad Sutras: Classroom Teaching as Sublime Vocation* (1993): "To be a *real* teacher, not just someone who takes the name, is to take up one's very life into speech, so that others may do the same." In this sense, all art seeks to teach, not just what is useful, but what is most personal—and does so in a way that is elemental for all other teaching. Artists take their lives and cast them into communicable media, so that they can be first melted and then recast by a multitude of others. When you wrote your "re-creation" of Levertov, the images and words that struck you did so because they somehow struck an inner nerve. You used those energies to construct an image of Levertov as your teacher that you could then use to construct a newer, better you, or at least a new possible you. And when you saw how at least eight other people had done the same thing, in very different ways, a personal bond was created between you and these eight other people, through your own response as well as to these variously constructed images of Levertov, even though you didn't even know the names of six of them.

We witness here a microcosmic democratic community where everyone's needs for meaning can be richly and variedly met, in some ways precisely because the act of reading and re-creating poetry renders the transactional response to poetry through purely aesthetic processes—bracketing out even the efferent question of what Levertov "meant" by her poem, other than as a gift that would keep on giving as others variously resonate with it. Because aesthetic meaning needs are the only needs that must be met here, we have a pure win-win situation. There is no "Darwinian" struggle for existence, no competition for the "right" meaning, just transactional coexistence among diverse meanings. Such is the value of "taking life up" into aesthetic speech: As we find ourselves able, in Inchausti's words, "to do the same"—to take our own lives up into speech as we have seen others do—we *all* become teachers. What Levertov called "writing in the dark" actually turns out to give us a pure vision of the path to mutual enlightenment!

TRANSACTIONAL RESPONSIVENESS AS SECURE ATTACHMENT

What Rico's "re-creation" exercise makes palpable is how art can at the same time both connect us to those who create it and free us to create on our own. In doing this, it is a form of what object relations psychologists call "secure attachment." Empirical studies have demonstrated that there are three basic patterns of parent-child attachment that have evolved in our species (Bowlby, 1969; Karen, 1994). *Avoidant attachment* evolved in environments where resources were scarce and caregivers needed to devote themselves to procuring material nourishment. *Anxious* or *ambivalent attachment* evolved in environments where humans were easily preyed upon and children needed to learn to subordinate their own instincts to those of their caregivers, to become strictly obedient and cling to parental authority. *Secure attachment* evolved in relatively secure environments, where children had room to explore, where there could be dialogue between parental and personal instincts and interplay between self and world. Linguist and cognitive scientist George Lakoff (1996) has famously shown how the latter two patterns of parenting have been translated into the opposing political frameworks of "strict parent" authoritarianism and "nurturant parent" democracy. However, we think, with Karen, that he has ignored the very real "avoidant parent" behaviors that permeate modern society, in which we are obsessed with production and consumption in the midst of material abundance, and often measure "love" in terms of material rather than human gifts.[4]

Testing students on measurable educational standards, when it is seen as central to education as a whole, intentionally socializes children to have anxious or ambivalent attachment toward the world, and often unintentionally socializes them toward avoidant attachment. As the film *The Race to Nowhere* (Abeles, 2010) powerfully documents, an overemphasis on standardized measures has produced a generation of students dominated by stress if they buy into this educational program and by apathy if they don't: either constantly second-guessing others' expectations or not caring what others think because they don't see that they themselves are being cared for through the education they are being given.

Art and literature are naturally evolved means for education that promotes secure attachment to others and the world. However insecure our outside lives are, the experience of art and literature can create a temporarily secure environment in which we can explore the meaning of life in the tacit company of the alloparent authors who created that secure environment for us, precisely to enable that exploration. They are the original and most powerful form of what George Hillocks has called "environmental teaching" (1986), the providing of an environment that safely scaffolds and guides exploratory learning. This foregrounds why teaching students artfully—whether the art we use is others' or our own—has such tremendous importance. It is a question, in Dewey's terms, of whether we seek to produce a nation and a world of competing "self-actors," of intelligent but unconnected "interactors," or of loving and wise "transactors" who seek, above other goals, to enjoy life, befriend others, and explore and better the world. The secure attachments and deep connections we establish with authors can help us overcome the avoidant or anxious attachments that have been established elsewhere in our lives and give us a fresh start in learning to imagine and make more secure attachments and deep connections in the real world. We hope you'll see something of how this works in the next two sections on classroom practice.

MAKING LOVE VISIBLE IN THE LITERATURE CLASSROOM I: TEACHING AUTHORIAL READING

In the "re-creations" of Levertov's "Writing in the Dark," we saw in microcosm how we conceive of implied authors bringing something essential to our attention, and how we use what we have been taught to create meaning of our own. As teachers, how can we tap into this process as we consider how to teach literature? How do we choose the best authors for our students' current state of being, and help them do the same for themselves? How do we encourage and assist students to connect with authors by inferring meanings constructed for us by the "intelligence behind the text" (Rabinowitz & Smith, 1998)? And how, once students have made this personal connection, do we get them to make new personal connections to their own world, to find new ways of *being* through these new ways of seeing?

Obviously, these are huge questions—questions that we can only begin to explore here. And they are questions, of course, that each teacher must ultimately answer for herself. To help, Jeff will share a number of techniques he has used to encourage what Peter Rabinowitz and Michael Smith (1998) have called *authorial reading*, a concept useful for promoting relationships with authors in the reading of any genre. Then Bruce will tell how he structured the readings in his teaching of a developmental reading/writing course at a Chicago community college, under conditions where a complete freedom of choice in reading materials provides an opportunity to maximize the transactional power felt through the course.

Authorial Reading for Shared Insight
and Deepening Interpersonal Understanding

The subtitle of Peter and Michael's *Authorizing Readers* is "Resistance and Respect in the Teaching of Literature." Wayne Booth's foreword for this book stresses that it teaches better than any other text he knew how to use literature for producing "full ethical and intellectual development in students" (p. xi). Our concerns here are with just one slice of students' intellectual and ethical development: learning how to infer meanings coded into a text and, through this, to develop the capacity to infer a conception of the author herself, and then how to respect, converse with, resist, and—if this process goes well—come to love that implied author, whose experiences and thoughts often differ radically from their own. In other words, we want our students to learn how to at least provisionally put on the glasses that the author seemingly calls us to put on, and to do so—as if we are on a first date—with a sense of wanting to get to know someone else's perspective and personhood, and with a sense of loving possibility for the relationship. This does not mean that using the author's lenses may not end up in resistance to the author's meanings, but this can also express a kind of love and commitment—for alternative meanings, different authors, and a particular but now newly tested sense of oneself.

Throughout our lives, we learn to move from more superficial to deeper and wiser forms of love. Authorial reading, akin to what Wayne Booth called "the rhetoric of assent" (1974) and Peter Elbow has called "the believing game" (1973, 2009a,b), can be conceived as steps in a "poetics of ascent" taken toward wiser and deeper forms of love. Here are a few techniques to help students on this journey to more consciously considered relationships with authors. It is easier to enter into relationships and conversations with authors if there is a topic for the conversation. This is why Jeff plans all of his work with students around inquiry units framed by essential/existential questions and the techniques featured here work best in contexts of inquiry.

Seeing Authors in Popular Culture. We are often attracted to authors because of our past experience and how authors speak to that experience (whether endorsing, extending, questioning or offering alternatives to it), and sometimes because authors provide a way to get experiences we might otherwise never have.

There are many teaching ideas that can build on these attractions. For example, students keep lists of favorite texts, books, movies, genres, and authors, and share their enjoyment and love of these in various ways, such as sharing their lists or creating posters, online fan websites, fanfics, fan videos, etc. to promote a favorite book or author (or video game designer, movie director, musician, artist, and so on). Every unit offers opportunities for sharing both our preexisting and developing passions and interests in ways that can connect to the unit as a whole while allowing elaboration on both the interests and the texts. For example, Jeff often asks students to bring in short video clips of a favorite character from a TV show or movie (many boys, for example, bring in favorite wrestlers from the wrestling shows they watch, or characters from video games). He then asks his students why they are attracted to this person as a character, what can be learned from the character, what we should emulate and admire and not emulate and admire, how this character is like or unlike us, how the character was presented (by an implied author) and with what effects. The unit should be one that will reward the consideration of character and the thinking of an author who created the characters, such as "What makes a good friend?" or "Who is a great leader?" (See Smith & Wilhelm, 2010.)

Think of the payoffs: The teacher gets to know the students and what engages them in popular culture. The students get to know each other and make connections to each other while seeing patterns among their tastes and interests. The teacher can connect what is learned from and about the students to subsequent instruction. This activity can assist with developing concepts, teaching strategies, and heuristics for understanding character such as exploring concepts and issues regarding heroes and antiheroes; investigating themes related to character (e.g., what makes a good relationship, the effect of context on character, and so on); and discussing genre issues like the hero and the hero-quest archetype. There are infinite possibilities and outcomes for this activity. Perhaps most importantly, it requires a level of inference about textual construction and meaning that can be extended to inferring the creator and elements of the creation of the various texts that are being read.

The same kind of activity can be done with any other literary convention (see Smith & Wilhelm, 2010) and with authors who use them by asking questions along the lines of, What does this author do for you? How does she do this? What kind of "work" is this author trying to get done (in general, or through the use of particular conventions or in terms of the inquiry)? What kind of change is she working for in you and in the world? All of these "moves" develop capacities required by the new Common Core State Standards.

Seeing Students as Living Authors

One immediate and concrete way to help students think about authors (and consider themselves as authors) and textual construction is something Jeff uses a lot in both school and National Writing Project work with teachers: the author chair. The author's chair is a special chair in the classroom and students are allowed to sit in it any time that they want to share their own writing. They can do this quietly during writing time with one or two peers, or they can do it during special times set aside for them to share their writing with the class.

When students share with larger groups, Jeff likes to use little rituals like having a friend introduce them as an author and introduce the piece they are working on. Then everyone claps. (Jeff calls this ritual "an appreciation.") There are no interruptions during the reading. Afterwards, the audience responds. Jeff likes to use response heuristics such as praise, question, take, and wonder. First the audience offers praise about the strengths of the writing, then they ask questions about the text itself, the process of writing it, how it was constructed and why, and so on. Next the audience offers what they took away from the writing as far as powerful ideas, images, or things to try in their own writing or living. Finally, they offer suggestions in a friendly, respectful way, by using stems such as "I wonder what would happen if . . . ." This kind of stem recognizes that the author is the boss of her own piece, and that authors have many options, and you are just respectfully highlighting another option in their writing repertoire.

Another idea is to have students, individually or in small groups, operate as a co-author or editor by providing alternative endings, writing a "what if" scenario for each other's writing or for literary texts themselves; for example, "Let's explore what would happen if Huck's Pa had not returned and write an outline for the rest of the book" or "Let's write a summary of a revised play based on the change that Hamlet had not seen his father's ghost." This kind of activity helps students consider why the author did what she did—and how that affected resulting action and meaning—and to explore how one's own proposed choices would change the text and transform meaning.

Students can also fill in story gaps, imagine new situations, characters, settings, events, or compose sequels or parodies. Jeff's students particularly like parodies, which typically imitate the parodied text quite closely, changing just a few salient details. These changes have profound effects on tone and meaning, which emphasize the power of authorial choice and single salient details in communicating meaning and providing a particular kind of experience and gift to the reader. Students also enjoy reframing a text into a different format (e.g., Emily Dickinson's "I Heard a Fly Buzz" into an MTV video) or genre (e.g., Edwin Arlington Robinson's poem "Richard Cory" into a story or film) and then exploring how this change transforms meaning and the effects of the text.

It's also easy to structure a consideration of the author into various discussion formats (see Wilhelm, 2007). For instance, Save the Last Word is a technique where each reader chooses a favorite quote or excerpt, shares it, and then waits to see what all group members say about that excerpt before telling why she chose it. As an adaptation of this technique, the teacher can simply ask the group members to consider and comment on why they think the author included that particular quote or excerpt, or why the author phrased the sentence in that particular way.

When using literature circles for discussions of texts, Jeff often assigns a role of Author Spokesman. The student playing that role stands in for the author, speaking for her or for herself if she were the author, explaining how particular details or structures were included to communicate particular effects and meanings, and responding to group questions for her. The lit circle members can play editors explaining what they would have done differently and why.

Rules of Notice Think-Alouds. Another great activity for promoting authorial reading is to pursue think-alouds that focus on "rules of notice" (Rabinowitz, 1987) for particular genres (stories with a twist, arguments of policy, ironic monologues, and so forth) and codings (for symbolism, irony, unreliable narrators, thematic meaning, and similar elements). What is it that the author wants us to notice? Why? How do we interpret these cues? Students work together to create anchor charts and flow charts of "rules of notice" and how to interpret them (see Wilhelm, 2001/2011a and Smith & Wilhelm, 2010 for full discussions). Rules of notice can be general (always notice a title, always notice ruptures and surprises, always notice emotionally charged words and events) or specific to a genre like ironic monologues or a convention like extended metaphor or irony.

Questioning. One of the unique powers of literature is that it doesn't tell you what it means—you have to figure it out. Readers must learn to

FIGURE 5.1. Thought Processes Involved in Authorial Reading

1.　Care for, pay attention to, and give respect to the characters you are reading about. This is called playing the "narrative audience."
2.　Consider what the actual text and how it is constructed (not to be confused with authorial intent) communicates about people, ideas, and issues.
3.　Consider *how* the text works, and how the reader must work to comprehend the text as it was meant to be understood, as it was constructed and coded to be comprehended on its own terms.
4.　Finally, decide how convinced you are of the appropriateness of the author's ideas and vision, and how these were realized by the text. Decide to respect, adapt, or resist the vision of the text, but only after having worked to understand it on its own terms. Authorial critics ask: What does this text mean to the audience it was written for (the authorial audience, who the author believes will have the respect, sensitivity, cultural knowledge and reading skills to understand the text), and how do I feel about that meaning?

figure forth by bringing their own life to the text, making connections like self-to-text, intratextual, extratextual (i.e., text-to-text), self-to-author, and text-to-world. Questioning schemes can be very helpful in assisting students to make these kinds of connections. QtA or Questioning the Author (Beck & McKeown, 2006) is a technique that obviously focuses on the author as the intelligence behind the text. Jeff has adapted this technique for guiding student questioning and promoting authorial reading in think-alouds by using initiating prompts such as the following: What does the author want her audience to know before reading and to learn while reading? Why? What might be her purpose and agenda in writing this text? What point of view or group perspective is being expressed? How is the author revealing her thoughts, beliefs, feelings through the writing? (For a full set of QtA prompts, see Wilhelm, 2007, pp. 135–141.)

The important goal with any think-aloud or questioning scheme is to get to the point where the students internalize the questions so they are the ones who ask and answer them without prompting, tweaking questions and responses for their own purposes and current life situation. This is the bridge between authorial reading in which we seek to connect with the implied author and reflective reading in which, based on the trust we've established with the author, we learn to connect anew with our own selves and outside lives.

Seeing Authors' Generalizations: Inferring Theme and Inferring Insight

Vipond and Hunt (1984) specifically address what readers must do to understand an author's generalization or thematic statement. Theme is understood as an insight that can be applied to the world outside of the text. These researchers explore what they call *point-driven reading* by considering what listeners do in conversation to figure out the gist of what a speaker is "getting at," how people try to understand the "points" in the context of conversations and daily interactions, and how they apply this process to literary reading. Their approach highlights the facts that speakers and authors matter, that they deserve and require respect to be understood, and that specific kinds of effort are required to understand speakers and authors communicating in particular ways.

Point-driven readings not only elicit a powerful, lived-through experience, but also attend to discourse level experiences and reflections: experiencing and considering a text constructed by an implied author who is trying to communicate something important to the reader. This is the crux move for the reader: People who read for a point understand texts as the result of intentional acts of other human beings in order to communicate through that medium. Since this is what expert readers do, it is crucial for students to understand that authors matter and must be specifically considered as part of the reading transaction. After all, who created the text, constructed its meaning, and did all the patterning to communicate these points and insights? (For a fuller discussion of thematic reading and point-driven understanding, see Smith & Wilhelm, 2010.)

Here's a quick activity that requires students to think about theme, how it was conveyed, and how the theme connects to their own lives:

> Imagine that the author of the story or book you are reading is also an advice columnist. How would the author of the book you are reading respond to the following letter focusing on an inquiry about choice and control? (Different letters could be written by the teacher or students about topics of other inquiries about any relevant subject. The trick is to pose a real dilemma and to respond in-role as the author in ways consistent with the text written by that author—and that can be justified by evidence from that text):

> Dear High School Helpline,
>   I am trying to figure out what I should do with my life after high school. I want to take a year off and go "to the woodshed" as we musicians like to say. I want to work on my chops, play with my band, work on my music right here in town, which would mean living with my parental units. I can get lots of local gigs. And then I want to see where things are in another year or two. My parents want me to go to college *no matter what* and want to help pay—they say I can study music and that they won't pay if I don't go now. I'm afraid they might make me miserable if I stay at home.

My best friends want me to take a year off and travel around the country together, an opportunity they say that we will never have again—and I can busk as a musician wherever we go. My girlfriend of 2 years wants me to go to the state university (not too far away) where she will be going even though they don't have a musical performance program. She says I can figure out what I really want and we can be together. My teachers and guidance counselor think that I need to continue my studies, probably in trade school for music production (they say my chances of making it as a musician are "slim to none"), and argue that "road leads on to road" and that I'm unlikely to ever go to school if I don't go now. I'm confused! What should I do?

Bad Note Music Man

Share your written response to this troubled teen with a partner. Justify what you wrote: Why do you think the author would respond in this way? What in the text makes you think the author would give advice about choice and control in this way? (This activity is modeled after activities from Smith & Wilhelm, 2010.)

Connecting with Authors through Dramatic Improvisations

Drama and action strategies offer some powerful ways to conceive of, consider, and converse directly with authors. Here are just a few ideas for doing so (Wilhelm, 2002/2011a).

Correspondence Dramas. Jeff's students often undertake conversations with authors through correspondence dramas, where they write letters, notes, questions, or advice requests to the author. Students can exchange these texts with one another and then respond in role as the author, while taking care to justify, based on evidence from the text and personal connections to the text, how or why they think the author would respond in this way.

Hotseating the Author. Hotseating is a more active drama technique in which a student (or the teacher, to provide a model) can be put in the "hotseat" in role as an author. (This can also be done in role as characters, forces, or a concept as well.) (While analogous to the author's chair, in hotseating you take on the role of the author of a piece that was not written by you.) A variation is to hotseat a character or force and have the author stand behind in the role of "inner voice," explaining her take on the character's responses, or how she constructed the character to respond in certain ways, or how she explored a particular force or idea through her text. It is often useful to have students plan and rehearse such work with this technique prior to using it more spontaneously, as a good deal of metacognitive awareness is required.

In one of Jeff's 11th-grade English classes, a student came into class and asked: "Why did Huck play that trick on Jim?" (i.e., Huck acting like he was a ghost because Jim thought he was dead). Before Jeff could answer, another student said: "Let's put Huck on the hotseat!" Jeff was pleased, because this meant that the students recognized that hotseating was a way to get inside a character's head and explore his motivations and feelings. After all, every drama technique is an externalization of an internal reading strategy. After 3 minutes of interviewing a student in role as "Huck," the class was satisfied that they understood Huck's motivations. In fact, they had created an elaborated text based on the one that they had read: a stream-of-consciousness monologue from Huck, prompted by questions from the class—an exploration of why we play jokes on others and their unforeseen consequences, the power we feel when we fool someone, and the humiliation we can feel at being fooled.

Though the students were satisfied, Jeff asked learning groups to consider why Mark Twain had included this scene and written it the way he had. This was in preparation for a hotseating of Twain. After they had prepared, several students volunteered to be hotseated as Twain. Students taking their turn in the hotseat as Twain had their learning group play the role of "lifeline" or "safety net" if they needed help answering any of the questions posed by the forum.

In hotseating, students in the "forum" (i.e., the classroom) took on various roles suggested by Jeff (e.g., reporters in a press conference, detectives, psychologists) or self-assigned roles as people who would have an interest in questioning or learning from the author, such as other authors from the unit or characters from other pieces of literature or popular culture. In role, students can then question the hotseated author who responds in ways justified by the text. The hotseating can be paused and students asked to justify (or question) responses based on the text. Other variations include having another student play an "alter ego" (providing an alternative perspective to Twain's, like being his evil twin), an "inner voice" or "shadow self" who stands behind the hotseated character/ author to reveal what the character or author is really thinking but not saying after each comment. (See Wilhelm, 2011a/ 2002 for examples and other variations.)

In Jeff's class, the initial hotseating of Huck and other similar drama activities like re-enactments and discussion forums were designed to get at questions like, What's going on in this scene? What is the character's experience here? The follow-up drama activities featuring Twain were designed to achieve something else: a considered relationship with Twain, including a consideration of his craft, what his craft created in terms of meaning, and an embracing, adaptation or resistance to this meaning. The hotseats and discussion dramas involving the author were for exploring questions like, Why was the text constructed in this way, and how do we, as the audience, feel about that?

During a hotseating of Twain toward the conclusion of the class's reading of *Huckleberry Finn*, Jeff saw a palpable relationship with Twain expressed on the part of many students. Several students, in the role of reporters, expressed disappointment in the end of the book. Some found it to "take a totally new direction" or a "new tone—it was hard to know how to read it." Several students resisted the gratuitous "horrible" treatment of Jim as anything from "mean" to "racist." The student in role as Twain had quite a time defending himself but did a fine job improvising an argument that he was showing how unquestioningly racist America was through Tom's treatment of Jim—showing that Tom did not think of Jim as a person fully worthy of respect, but as an object to be used in his "games," much as he had seen adults like Miss Watson do. The student playing Twain's alter ego revealed that he had gotten tired at the end of the book, that he had written the ending at a different time (this is true), and he just wanted to "get it done" and "be amusing": "I just lost my mojo, I guess," he said. This led the class to a discussion about when a piece of writing or any task is truly done, and if we should see *Huck Finn* as not yet complete, and whether we could reconcile the ending with the rest of the book in a way that made sense to us. The discussion was very rich and Twain, as well as his writing, was at the absolute center of it. The students were engaged in authorial reading, and considering themselves as authors in relationship to Twain as an author.

To Tell the Truth. In this hotseat variation, three or four people play the role of the author. Small groups brainstorm questions that they want to ask the author. As the game begins questions are fielded by the panel of three or four possible authors. At the end, the students in the forum vote for who did the best job playing the author and must justify their vote with evidence from the responses and from the text that has been read.

When Jeff did this activity at the conclusion of Huck Finn, the votes and justifications were moving examples of authorial reading. One boy, typically the class clown, wrote with unusual seriousness: "I vote for Tom as the best Twain. He was pretty clear about not only what he was attacking by making fun—things like slavery, false chivalry and politeness, scam artists, gullibility and all kinds of other ways of being mean and stupid. He knew more of what Twain was making fun of, and how he did it. I loved how he talked about Emma Grangeline's [sic] poem and how he loved writing it to make fun of being overly sentimental and all that. When he was talking I could almost believe he was Twain himself, especially with his bad hair!"

The point of these activities is to take the first steps toward authorial reading by simply getting students to begin thinking of texts—and the elements and conventions of texts—as authorial constructions. Through accomplishment of this, students will begin thinking of and relating to the authors behind these texts, as well as the characters and events within them, with increased care and respect.

Teaching Caring Reciprocation Through Authorial Reading

Reciprocation is necessary in any relationship, including that of reader and implied author. Care cannot exist fully without reciprocation, without an attempt to fully recognize and appreciate each other, to hear one another in the language and terms that one uses to define oneself and to communicate.

Jeff had a powerful experience with reciprocation during his teaching with Rachel. At Boise High, students shuffle their scheduled class periods at the end of each semester, meaning that every class roster was filled with about 50% new students. His 2nd-hour class, which had been the most enthusiastic, caring, and mutually supportive class of the day, was suddenly unsupportive and dull. The students had to relearn reciprocation and appreciation for each other as a reconfigured group. They had to get to know and trust each other. This did not happen by magic but through several weeks of joint productive activity that required them to share, listen to each other, and work together on significant projects. At the end of several weeks, Jeff thought that this class was an even stronger community than his favorite one from the previous semester.

Reciprocation is necessary in learning how to recognize an implied author, building an awareness of the author, caring for and trusting that author, and learning their codes and languages of communication. It takes time and continued, conscious effort. Being an author oneself, and considering oneself to be an author, greatly assists in forging such relationships. This harkens back to the Laura story from Chapter 1. Laura was aware of her capacity to evoke responsiveness in others—the other kids were aware of her as an author behind the text—and this is what mutuality is all about. Even after her death, her classmates perceived and felt and learned from her presence through her writing.

Authorial reading requires the reader to enter into the perspectives of authors by reading any text in the way it was coded and structured for reading by the author. (This is not to be confused with *authorial intent,* which is unknowable in any finally determinable sense.) Its focus is on attending to the coding and forming of text, and how a particular coding asks us to read. Rabinowitz and Smith (1998) argue that while some textual critics (such as the New Critics) ask, "What does this text mean?" and subjectively (rather than transactionally) oriented reader response theorists ask, "What does this text mean *to me*?", neither question considers either the author or the specific kind of reading the text requests from a reader—that is, coming to understand how to read in the specific way that the text construction indicates that it should be read. Further, Rabinowitz and Smith explain that the authorial reading question is "How did the author expect her audience to read and understand this text and how do I feel about that?" The authors argue that we must first respect authors—seeking to read their text the way they want us to read it—before we decide to what extent we want to embrace, adapt, or resist their visions. We are not arguing for an efferent or a purely objective respect through the isolation of code/form, but rather a transactional empathy through an attentive consideration of code/form as the result of authorial choice, recognizing that just as we can never finally know an author's intent—and that's not the point of seeing writing as a gift to us—we can also never judge culture codes that differ from our own background, biases, and interpretive frameworks.

We find this notion of authorial reading very valuable on at least two important levels: first in the teaching of literature, but also, through preparing students to respectfully relate to others as a community. When reading authorially we seek to understand an author and her views on her terms before we begin to critically differentiate the authors' views from our own. Both moves are necessary for a relationship. Authorial reading puts an emphasis on relating to authors by inferring and considering the meanings in the texts they've made for us and it posits that we read mostly to be connected—to characters, to implied authors—through these ideas. Eventually, reading in this way can connect us to the world and to our communities. We learn which authors to trust through our concerted attempts to understand them and to use what they are teaching us in our social interactions and conjoint living.

When we read for love and wisdom, we read first to understand, then to acknowledge both alignments and disconnections. To outgrow one's current self, to become a better self, we must fully entertain that which is not yet our own; we must attempt to connect to what we are disconnected from. How can we meet this challenge?

What follows is one example illustrating how, by and large, this personal reconnection was drawn by a group of students with an author and a work Bruce selected specifically for them, to help them negotiate a specific life transition through a specially chosen transitional object.

MAKING LOVE VISIBLE IN THE LITERATURE CLASSROOM II: AUTHORIAL READING AND THE REREADING AND RE-CREATION OF THE SELF

In connection with writing this book, Bruce recently went back to teaching English at a Chicago community college with a course in developmental reading and writing called Integrated Communications —a title he loved, as you can imagine. Since for most of his students this course marked their entry into higher education—and almost all were the first members of their families to attend college—he chose to structure the entire curriculum for the semester course around the topic of "education and hope." Here is how the course was described on the syllabus:

> Throughout the semester, we will be reading and writing primarily about how education, when it is truly and dedicatedly pursued, can give us the energy and purpose to pursue and persist in realizing our dreams: for ourselves, for others in our lives, and for the world. Your personal hopes and dreams—the reasons for your coming to school—will be our primary texts, and will be interwoven with most of what we read and write together.

The literary readings were structured in two stages. In the first stage, students read short selections by authors whose social situations were quite similar to their own, and they had a degree of choice in selecting one of those authors to help assure that they could find one with whom they very closely identified. In the second, they read a long work—far longer than any book most of them had ever read before—written by someone whose background was very different from their own, but about someone who, through a very difficult educational struggle, negotiated with flying colors the transition they themselves had decided to try to negotiate—a transition from a static and often violent life on the social and economic margins, in the company of many cynical "dreambusters," to a mobile new life of their own choosing, pursuing their personal hopes and dreams along with others on similar hopeful paths. In other words, they started with a short look in a literary mirror and proceeded to a quite long look through a literary window, through a transitional object selected precisely to help them more easily negotiate—in the company both of an insightful authorial friend and of other readers in a similar life situation—a particular existential *life* transition, portrayed with deep richness and complexity in the book.

The class started with 2 weeks of readings from an issue on the theme of education of *The Journal of Ordinary Thought*, a wonderful publication of Chicago's Neighborhood Writing Alliance, a grassroots organization founded by Hal Adams of the University of Illinois, Chicago. Most of the work of this journal is produced at workshops in libraries and community centers in impoverished neighborhoods of Chicago. You can only imagine how excited Bruce felt in finding the following on the masthead of the journal, in conjunction with using it to teach a course alongside the writing of this book:

> *The Journal of Ordinary Thought* publishes reflections people make on their personal histories and everyday experiences. It is founded on the propositions that every person is a philosopher, expressing one's thoughts fosters creativity and change, and taking control of life requires people to think about the world and communicate their thoughts to others. *JOT* strives to be a vehicle for reflection, communication, and change. (Warr, 2007)

The students were going to start their struggle toward claiming new authorship of their own lives in the friendly company of authors quite similar to themselves, showing themselves engaged in the very same struggle.

On the first day of class, the students read two short pieces: "The Granny Course" by Mary Gray Kaye, about various humorous lessons a wise grandmother learns from her granddaughter, and "The Bright Future of Everyone: Thoughts on Education," a group poem written by the Albany Park Community Center. The latter became the jumping-off point for a composition called "GH: The Section of Good Hopes" (GH was the actual section name), which Bruce compiled from their responses to "The Bright Future of Everyone." It began like this:

> I have come from intelligence and succeeding—the place that
> I come from is everywhere—from the westside, the southside,
> the eastside of Chicago, Mexico, Virginia, Seattle, Alaska, the
> Army, the Navy, Iraq, Korea, cease-fire, war—I have come from
> nothing to something—I have been through a lot and I just want
> things better—I have seen many things, and now see I have to do
> something for me.

The next day the students chose a different piece from the journal that they liked and wrote a brief essay about it the following week. They found pieces about other wise grandmothers, about the difference between "street smarts" and "school smarts," about the challenges and freedom of being an unmarried 30-year old woman, about the deep ambivalence of meeting a parent who once deserted you and now wants you in his life again, about living "awe-thentically," and about confronting fear. In each case, they found people much like themselves who wrote "literature," in the terms we encountered from the "wholistic/Joy" group

at the Wye conference: "the honest and eloquent re-creation of experience through language." It was very easy for them to see these authors
as friends, and Bruce asked them to write about how they regarded the
author as part of their essays:

> I think the author was independent, a realist, and accomplished.
> The author gives an inside view of a group of people that are
> invisible, outcasts in a sense because of the societal stereotype of
> marriage and the family as the only option for a woman.

> I think the author is a wise, inspiring, meaningful, caring, well-
> rounded, driven, and educated individual who has taken all that
> education has to offer and has made it his mission to spread and
> touch as many people with it as possible.

> I think the author was a strong and brave person because a lot
> of people cannot or will not write or discuss their feelings or things
> about their lives.

Over the next 7 weeks of the course the class read Ron Suskind's *A
Hope in the Unseen: An American Odyssey from the Inner City to the Ivy League*
(1999), which told the story of Cedric Jennings, who made his way from
being an outcast for his pursuit of intellectual success at what was known
as the worst high school in Washington, DC, to become a half-successful
student at a summer program at MIT, and then, ever so gradually, a fully
successful one at Brown. Cedric's struggles were painfully close to the
struggles most of Bruce's students were undergoing—many of whom had
undertaken long commutes in order to attend this particular community college, for the main reason that it was far away from the "friends"
they'd grown up with whose proximity could easily dissuade them from
furthering their education and starting a new life. And the insight and
compassion with which Suskind portrayed those struggles—and the fact
that he'd clearly given up so much of his own life in order to portray
them accurately and compassionately, so that others both like and unlike Cedric could see them clearly and feel how hard, how fraught with
ambivalence, and yet how heroic they were (as heroic as any other literary "odyssey")—gave these students a powerful sense that such personal
struggles really mattered, not just to them and their loved ones, but to the
broader world.

Mary Rose O'Reilley (1998) in *Radical Presence* says, "You can listen
someone into existence" (p. 21). Suskind, as an author, did this in an
intense and prolonged way for Cedric, someone so very like the large majority of Bruce's students, in ways that validated those students' choice to
enter higher education, encouraged them to persist in all the intellectual

and social challenges they would face, and enlightened them about how it might definitively change them for the better, helping them become, not just successful in terms of outward achievement, but better people, as Cedric clearly became by the end of his long struggle. One of the students, upon finishing *A Hope in the Unseen*, commented, "I never even imagined I could *enjoy* reading a book before!" It was far from easy for these students to read a book of over three hundred pages. (And Bruce *knows* that not all of his students were able to read every word of it.) But most of them were able, to a meaningful extent, to "be" this particular book precisely because its author worked so very hard in writing it to learn what it was to be someone very like them. What better kind of friend is there than that?

Alex Sanchez, the author of *Rainbow Boys* and other works of young adult literature about adolescent gay men, said at the 2010 NCTE convention, "Birds need to hear their parents sing in the first month of life. If they don't, they never learn to sing themselves. Humans have more time. But many of us need *books* to discover that we are a person worth *being*." In the next chapter we'll show how Bruce's students used Cedric Jennings's story as told by Ron Suskind to reflectively reimagine the individual stories of their own lives. And in the last part of the book we'll show how Cedric's story became the centerpiece for a classroom community woven by the sharing of those individual stories. But it is important to see that what opened the door for all that lay in students' being helped to find literary authors with whom they could become friends, who sought to transact with people like them. In particular, Suskind's finding prolonged value in the song of Cedric Jennings's challenging life was instrumental in *their* coming to find value in the songs of their own and one another's lives. It became the common ground for shared being. Because they had felt "listened into existence" in their reading, they were able to compose new stories for themselves and to compose a classroom community composed of those new selves. Suskind's authorship was the ground for this reauthoring; his imaginative "re-creation," the ground for *their* re-creating reality.

ENDLESS LOVE:
IMPLIED AUTHORS AND THE TRANSACTIONAL
PEOPLING OF THE PAST

We are not done plumbing the depths of the connective dimension of transactional response, though. Those depths are, in fact, endless. Authorial reading shows us how to draw relational lines between authors and ourselves, how to make friends (or not) with particular authors. But these, after all, are just line segments. As in geometry we learn that implied by every line segment is an infinite line, so relationships with im-

plied authors extend ad infinitum. The story of Cedric Jennings that Suskind tells is, after all, as its title says, an *"American* Odyssey." And reading
it helps us identify, not just with the struggles of Cedric, but also with
the larger struggles of our nation. There is a very clear way in which the
story of the book is the story of America struggling with itself, to realize
its kinder, gentler, truly democratic potential, in which the hero and the
implied author both serve to channel for readers a compassionate, truly
democratic spirit, or poetic muse of our nation, seeking to rewrite human
history so that all human beings are *re-created* equal. What is more, it is an
"American *Odyssey*," not just an updating of Homer (the implied author
behind Suskind), but a democratic broadening of the very notion of a
heroic journey to reclaim one's spiritual home.

By connecting with Cedric Jennings and Ron Suskind, Bruce's students learned to better connect with America and, in a way, with the
whole of humanity. They learned to feel better, not just about themselves,
one another, and a few other people whose shoes they learned to imaginatively walk in, but about a nation and a world that had in some ways
betrayed them. The book's title, *A Hope in the Unseen*, refers not just to an
unseen personal future. It also refers to the unseen human presences from
our past that we learn to feel supported by—the presences of the individual parents, teachers, and authors who have, in Robert Inchausti's terms,
"taken their lives up into speech so that we may do the same," and who,
seen together, also provide cultural support, secure *cultural* attachment.

To sum up, the evocative dimension of transactional response brings
us momentarily alive, brings us to the experience of "flow." But its connective dimension ties the flow of our individual experience to the flow
of experiences larger than our own. We see ourselves as beings connected
to others through their initial creation and our subsequent re-creation
of experience. The ancients spoke of created nature as a "great chain of
being" that was fixed for all time. The ultimate effect of the connective dimension of aesthetic response is to bring into view a great chain of being
that can and must be re-created time and time again, by each one of us.
The company of the implied authors we keep, with whom we establish
relationships, establishes—differently for each one of us—a human family, a chain of beings we have made loving connection to. The evocative
dimension of response brings forth a temporary story world; but the connective dimension enduringly peoples the world through the sharing of
created and re-created stories.

And as we transactionally re-create a beneficent past, so are we empowered to transactionally create a better future. The company of authors
we keep, the band of companions whose rendering of experience we deem
to have "augmented" our own, opens up vistas to the past as a nourishing

ground for the re-creation of the future. The secure cultural parenting offered through the connective dimension of aesthetic experience becomes the ground for the self-reauthoring that occurs in the reflective dimension, which we have already seen in the eight "re-creations" of Levertov's "Writing in the Dark," but will be exploring far more thoroughly in the next chapter. And reflective re-creation within the secure environment of art, in turn, can become the ground for transactional, artfully lived life beyond the secure space art provides for psychological nurturance, the ground for selves to meet and grow together in the real world, which we will be exploring in the last part of this book.

CHAPTER 6

The Reflective Dimension
Response and Responsibility, Love and Loving Wisdom

. . . for here there is no place
That does not see you. You must change your life.
> —Rainer Maria Rilke, "Archaic Torso of Apollo"

Never am I more active than when I do nothing; never less alone than when by myself.
> —Cato the Elder (epigraph to Hannah Arendt's
> *Thinking, Volume One of The Life of the Mind*)

The place of stillness that you have to go to to write, but also to read seriously, is the point where you can actually make responsible decisions, where you can actually engage productively and responsibly with an otherwise scary and unmanageable world.
> —Jonathan Franzen, *Time* (August 12, 2010)

"The great secret of morals is love," said the poet Shelley in his *A Defense of Poetry* (1820). He then defines "love" first as "a going out of our own nature" and second as "an identification of ourselves with the beautiful which exists in thought, action, or person not our own." The evocative and connective dimensions of responsiveness echo this understanding. First we "go out of our own nature" by entering the flow of immersive story time in the third space in which the boundaries between self and world partially dissolve. Then we come to identify ourselves with an implied author, through inferring shared insight into the experience of life they shaped and gave to us. Yet more is required of us than immersion and identification if we are to fully receive the gift of shared life that is given to us through art. We need to consciously make that gift our own: in Shelley's terms, to reclaim and renew "our own nature" *after* "going out of it"; in our terms, to find new wisdom that is ours to give, through finding life and love in the gift of art.

To read only to be emotionally touched and feel affection for others would be to read only fancifully and sentimentally. It is only through the final, reflective dimension of responsiveness that the deep emotional pathos and authorial ethos evoked by literature are justified: literature draws us into a feeling conversation—into "living discourse" as Moffett would have it—about the meaning of life, in which we are passionate, morally insightful participants, not just vehicles for sensation and affection in imagined experience but thinking actors in the drama of real life. Story time is not just time for pleasure, and for love. It is also, existentially, *our* time, time we are called to make special (in Dissanayake's term) within the particular horizons of the stories of our own personal lives; the stories of enduring cultural, national, and historical life in which our personal lives are immersed and enmeshed; and, through these, in what Rachel Remen calls the One Story of life itself. Story time is not just dream time in which we are submerged in fantasy (though it is that in part). Fully experienced, it is time when we grow awake to the meaning of our own story within the story of life. Through the reflective dimension of responsiveness, we are moved to see, consider, and live our own lives anew. And if we are not so moved, the central educative and transformative function of art has not been fulfilled—and a large part of its evolutionary survival value is lost. Put another way, as emotionally and interpersonally fulfilling as art may be in connecting us to the present and the past, if it remains sterile in respect to the future, it is transactionally and transpersonally incomplete. A complete mimeme is an opening of present experience to *two* new temporal horizons: one to a creative moment in the past that has been given to us, another to our own newly creative power to resee and remake the future. The greatest gift of aesthetic response is the desire to take new responsibility, to somehow live more artfully and meaningfully in the real world.

WHAT IS TRANSACTIONAL, AESTHETIC REFLECTION?: MAKING RE-CREATIVE WISDOM VISIBLE

The poet Rilke perhaps best crystallized the reflective dimension of aesthetic experience at the end of a long poetic meditation on an ancient sculpture: "[H]ere there is no place / That does not see you. You must change your life." What Rilke beautifully captures is how art is a form of light. "You must change your life," precisely because this new light has prismatically bent that life in new directions, *literally* "reflected" it by placing it for a time in a different medium.

Again, let's start to see how this works by examining it in microcosm, through Bruce's, Jeff's, and your own reflections on the process of our "re-creation" of Levertov's "Writing in the Dark" (see Chapter 3, Figure 3.2).

Bruce's was written in early morning darkness (though he did turn the light on). As he wrote his poem, some of the unqualifiedly positive words that had called to him in Levertov's poem—"the vision," "to make the sun rise again"—were neglected in favor of more tentative ones. Levertov's opening flowers became a possibly opening door, with someone possibly behind it. Levertov used the word "words" once toward the end of her poem, but Bruce used it seven times, including the title, "Words Before Morning," the title coming to him right after he finished writing the poem itself. As you might guess, this poem came to be during the process of writing this book, a project one undertakes "in the dark," as an act of faith, without knowing how one's readers will receive it. And it came to be about the process of transactional knowing, the subject of this book: how we need words to make friends with strangers, but to do so we need to let the words, in part, choose us, rather than bending them to our will; and how this process of letting words befriend us is similar to how we let people do the same. As someone whose customary persona is of being a visionary, Bruce liked how he was able to take on a more tentative persona in writing this, one more concretely hopeful in being less wildly visionary; and how he did that by first being attracted to Levertov's visionariness in his notes, but then realizing he was out for something more for himself. He was particularly pleased with the growth in meaning between the two uses of "Who knows?" at the end of each stanza: both expressing tentativeness, but the first dissatisfied with the tentativeness, the second not just reconciled to it but maturely and hopefully embracing it. And he is also particularly pleased to now have a meaningful part of his own life and personal growth inscribed within this book about the journey of existential inquiry.

Jeff resisted writing his re-creation poem for some time. He was busy and preoccupied. His wife Peggy was in the hospital in the direst of circumstances, and for some time there was discussion whether she would make it through. When the life-threatening phase was through, she entered into a long coma. Jeff felt that he was "stumbling in the dark" and didn't know how to express all of his jumbled feelings. He knew the poem would be about his intense emotions about Peggy, and he didn't feel up to expressing his feelings about it. Jeff eventually wrote the poem during a workshop with Bruce as what might be considered a "forced memo" or poem; he had to do it as a participant in a group. Once he started, though, it was all good and flowed from him. He also was supported emotionally and as a writer by his group in ways that were uplifting to him.

Jeff picked up on images and feelings that resonated with him at the moment of the writing, that connected to his wife's being in the hospital and not being sure if she would survive, but believing very intensely and perhaps somewhat irrationally that she would, maybe in some way he could not yet understand. Though the meanings, like all artistic meanings, are such that they cannot be expressed literally, they might be crudely named in the following way. He begins by expressing how much he wishes the ordeal was over and done with. Next he expresses his fear of "the night," both real and symbolic (he disliked going home to an empty house and bed, and is fearful of death and the unknown), yet acknowledges that this fear has uncovered many feelings and realizations that he would not cover up again: the depth of his love and appreciation for Peggy, her personhood, and for life itself. In the next stanza, deep in his unconscious a falcon (the ego; rationality; a control complex) releases its talons from his heart (his feeling center/True Self), which becomes a flower (repressed feelings coming to light, pure spirit/one with God) and bursts into blossom (rebirth into a new being and Self), which by its very flowering and need calls the sun to rise again for a renewal with life (Peggy's survival on one level, but more than that a new kind of consciousness and living no matter what happens).

In many ways, artistic creation and response makes us into a "better self" and Jeff wrote afterwards that writing the poem "place-held and clarified" feelings and helped him to be "wide awake to both the negative and the positive" about a very difficult experience. This in turn helped him to be a good support for Peggy and a best possible self for assisting himself and his daughters in the difficulty of the current circumstances.

Several weeks later, Jeff felt some enduring effects on his life, small though they may be, from doing the writing. He wrote the following entry in his journal:

> It reminds me and makes me conscious of my own feelings while
> Peggy was sick and in the hospital. I gave her the poem when
> she awoke from her coma, and it was moving to her. It expressed
> something between us that is difficult and maybe impossible to put
> into more prosaic terms. It reminds me of what it was like to go
> through that and maintain hope in the face of it—particularly since
> we know it is likely to happen again. Reading it, I feel stronger
> that I can face the challenges of the future. I am reassured that
> night is followed by day and that the way we live can bring the
> day into being, make the sun psychically rise for ourselves and
> others around us.

And you? How did you move from the response notes on first hearing Levertov's poem to creating your own poetry? What did you need to bring to awareness or change about yourself to write what you did? And how do you see yourself anew or differently after writing it? What new aspects of yourself, what new prospects for your life, can be observed after this writing?

If the exercise was successful for you, we're guessing it gave you a new sense of personal freedom, the freedom to securely create, to find new insights into your own life through Levertov's insights into hers, though it's not always as easy as Gabriele Rico's re-creation exercise tends to make it. Consider the words of Jonathan Franzen, the author of the much acclaimed novel *Freedom:* "The place of stillness that you have to go to to write, but also to read seriously, is the point where you can actually make responsible decisions, where you can actually engage productively and responsibly with an otherwise scary and unmanageable world." This highlights that aesthetic, transactional reflection is different from analytic cogitation. Because this reflection is grounded in transpersonal communication, in shared life, it creates, in a context of outward stillness, a feeling of inward flow, from insight to insight. The author's and our own wisdom are related as secure parents and children are: We see the world for ourselves in the context of a loving environment, in a world whose deepest problems we can freely explore while knowing that nothing utterly destructive will happen to us, as long as we are *here* with *them*. And when we take independent responsibility in the real world for the problems we've explored in the secure context of art, we take that sense of security and shared insight with us: We're not existentially alone, but existentially together with others who have confronted and learned to claim responsibility for similar problems.

FROM MICROCOSMIC MIMEMES
TO THE BIG STORIES OF REAL LIFE:
RESPONSE TO LITERATURE AS EXISTENTIAL EXPLORATION

Understanding how aesthetic reflection works in microcosm, though, doesn't yet give us an idea of its complete power. An individual transactional experience, or mimeme, is a unit rather like a contained cell of a living organism. It needs to be understood in terms of its meaning within a larger whole, networked to a larger and more complete set of meanings. The whole organism of which the mimeme is a kind of cell is the journey of a meaningfully led life. The reflective response to a work of art, or other aesthetically conceived experience, is an organic moment in the course of a life dedicated to the organic growth of personal moral responsibility toward the world in which that life is found. This, we think, is what we really want when we say we want to help our students become lifelong readers: We want them to continually seek a meaningful life of loving wisdom.

So, before we talk about how we bring the reflective dimension of transaction into our classrooms, we need to try to give you some idea of how it can affect our lives as a whole. To do that, we'd like first to go a little deeper into the stories we told in Chapter 5 about our relationships with Hesse and Shakespeare, as a way of tracking how the two of us can see we have gradually grown as human beings through these relationships. Then Jeff will share a major transformation that occurred in his daughter Fiona's life through a recent literary encounter. We're moving, in other words, from the microcosmic directly to the macrocosmic level before we move to the level of practice. Like good physicians, we're getting a view both of elemental cell structure and overall organismal function before we discuss how we as teachers can best help move the life process along. Since we can't see our *students'* whole lives, we need to look at ones we're very familiar with to get the macrocosmic view.

FRIENDS FOR LIFE: AESTHETIC REFLECTION AS THE LIFELONG MARRIAGE OF TRUE MINDS

The concluding passage from Jeff's favorite Hesse poem reads (in Jeff's translation from the German) "over the fields, across the rivers and hills/ The lost child of my mother wanders, searching for home." The line always gives Jeff a frisson of pleasure. It's simple but so deep and complex. Jeff sees the fields as work and the fruits of labor, the rivers as life boundaries and transitions, the hills as personal life challenges. He loves the phrase "the lost child of my mother," and though he knows the phrase well, it always surprises him a little that the lost child is revealed to be—himself. These lines summarize Hesse's work to Jeff: his unflinching dives into the depths of the unconscious, with all its complexes, to help us navigate the journey of our lives in more worthy, wide-awake, and satisfying ways—to find, in other words, our home. This notion of a search for home is at once physical, symbolic, and psychic to Jeff. He is the child of a first-generation immigrant. He has lost both his parents, his mother at a young age. He sees his life journey as finding and fulfilling his destiny to become a whole person in some way he does not yet fully understand. This process of crossing fields, rivers, and hills likewise summarizes Jeff's fascination with Hesse, and his relationship with Hesse and his body of work.

Hesse has served as a kind of archetypal spirit guide or "god teacher" to Jeff throughout his adult life. He has explored with Hesse the navigation of the "fields" or the world of work with Magister Ludi of *The Glass Bead Game*. He has waded the "rivers" of personal transitions with *Demian* and with *Narcissus and Goldmund*, dove to the depths of those rivers and into an exploration of the "unconscious" with *Steppenwolf*, and climbed the inevitable hills with *Siddhartha,* eventually winding up at the river again, with the river as his symbolic teacher and guide. Like Siddhartha, he sees himself as a "boatman" gaining personal depth, if not wisdom, from ferrying others through their life challenges and across their current boundaries, which is how he considers his career as a teacher. When there is no one to ferry, he reads, again like Siddhartha, the river of life (the literature and art he so passionately loves) in moments of treasured quiet and reflection.

Bruce wants to focus here on just one small part of his relationship with Shakespeare: his growing understanding of the importance of the idea of "the marriage of true minds" from Sonnet 116. When given the assignment to memorize a favorite poem—by a creative writing teacher he was studying with in his late thirties, to help prepare him to be the advisor for a high school literary magazine—this was the one he alighted on. He hadn't been aware before being given this assignment that it *was* his favorite. But it was quite clear once he'd chosen it why it was. Bruce's life has been filled—and fraught—as Shakespeare's also evidently was, with rich, yet problematic relationships of many kinds: familial, romantic, intellectual. What this poem taught him was how and why to hold onto the good, secure parts of those important relationships. To cut others off, as they might have done to you, is to betray, not just your love, but love itself, and the life it gives.

In the course of writing this book with Jeff, Bruce has also come to see the thinking of this poem to be interwoven with a long history of human thought on this topic—and on its social, political, and philosophical, not just personal importance—that our book seeks to pick up and continue. This notion of an ongoing conversational thread has been picked up on by many of the poem's commentators (e.g., Booth, 1977): how it takes up Plato's understanding that the true divinity of love is not, as we tend to imagine, in the worshipped object of love, but in the heart of the one who loves, and thus can survive the loss of the loved object through one cause or another. As he thought more about his relationship to Shakepeare though, Bruce lit on the fact that there is a very clear echo of Sonnet 116 in Matthew Arnold's "Dover Beach," the poem that became one of the seminal influences on the creation of the discipline of democratic humanism that came to be called "English" (see the discussion in Chapter 2). At the climax of that poem, Arnold says to his beloved, "Ah, love, let us be true / To one another!" As there is no objective truth in the world that we can gain, this effort to "*be* true" is the only solution open to us. In the modern world, in which we live "as on a darkling plain," a flat world, there is no clear source of higher authority, and thus "ignorant armies clash by night." To compare "Let me not to the marriage of true minds /

Admit impediments" in Shakespeare to "Ah, love, let us be true / To one another!" in Arnold makes it clear that, whether Arnold was consciously aware of it or not, Sonnet 116 was very likely a poetic germ of the central moment of "Dover Beach," the writing of which was the key existential event for his eventual shaping, nearly 2 decades later, of the theories of democratic humanism in his *Culture and Anarchy*—which were, in turn, instrumental in the shaping of what came to be called "English" (see Novak, 2002a, 2002b, 2003).

What is more, something of the understanding of the critical importance of learning to *be* true seems to have rubbed off both on Gandhi and on Dewey in their understandings of "being the change" and "aesthetic transaction," also seen by them as what is primarily needed to save the modern world from "chaos," Arnold's "ignorant armies clash[ing] by night." Shakespeare's "marriage of true minds" and Arnold's "being true" have thus exerted a tremendous amount of what we in the last chapter called "transactional authority": the reflected-upon rather than commanded authority which art evolved to teach us and which Robert Inchausti's "real teachers" seek to exert through their artful teaching. Transactional authority *is*, in fact, "the marriage of true minds," "being true," and "being the change."

Here we also come to a clearer understanding of what aesthetic, transactional reflection is: a blossoming of the love one has felt for an implied author through a transitional object in a meaningful understanding of how the power of that love is in very large part the accumulated power of one's own life force and how this needs to be exerted in one's actual life. Through being immersed, partially dissolved, and softened in the flow experience of art, and lovingly connected to the alter ego of the implied author, we are newly able to feel the flow of the meaning of our own lives as coming from somewhere other than our own egos. In *The Ego and the Id* (1923), Freud posited the existence of a strict, punishing conscience, which he called the "superego" (in German, "*das Über-ich*," literally, the "over-I"), constantly demanding moralistic compliance with its strict moral standards. Transactional authority provides us with a kinder, gentler form of conscience, a reflective "trans-ego" or connected "beyond-me"; a nurturing presence, a transpersonal secure base that helps us reflectively discover new personal possibilities and meanings in life; a *secure* rather than an anxious, ambivalent conscience, freely creating new life with the blessing of the past rather than clinging to old forms of life in fear of it.

With this we are ready to go to Fiona for an example of how aesthetic reflection can lead to aesthetic action: the impulse to make the world a better place that arises organically from the transactional process.

FIONA :
AESTHETIC REFLECTION LEADS TO A LIFE QUEST

Fiona, Jeff's older daughter, is known for many things. She is tremendously funny and irreverent. She is caring and deeply spiritual. She is very divergent, creative, artistic, and musical. She doesn't compromise when she feels her identity or anything else of significance is at stake. She is truly and utterly herself.

Despite all her numerous and various strengths, Fiona can be disorganized and very resistant. She has, in fact, been resistant to school throughout her life. She finds lots of words to describe her schooling, but few are favorable. One of her favorite quotes, which she often spouts when asked about school, is: "School is for babies! Life is for grown-ups!" She sometimes elaborates, along the lines of: "School is a playpen! Life is a mountaintop! Let us out!" Just as with the boys in Jeff's studies of literacy and young men (Smith & Wilhelm, 2002, 2006), we see the bifurcating of school from life in her attitudes.

In her 12 years of formal schooling prior to university, there was only one occasion where Jeff can remember Fiona really getting fired up for sustained engagement on a school project. It was her senior year, and her class was pursuing the inquiry, Whose story gets told? Readings included *Things Fall Apart* by Chinua Achebe and *The Awakening* by Kate Chopin. Fiona was particularly taken with a subquestion: Who gets silenced and why? Fiona rephrased this for herself into a slightly different question with a social justice angle: How can we give voice to the voiceless?

At the time of the unit the students were required to devise a social action project that helped them address the problem-orientation of the essential question in some way. For her project, Fiona joined several other students in working with refugees at the Center for New Americans in Boise. While there, they interacted with new refugees and videotaped several of them telling why they came to America and what challenges they faced here. These videos were shown in class and in various other venues.

The group didn't stop there though. When hearing that the refugees had no good transportation options, they organized the collection and repair of bicycles for both adults and children. Upon hearing that there were few ways for the refugee children to interact with native Boiseans, the students helped organize a soccer league that would include the refugee kids. Suddenly, Fiona wasn't saying that school was for babies. She positively beamed when she talked about "her work."

It seems to us that every humanities class affords many possibilities for such discoveries, renewals, and reflections through projects, both small and large, and so do science and math classes if we are willing to stretch just a bit. In fact, if students are truly inquiring, and we are teaching toward understanding and application, then such projects seem both obvious and necessary. And if we are teaching for love and wisdom, as we argue we must, then working for social justice in the world is compulsory.

Curious about his daughter's sudden interest in school, Jeff asked Fiona why she was so fired up about her senior projects. "Because I see what happens when you don't have a voice or possibilities and I could see it happening to me. So I want to do something to exercise my voice and at the same time help others use theirs."

When asked what helped her see this, she went on about *Things Fall Apart* and *The Awakening* and how the major characters, as well as many characters around them, were destroyed by having their true selves and voices suppressed and denied them. "That made me really think," Fiona professed. "How am I being socially constructed? How am I being told what to be instead of being helped to discover who I am and need to be?"

Interestingly, Fiona revealed that she did not like either book that much: "I think they are too hopeless." Then she continued:

> In fact, what helped me with the unit and the projects were really books that I'd read before that provided more hopeful possible answers to these books, because they offered the positive alternatives. Like *The Secret Life of Bees* [by Sue Monk Kidd], the main character and the women who helped her—they were all standing up and making the best of bad situations. They resisted the status quo. They made new and really radical meaning for themselves in the face of challenges. So at the end of *Things Fall Apart* and *The Awakening* I asked, how could they have been more like the characters in *The Secret Lives of Bees*? And that really was my project, to be like the family of beekeepers and do something positive to keep the silencing and oppression from happening.

Now Jeff has heard Fiona complain so bitterly about school reading for so long that he was surprised by her positive reaction to *The Secret Lives of Bees*, which was a required text in the 10th grade. He asked her about other books assigned in school that spoke to her. She immediately ripped off: "*The Odyssey*—I loved that! And *The Alchemist*—that was an awesome book—and *Siddhartha*, *Antigone*, the Greek myths—I loved all of those!" Fiona then elaborated a bit on *The Alchemist*:

> *The Alchemist*—I loved the idea that your life has a destiny—he kept teaching himself to be better, to do more things, to help people and he eventually found and fulfilled his destiny, and it was right where he started but he couldn't have found it if he had not gone on his

journey. This turned me on to quests and I have talked and thought about quests ever since. I see my whole life and my life's little episodes as a giant quest. And that really helps me think about my challenges, my goals, to live with some more intention.

When asked what books she had read on her own that spoke to her, she immediately replied: "All the Harry Potter books! I read all of them twice!" And when asked what these books had in common for her, she explained:

If you see yourself in the story, or your quest in the story, then it means something to you—you can use it to live your life, to think through your problems. Most books don't do that for me, and teachers never give that any attention, but that is the crucial thing.

I know I get self-satisfied or distracted—thrown off my quest—like Siddhartha when he was rich or the Alchemist in the desert—but you have to keep going on your journey. You have to keep at it.

I think all the books I like are quests. All quests of finding your true self, overcoming challenges, doing what is right and true, which always involves shedding your socially constructed and pleasing-others self and being true to your true self and your real destiny.

Jeff realized as he talked to Fiona that he could usefully define his own life quest as helping those around him become more fully themselves—this has certainly been his wish as a husband and as a father. His professional quest is in line with this: helping teachers help kids through literacy—and now he would say: helping teachers help their students on their life journeys through existential inquiry and literacy.

TEACHING TRANSACTIONAL REFLECTION I:
FOSTERING PERSONAL RESPONSIVENESS

Reflection, because it is personal, cannot be uniformly taught. But if we see that it is the central reason for teaching literature (and, as we'll see in the next chapter, for teaching in general), we learn as teachers to center our teaching around it, to create situations that invite, encourage, and nurture reflective responsiveness.

First, since reflection is a habit of hearts and minds, it can be incorporated into just about any curriculum through regular rituals. Bruce, for instance, asks his students to write, after everything they read, the answers to two questions, relating authorial reading to responsive reading:

- How do you think the author was trying to change how people think and feel by what he or she wrote?
- How was your own thinking and feeling reinforced, challenged, or changed, in small or large ways, by what you read?

This transactional journal, submitted online the night before class, gives Bruce the means as a teacher to prepare for discussions that will encourage students to transact with one another. When we know beforehand how students have responded differently to texts, it is far easier to bring them into productive dialogue with one another. And when they see how they have read authors differently, by pointed contrasts the teacher can make between various journals, they also see how they are reading themselves and their worlds differently, and how they might reread them.

Second, we need to recognize that what Gabriele Rico called "re-creating," the shaping of literary and artistic responses to literature, is not just personally and educationally valid, but often the most complete way of eliciting and gauging reflective response, and the fullest way of internalizing response to literature. It turns the evocative power of the drama activities we highlighted in the last two chapters into transactional reflections—stemming directly from responses to texts and their implied authors—within the ongoing dramas of students' own lives.

Thinking Through Life:
Re-Creating Literature to Foster Reflective Responsiveness

After Bruce's first week teaching AP English, he collected his students' essays. Many of them exhibited a common problem. The abridged edition of *Anna Karenina* he had assigned for summer reading had shortened all the Russian names from three to two components. But the majority of student essays had all three components—a pretty good indication that what they had read was neither the assigned edition, nor any of the complete ones, but the CliffsNotes. The next day of class, he asked them to start reading the book and then redo their essays. One of the essays had a different problem, though. The student, Brad, had used the same naming system as the assigned edition, which indicated he'd actually read the book, but he hadn't bothered to type what he wrote, or even to pretend to care much about the assigned topic. Since Brad was already one of the more engaged students in the class, Bruce asked to talk to him for a moment at the end of that second Monday to see if there was a problem. Indeed, there was—a pretty big one for an AP class:

"I just don't *like* writing essays," Brad told him.

"Oh, boy," thought Bruce to himself. "An AP Bartleby the Scrivener, who simply 'prefers not'!"

"Well, buddy," Bruce said, "I'm afraid I can't help you a whole lot there. This is an AP class, to prepare you for an AP test. Writing essays is a pretty big part of what we do here. I'm going to try my best to make the topics interesting for you, but I think that's the best I can do. I'm sorry. I'd like to keep you in the class, but have you thought about not being in AP?"

"I like the book," he said.

"I'm glad. I hope you can eventually turn that liking into liking to write essays about books, too. We'll see."

That night, though, Bruce started to think: "Is writing weekly essays about literature my favorite thing to do in the world? Maybe not, believe it or not, even though I'm now proud to be an AP English teacher. I do want them to write something every week, but maybe that something doesn't always have to be an essay."

He thought back to his freshman humanities course at the University of Chicago—an experimental course offered that year by Jerry McGann, a scholar of Romanticism—focused on the question, What is wisdom literature? In that very important class for him, his favorite assignments were ones like, "Write the sermon Father Mapple would have given to his congregation on Nantucket after the demise of the Pequod at the end of *Moby Dick*," or "Write the letter Darcy would have written to his aunt to explain his affection for the low-born Elizabeth Bennett in *Pride and Prejudice*," or, his favorite, "Write a story about a chair thinking to itself" (an idea from Ludwig Wittgenstein's *Philosophical Investigations*). These were memorable and intriguing assignments, not just because they evoked secondary literary worlds in the writing process, but also because they provoked deep personal reflection, not a regurgitation of what was read, but a direct application of it to a creative endeavor in life. In particular, Bruce remembered how hard it was for him to summon up the reticence, probity, and respect he knew Darcy would display toward his aunt, how these were not just useful but admirable qualities that he, a member of the "let it all hang out" generation, could well consider developing in himself. And what he now sees as the "transactional, aesthetic" process of writing that letter did help him *start* to develop such qualities (though certainly, even at his very advanced age, he still has a long way to go with them!).

The next week in his AP class Bruce asked his students to write a parody of *Anna Karenina*, set in their high school around the Homecoming Dance that was coming up. Everyone loved it and wrote memorable stories. Brad's "Love Stinks" was *particularly* memorable. (Bruce gave it to a lady friend he was having dinner with, whose immediate response after she read it was, "Do you think Brad would consider inviting an *older* woman to Homecoming?") What was more, their essays the next week grew much livelier and more insightful. Their engagement and reflection in literary form improved their engagement and reflection in conventional essay form. Even Brad started to like writing essays, as each essay assignment Bruce gave after that was preceded, as a kind of frontloading, by an assignment in some literary form regarding the text in question.

Bruce believes that the students came to love literature much more that year, through regularly writing it themselves in a way that connected them to the literature they were reading, and that in turn helped them reflect upon it; and he believes that that love affected the quality of their lives in dramatic ways. For instance, at the end of the year many of them said they would never forget how *Anna Karenina* taught them that "trust" was even more important than "passion" in relationships—something if you just say it in an essay sounds right, but when it is lived by telling a story about it is driven home.

Two other assignments he gave in literary form come immediately to mind. The first is the final exam of his remedial junior class. Their last unit, at their request, was on Chicago. Bruce put together a number of readings, including *The Jungle, Native Son*, and finally, *A Raisin in the Sun*. He saved that for last, because the suburb he was teaching in mirrored the 1950s Chicago neighborhood of the play: Many Blacks from the city were moving into its traditionally all-White enclaves, a fact that was directly reflected in the population in the room. The "final exam" involved each student writing, in dramatic scripts, what they saw happening to the Younger family 5 years after the end of the play, and then the whole class tying their scenes together into a coherent drama. This they performed on the very last day of class, as most of the students at the school were sitting at their seats filling in bubble after bubble on multiple-choice exams. Most of what they wrote did not reflect well on what they thought of their local community—many of their scenes were horrifyingly violent. But the way they took to doing this assignment together showed them as directly as possible that they themselves had become capable of forming a kind of community their neighborhood had not. Quite a final exam, showing how they had collectively "passed" into a more genuinely democratic form of life!

Another activity is one Bruce talks about often when he refers to the power of narrative assignments to stimulate deeper *thought* than traditional argumentative ones. Bruce's first unit for his regular-track sophomore classes was on "school." The textbook he was using conveniently included a well-known story entitled "Barrio Boy" by Ernesto Garza, about how a young Mexican immigrant, a refugee from the 1910 Revolution, was kindly taken into a school in Sacramento, California. In a strange historical turn of events that became a "teachable moment," California had on the ballot that year the infamous Proposition 187, which was going to bar all undocumented immigrants from using its schools and hospitals. What

a terrific opportunity this seemed to be for teaching the skills of argumen-
tation—claims, evidence, warrants! Well, yes and no. The students *were*
all engaged in the assignment and generally used the tools of argument
that they were taught quite powerfully, but in a way that made Bruce feel
deeply uncomfortable with the assignment he had given. The Black students in the room were all strongly convinced that it was wrong for illegal
immigrants to take jobs away from *their* people, that this was another new
form of their age-old oppression. They had very strong warrants—it was
the law, after all, and for a change it was on *their* side! But they were using those warrants as sledgehammers. The one Latina student in the room
was equally eloquent, but the debate in this issue-centered class could
never get beyond an "us" versus "them" mentality. And the arguments of
the White students, though they tended to side with the immigrants, also
tended to be more tepid and abstract, as neither their people's jobs or their
basic quality of life were being directly threatened.

Then Bruce came up with an idea: "Let them all write a story called
'Barrio Boy 1994,' in which they depict in some fashion a young child
being forcibly denied education and medical care." After the students had
done that, and he read some of those stories to his classes, he asked the
students where they then stood on the issue of Proposition 187. Not a
single one, at that point, would publicly say they supported it. The force
of their warrants, the force of the law, even the force of past oppression
melted away, at least for a moment. Bruce does not recall a more powerful instance of what Rachel Remen (1996) calls the "power of story to
touch us in this place of common humanness, awaken us, and weave us
together as a family once again" (p. xxvii). He is not in touch with any of
those students now, but feels this lesson was an invaluable one for them,
teaching them to see at some level the existential fact that, no matter the
laws of their country or the history of their people, they are also part of a
worldwide human web.

The "Barrio Boy 1994" stories they wrote and heard brought out what
Matthew Arnold called their "best selves" and what we have called their
benign "superegos": their personal "connected-beyond-me's"; their own
inner, nurturing implied authors. And this, in a way, crystallizes the goal of
teaching transactional, aesthetic reflection. It instills and cultivates in students their own inner teacher, an inner alloparent who will help them see
how to affirm, preserve, and promote life through the course of their lives.

Thinking Prospectively About the Journey
of One's Own Life with the Guidance of Literature

Besides instituting regular rituals of direct reflection and designing
re-creative reflective assignments, we can also teach aesthetic reflection

through the writing of retrospective and prospective autobiography, asking students to directly imagine their lives in terms of story time. These assignments can take narrative, dramatic, or essay form.

Bruce believes that the most important AP assignment he gave was the last of the year. After reading Joyce's *A Portrait of the Artist as a Young Man*, the students were asked to write their autobiography in three parts, concerning the distant past, the immediate present, and some point at least 5 years in the future, using Joyce's technique of intense, image-filled "epiphany." (Realizing that students might not want a record of what they wrote in his files, Bruce agreed to sit down with students, read what they wrote, and immediately respond and assign a grade, if they asked him to.) This assignment was very much based on the tripartite understanding of human time advanced in Ricoeur's *Time and Narrative*.

The formal assignments for his university-level Philosophy of Education class (which will be discussed in Chapter 7) were all at least partly autobiographical—on the basis that if teaching is centrally about wisdom, one's thinking about it should always be at some level explicitly personal.

Most recently, in a developmental communications class at a local community college, Bruce assigned an essay that was at the same time autobiographical and involved literary interpretation. Along with reading Ron Suskind's *A Hope in the Unseen*, Bruce assigned them his friend John Creger's "Personal Creed Project," a beautiful, elaborately sequenced autobiographical activity (which we'll come back to in its own right in Chapter 9). They completed this assignment both assuming the role of the book's protagonist, Cedric Jennings, and for themselves. And their major assignment was to write a comparison/contrast "personal creed" through which they could find "hope in the unseen" in the odysseys of their own lives through Cedric's story. Here is a portion of what one student, Carlos, wrote:

> Beep! Beep! Beep! That was the sound of the metal detector when a student walked through it, as they were entering Roberto Clemente High School. Yes, they could take the guns and knives away when you went in, but they couldn't take away the violent and fear-filled thoughts from the minds of the students. My high school experience was a blur. I really do not remember doing any work. I never brought a book home. The teachers at the school never really cared about the students. And the students, all they did was fool around, fight, and smoke weed. A lot of people there, even some teachers, had that "screw the world" attitude.
>
> I am writing this spiritual journey of mine because I would like to be able to give the next generation some advice on life and education, through my experience, and the similar experience of one other person, Cedric Jennings. I also think I still have a lot to

learn from Cedric. Like him, I attended a neighborhood high school that had a bad reputation. But unlike Cedric, I didn't understand until a little later in life how much I wanted to live a different kind of life than the one I found in those surroundings. I don't live there any more, but I'm still struggling to escape. I'm trying to escape the violent and fearful thoughts, and the lack of care about life. . . .

First, [Cedric] learned never to see himself as a failure, even when he did fail on the outside, and he felt totally bad about himself: "It's always the same: he's thrown himself into a deep gulch. All alone at the bottom, he shouts for help. There is never an answer." Even with nightmares like this troubling him every night, Cedric buckled down, did his work, and "showed improvement up to the last day." I think I need to just schedule time to study and to not do anything else in that time, even when I find it hard to focus. As one of Cedric's teachers said, "Don't be so hard on yourself. A lot of the material is new to lots of the kids. Just keep at it. It will get easier. . . ."

A friend once talked to me about "metamorphosis," that we can change from one kind of thing into a totally different kind of thing, like a caterpillar turns into a butterfly. That's what I'm trying to do with myself right now, but I think I'll only be successful if I learn somehow to take the bad luck that often gets thrown my way into chances to become stronger, instead of plunging myself in weakness, shame, and insecurity. I have my tests scheduled for me at school this week, but I also have life tests I need to schedule for myself. I need to move out of my old apartment, be honest with my lover about what's happening, and schedule time to study, read, and write while all this is going on. Only time will tell.

TEACHING TRANSACTIONAL REFLECTION II: FOSTERING TRANSACTIONAL DIALOGUE ABOUT LITERATURE

The whole of his adult life, Jeff has belonged to book clubs. Whenever he has moved, he has almost immediately organized a book club. It's one of the few activities he feels he really needs in order to feel at home in a place. Over time, he's learned what makes a good book club: a group of people willing to read books suggested by each other, who are willing to share their responses, and listen and respond to and learn from each other. He feels that the best book clubs are truly diverse—bringing very different people with different backgrounds, attitudes, and ideas to the table.

Jeff and Peggy are currently in a very good book club, including a local musician named Mark and his free-spirited British wife, Gemma;

the irrepressible Polish retirees and world travelers Wita and Gregor; an economics professor—the very honored Herr Professor Doktor Meister Meister Meister Black (so called because of the German tradition of listing all degrees in one's title and he has three masters degrees); a fabulously well-read former English professor, Helen; a local hydrologist and Jeff's ski partner Dale and his polyglot wife, Meg. The boundaries of the club are permeable and guests are often invited in for a meeting or two if they are in town or have a special interest in the book.

As Jeff considers the incredible vitality of what the group actually does in their meetings—besides eating and drinking copiously (one member describes the group as an eating club with a reading problem)—he would argue that their activity comprises what we would call "public aesthetic reflection" along the lines of what he has described as the "reflective dimensions" of literary response in *You Gotta BE the Book*. As the group gathers, there is friendly conversation and lots of catching up. There is food and drink that is either directly suggested by the book (the group ate goat after reading *Cold Mountain*) or that captures a theme of the book (wingless Cornish hens after reading *Birds Without Wings*). Typically there is music that speaks to the reading, and often members bring in poetry or excerpts from other books that somehow connect to the book at hand.

At some point, one member, usually Gemma, will whip out her copy of the book and read one or two passages that spoke to her and then speak eloquently on the significance of these lines. Someone else will take up Gemma's comment, often giving a different interpretation. Frequently, a recasting or "what if" of the passage or scene will be offered.

At some point Wita will ask (and this really does happen every single meeting): "But is it LIT-ER-A-CHUR?" What ensues is a discussion of the quality of the text, of the constructedness of the text— its use of conventions and moves to create an experience for us—of what kind and quality of experience we each had reading the book. Often people disagree vehemently about the quality of the text and their experience with it, arguing, "you liked it because it speaks to you because . . . " which is the recognition of reading as a transaction. There is always a consideration and evaluation of the author as a real human being, and of the individuals as readers, and of the various "readings" and what work they have done for each member, or not done.

This is one of Jeff's favorite episodes in every meeting: the taking on of relationships with authors, and through them with each other. By the end of the night Jeff is feeling very close to all of his fellow book club members, even those whose opinions he disagrees with. The meetings are intensely communal.

Another thing always happens in every book club meeting—the book is no longer being discussed per se, but is being used as a springboard to think about and apply what has been learned to real life. There is often disagreement, but there is a lot that is learned from these disagreements— Jeff typically feels that the group is becoming something new together— learning to love each other's differences and at least respect them, sometimes adapt and integrate them into their vastly different selves.

Jeff has often considered how he can work to create this same kind of atmosphere and exchange and public aesthetic reflection in his own classrooms at the middle school, high school, and university levels. How can he create a classroom that is somewhat like the sharing community of his book club?

We've already explored many of the ways to do so in this chapter, but they are worth repeating here, and adding a few more ideas, naming how the different techniques develop the different interdependent dimensions of reflective response from *You Gotta BE the Book*.

First, students need to be encouraged and assisted to create a personally meaningful and compelling response to the text. This can be done as individuals or in a group, through writing or through art or drama. It often involves recasting the text, exploring and manipulating it for the fun of parody, the critique of satire, the exploration of "what if" that gets after how the construction of a text contributes to its meaning. It involves sharing this personal response and making it a stimulus and a source of dialogue about what the text means to each as individuals and as a group. It means reflecting on each other's responses, taking them up respectfully, and creating community responses that accommodate in some way the different responses of the groups.

First and foremost, the classroom needs to become a dialogic space, where students' thinking is encouraged, assisted and privileged (see Nystrand, 1997). In his book *Engaging Readers and Writers with Inquiry* (Wilhelm, 2007), Jeff explores many ways of doing this through different kinds of group structures—and that book, in particular, can be considered the practical, pedagogical extension of the personal observations and philosophical/psychological understandings we've mostly offered here.

TRANSACTIONAL REFLECTION AND THE GIFT ECONOMY: ALL THE WORLD'S A BOOK GROUP

Consider again the vivid exchange between Marie Bunscombe and E. D. Hirsch from the Wye Conference, which we related in Chapter 1. She asked him, "Can't I be literate and *different* from you?" and he essentially said, No—diverse literacy had to be sacrificed on the altar of monocultural standards. Bunscombe, understandably, preferred anarchy to compliance with the tyranny of Hirsch's standards; but her membership in the three-woman "wholistic/Joy" group of the College Section also indicated that she ultimately sought something beyond *sheer* difference and diversity and the anarchy implied by it. Neither the issue-centered curriculum advocated by the College Section nor the sheer Joy/life/student-centeredness of those who advocated "the power of softness" are in themselves adequate to overcome the monolithic educational agenda in the public mind. They oppose mere compliant, conceptual, and procedural unity with intellectual diversity on the one hand and momentary, joyful, emotional unity on the other—when what is needed is a road, both feeling and thoughtful, to secure, lasting unity.

The key to moving beyond tyranny, anarchy, and merely momentary joy altogether, we think, lies in seeing joy *holistically*, within the *whole* of story time. The framing of the prerequisite, evocative beginning of story time within the real stories of our real lives opens the way to sustainable reflective unity among persons and groups. This brings transactional authority to the real world, freeing us at the same time—to whatever extent it prevails—from both tyranny and anarchy.

Aesthetic reflection is the first step toward envisioning and enacting the human reality of "multeity in unity." Emerging from issues raised within the self by the encounter with the implied author of an evocative text, it enables connection through mutual vulnerability. Readers who have been separately opened by this experience can then connect reflectively with one another, as well as finding renewed visions of themselves and the future. This is how good book groups and literature classes also provide good group therapy. We inhabit *shared* transitional space; our varying reflections on the meaning of what we have read are offered as implied authors of the reflections of others. Just as author and reader grow alive in one another in transactional reading, groups of readers also grow transactionally alive in one another through reflecting together on the meaning of the holistic experience they have shared, but reflected on in various and often very diverse ways.

You'll see a lot more about how this works in Chapter 8, where we'll show how the dynamics of aesthetic transaction can actually help us re-see the dynamics of democracy, both the microcosmic democracy that takes place in classrooms and the macrocosmic nature of democracy itself. For now, though, we want to give you an image for the meaningfulness of communities, both large and small, that are formed in the space of shared transactional reflection.

One of Bruce's very favorite books—you'll easily see why by the title— is poet/anthropologist Lewis Hyde's *The Gift: Imagination and the Erotic Life of Property* (1979). Hyde maintains that supervening on all interactive market exchanges, or trades, is a "gift economy" in which what is given is not exchanged for something in return, but transformed and given again, ad infinitum. This gift economy is like a big potluck reading group: everyone gains and is enriched from what everyone brings. There are no winners or losers. Everyone augments everyone else's being. Just as we saw all the "re-creations" of Levertov's "Writing in the Dark" fed into each other's meaning.[1]

For now, we just want to leave you with this image, and with the idea that in a time—after the crash of 2008, the worst since 1929—when the interactive markets we have organized our society around have gone wildly awry, there seem to be very pressing reasons to create transactional democratic spaces. These are also spaces of what Dewey (1939/1988) would come to call *"functional* socialism" (as opposed to "State socialism")—where responsiveness and responsibility combine to create self-governing, aesthetic "multeity in unity." Could it actually be that our economic crises are brought about, in very large part, through lack of aesthetic, feeling responsiveness, and attendant responsibility? Even if this is not the whole story, films like *Enron: The Smartest Guys in the Room* (Gibney, 2005) and *Inside Job* (Ferguson, 2010) make a good case for it. And we think we could make a pretty good case that we could eventually save ourselves many trillions of dollars by investing in good book groups!

FROM BEING THE BOOK TO BEING THE CHANGE

Art and literature evolved to serve, in a way, as a cultural womb: a contained environment in which hearts and minds can be nourished and grow in a relatively pure state, protected from danger, able to experiment with different possible selves, different ways of being and of relating. The questions we will concern ourselves with in the last major section of this book move from the safe confines of a nurturing artistic or classroom space into ways of seeing how such spaces can connect to the often unnurturing "real" world in transformative ways:

- To what extent can we come to see the world as a whole as a nurturing environment? To what extent is the world we have inherited from the past "good enough" for us to live and thrive in, despite all the dangers and malevolent forces that exist in it?
- How can we promote democratic living within a "gift economy," and so help make the social and political world an aesthetic one of shared life?
- Most personally, to what extent can we reflectively turn the stories of our lives—both individually and collectively—into wiser and more beneficent ones?

Here we find the consilient bridge from the reflective dimension of art back to life, the bridge from insight into the finished stories others have made for us to the incomplete ones in which we find ourselves enmeshed in reality. The latter are lacking the protective safeguards of the contained experiences provided for us by others. But the central purpose for which those safeguards have been given to us is precisely for us to be able to learn to live well beyond and without them: to negotiate transitions in life for ourselves through the prior experience of transitional objects. We move from aesthetic reflection through art to wisdom exercised in real life.

Aristotle distinguished between "theoretical" and "practical" wisdom, a distinction that is very much with us today, though the word *wisdom* is usually dropped from it. Yet, just as there are three forms of friendship for Aristotle—friendship for pleasure, friendship for mutual benefit, and friendship for its own sake—we can find three parallel forms of wisdom: wisdom for pleasurable contemplation, wisdom for interactive social use, and wisdom for loving transactional companionship. And it is the last form of wisdom, unnamed by Aristotle, that we might call transactional, loving wisdom, the wisdom of aesthetically shared *being*.

We are all implied authors and readers of ourselves, of one another, and of life itself, insofar as we live artfully. Implied authors offer us their companionship, so that, nourished by them, we can in turn offer ours to others, to increase both the quality and the quantity of companionship that exists in the world. Our task is not just to *acknowledge* diversity, as the Wye Conference had it, but to understand it, revel in it, and learn from it; to be transformed by the differences we see in the world, by being open and respectful to them; and to seek to integrate those differences, to create "multeity in unity" out of them. The largest question of transactional, existential, narrative inquiry is: To what extent can we deliberately turn our separate stories into the "One Story" Rachel Remen refers to? That One Story that we so often get a dim sense of when we reflect feelingly together in public?

This task, the real-life "marriage of true minds," has always existed, but now appears to be a necessity for us to undertake. If, as Dewey claimed, the development of aesthetic transaction is both the summit of human evolution and what we need now to decisively evolve and spread to save the modern world from chaos, can we, the collection of existing and yet-to-exist human beings, arrive at a transactional worldview that can be broadly shared—fulfilling our evolutionary potential in ways that may yet save both our own species and much of the natural world we are now rapidly destroying? Can we discover an encompassing narrative, based on real natural and cultural history (our collective mimesis$_1$,the present-past); calling us to educative action and the creation of a cultural gift economy with stronger appeal than the competitive struggle for commodities and narcissistic glory (our collective mimesis$_2$, the present-present); to envision a wisdom revolution (our collective mimesis$_3$, the present-future)? Can we, individually and collectively, through learning to *be the book, also* learn to *be the change?*

Let us see.

Part III

READING *BEYOND* THE BOOK

Moving from a Transactional Worldview to a Transactional World

On the seashore of endless worlds children meet. . . . and play.
—Rabindranath Tagore, "On the Seashore,"
cited in Winnicott, *Playing and Reality*

Not only is history not dead, [it may be] about to take its first unfettered breath. . . . Time does have a future. Longer than the past and infinitely more hospitable . . . to the human race.
—Toni Morrison, "The Future of Time"

PRELUDE:
FROM ART TO LIFE, PLAYING IN REALITY

One of the epigraphs to this section comes from the great Indian poet and educator who was the central influence on Gandhi, therefore a perfect implied author for the transition we are making here from "being the book" to "being the change." This section is about bringing the "third space" that art and other transitional objects create between self and world into play without the use of these objects as props. We will see how to make the processes of the transactional reading of literature explored in the last section a secure base for seeing and living the whole of life transactionally. Through this we hope to begin to show how we can bring alive Lisa Ruddick's vision that "our profession may in time develop a culture that somehow uses literature as the basis for a complex exploration of the art of listening that is one of the creative forces of the world."

An experience of art flows from beginning to end; but it *has* a beginning, a middle, and an end to help it do so. The book or the stage curtains are opened; we experience what lies within or behind them; then they are closed. Art is finite; it it serves to contain a meaningful part of life. Life itself is infinite; but it, too, can be brought to flow as art does when we apply the lessons of art to it—the lessons that art evolved precisely to teach us. This is what Tagore's mystical image conveys to us: the idea that the spirit of creative play can create transitional space that is not just temporary and contained but permanent and infinite, if we can imbue the whole of our lives with that spirit.

Our lives—both our individual lives and the communal life we lead together with one another—are themselves a form of literature: needing to be well-shaped, to be heard and responded to, and to be revised and elaborated upon. The stories we see in life also contain life, and can guide its flow in the way that art does if we become awake to their meanings. The existential question we'll be asking in this section is the fundamental one: How are we to bring the stories *of our lives* into play with one another and with life itself for the mutual benefit and growing together of everyone and everything?

The answers we'll be offering come in three parts, in the form of ever larger real-life containers for nurturant play: the container of teaching, the container of democratic community, and the container of human history. The first takes the form of the relationship between teacher and student, which we have already noted is very like that between author and reader, where the gifts of the former serve to freely nurture those of the latter, to help bring latent possibilities into emergence over the course of a contained time. The second takes the form of the community where, over time, people seek to come into play with one another as equals; here the intentional development of democratic community in classrooms and schools becomes the prototype for the large ongoing story of the evolution of democratic life as a whole into a new, transactional form, whose overriding purpose is not just mutual benefit, or enlightened self-interest, but full human fellowship and mutual enlightenment.

Teachers educated in the progressive tradition tend to have the two transactional ideals of the caring pedagogical relationship and the authentic democratic community already in view. But the complete transactional worldview has a third dimension, a deeper story that must be told, that we believe also needs to be thoroughly embodied in the education of teachers.

The third dimension of transactional life, beyond particular relationships and communities, is wisdom in general—presence to, reverence for, and responsibility toward life as a whole—which both antedates democracy and needs to be seen as the largest and fullest goal of democratic life. The establishment of democratic fellowship among diverse persons needs to be seen as part and parcel of the establishment of the integration of the human species with life and our natural environment as a whole—surely the greatest challenge of the present time, and one requiring all our help. So the subject of the last chapter of this section (Chapter 9) will be the narrative container of the human story as a whole: the horizon of the human past insofar as it has fed meaningfully into the present; and the horizon of the human future that we can, and now must, meaningfully transform and re-create, precisely by seeking to be as fully, wisely *present* as possible to ourselves, others, and the world. What we will seek to show here is how the story of human history can actually be seen, as Toni Morrison has said, as "perhaps about to take its first unfettered breath"— despite, and in some ways precisely because of, the many deep dangers that now threaten us—and how we need this story clearly, vividly, and publicly told to have real hope for teachers to communicate it to those who need to live it.

CHAPTER 7

Aesthetic Education

The Artistry of Transactional Life in Classrooms

In Chapter 5 we spoke of artists as teachers; but teachers, of course, are also artists. Teaching—real, humane, vital teaching which, of course, doesn't just occur in classrooms—could be considered the literature of life. All of us, insofar as we are aware of our lives transacting with others around us for mutual benefit, are teachers and learners.[1] And it is the highest privilege of professional teachers to engage in the process of sustained personal intercourse, the development of what James Moffett called "I-You" relationships, with an eye to the fostering of personal growth. This is the key difference between transactional teaching and purveying of information—the merely efficient, efferent, "I-It" instruction in facts and skills, in which the beings and relationship of those engaged in the practice do not necessarily enter in.

In this chapter, we will treat three dimensions of teaching that are transactional in nature, whatever it is we teach:

1. Its direct interpersonal aspect
2. Its interpersonal aspect mediated through the transitional objects of the curriculum we artistically shape so as to help students transact with the world
3. Its aspect of offering a transactional view of the world itself, which grows from the first two and is unable to take full effect without both being evoked

We refer to these transactional dimensions of teaching as being the "good-enough teacher," the "implied teacher," and the "philosopher teacher."

Our argument here is that all teachers—not just English teachers—need to be sensitized to the transactional life of teaching and learn to consciously enact it. At the end of the chapter we'll give you some examples of how Jeff's National Writing Project teachers in Boise embody these dimensions of teaching in their classrooms, as a way of helping you see how you yourself already embody them, how you might better do so, and how you might help mentor others along these lines.

THE "GOOD-ENOUGH" TEACHER, WHO REACHES OUT TO OTHERS' SEARCH FOR MEANING

In *"You Gotta BE the Book"* Jeff spoke of how deeply aware he was that he would always be each of his students' seventh-grade reading teacher for the rest of their lives, and how humbling a fact that was. The fundamental fact about teaching, considered transactionally, is that we are ourselves personal figures in the dramas of our students' lives, and the way we play the parts we are given in those lives may make all the difference to them.

Mark Edmundson, Professor of English at the University of Virginia, has written a beautiful book, called simply *Teacher: The One Who Made the Difference* (2002), about how both his love for literature and his love for thinking were brought about almost entirely by the personal presence of a single high school teacher, who taught an experimental philosophy class for exactly one year at the lower-middle-class high school he attended in Massachusetts, a course he enrolled in almost as a fluke.

In his essay "Ego Distortion in Terms of True and False Self" (1965/1960), Donald Winnicott speaks of the crucial role of the "good-enough mother," characterized by the ability to regularly, if not perfectly, "meet the infant gesture," to "read" the inner life of the one in her care from its outward signs. The parent's ability to "listen" and to "meet" the nonspeaking infant partly on her own terms leads to the formation of what Winnicott calls a "True Self," who in further development keeps learning to become attuned to her own inner life, listening to this inner life and developing it, now, independently of the parent, who has been internalized as a mentor of the listening process. A parent, on the other hand, who expects total compliance, failing to listen to and meet the child halfway, leads to the development of a "False Self," who will either be a slave to others' wishes or pretend to be such a slave so as to manipulate them to do what they want: hiding herself from the world rather than reaching out to meet it, and also hiding herself from the depth of her own real inner life as the drive to manipulate supplants the capacity to connect. This is the familial origin of the tyrannical mentality which transactional mentality seeks to redress.

Bruce's first published essay took its cue from Jeff's remark about the relational dramas teachers craft with their students and from an essay in Jerome Bruner's *The Culture of Education* (1996) called "The Narrative Construal of Reality." "Seeing Student/Teachers Relationships as Hidden Dramas of Personal Development" (Novak & Fischer, 1998) was a study he conducted with a teacher who was a friend of his, a fellow student of George Hillocks named Brian Fischer, containing a story of how Brian learned to become a "good-enough teacher" to a deeply troubled student, Angel: as is readily apparent in Angel's responses on his September pretest and his June posttest to the prompt, "What is your philosophy of life?"[2]

September: I think the world shouldn't be the way it is today. In this life you have to make choices that determine what your life will be like. I think that the reason why I act crazy is because of the neighborhood I grew up in.

June: My philosophy on life is to grauate [sic] from high school. After I grauate from high school I wanted to go to MCI, to learn on how to fix modern cars of today.

I want to be somebody. Somebody who people recognize. So people look up to me. Like President Bill Clinton, who is known very well. His name is known in the Eastern & Western Hemisphere.

But it will be kind of hard for me to do that because of my race. I'm a very troubled Puerto Rican young man who's had lots of problems since the age of 6 years old.

It's going to be hard for me but I think that I'll be able to manage to do what I got to do to be the person that I will and always wanted to be.

I'm taking life serious now because I have opened my eyes. When I was 15 and 16 I was blind. I took my life & life for granted. But I finally realized that life isn't a joke.

People have told me lots of stories about life but it went in one ear & out the other. But when I finally sat down and thought about it they were telling the truth.

Most of the stories people told me were true. But I still wasn't convinced, so I wanted to know. What I did is I read some books about life and I even found some stories that people told me and they were in those books.

So my philosophy on life is to set an example for the younger kids today, because if I don't, then who will. It's all up to me and the others who have opened up their eyes.

What Dewey said about transactional mentality is right there is Angel's philosophy: "The world shouldn't be the way it is today," but the key to making it different has to do with each of us learning to exercise the right to open up our eyes to see (Dewey & Bentley, 1949). The good-enough teacher reaches out to see others and to listen to them, so that they can in turn reach out to others and the world.

THE NEED FOR GOOD-ENOUGH SCHOOLS
AND A GOOD-ENOUGH SCHOOL SYSTEM

The large question we can only raise here is, How do we structure our educational system as a secure base for our children to learn how to form secure attachment to themselves, to others, and to the world?

Obviously, a big part of the answer is by educating teachers at all levels and of all subject matters to recognize that reaching out to students is a big part of their role. But we also need to see as a society that, although we certainly have many caring teachers out there, we have not structured our educational system at any level to promote the secure attachment of our young people to the world they will inherit from us.

In K–12 education in particular, the standards movement has tragically made education into a vast system of enforced compliance, teaching children that they count to the world only insofar as they fit its preset standards. Through this we have systematized a pedagogy of the False Self!

This is not to say that we don't need *any* measurable standards—standards of the "efferent," in Rosenblatt's terms—only that we need to recognize that education is centrally a transactional, aesthetic activity, an activity of felt life, that needs to be centrally geared to educing the evolution of new possibilities and new life. We have a horror of biological cloning, but we have become inured to pedagogical efforts at cloning, which have been around much longer, and are now being horrifyingly systematized (Botstein, 1997). Evolution would never have occurred if species continued reproducing themselves *exactly*. We need to clearly see that the False Self is also in many ways a Dead Self—one whose growth and life have been intentionally stunted, to serve the past, not the present or the future. When enough of us clearly see that, testing mania will go the way of "baby swaddling and the binding of women's feet" (see Appiah, 2010). What we now see as normal—and, in a way, it is just that, *pathologically* "normotic" (Bollas, 1987)—will come to be seen as cruel, outdated, and barbaric.

THE IMPLIED TEACHER: THE TEACHER AS CURRICULAR ARTIST

In some ways, the central means for education to become centered on the aesthetic rather than on the efferent is not the centrality of art to the curriculum, but our seeing the centrality of artistry to teaching. Teachers are authors whenever they have the freedom to devise some version of curriculum for their students and to use that freedom creatively, as artists do: embodying meaningful parts of their own experience so that others can imbibe it holistically and make their own meaning out of it. The word *curriculum* is not one we particularly like: as we've noted already it's Latin for "race course." But it is the best word we have for the way we construct cumulative, aesthetic, transactional experience through the courses we teach, as artists do though their works. Maybe one day we can change it to *amiculum*, the course through which we seek to befriend one another through mutual learning, and also change *syllabus* ("working together") to *sylludus* ("playing together"), but for the time being we'll content our-selves with the word we have.

When George Hillocks asked his students, as the central task involved in their becoming English teachers, to devise and teach an 8-week unit of conceptual inquiry through carefully constructed sequences of litera-ture and writing, he was asking his teachers to become creative artists of personal growth and classroom community. The power of the inquiry method, we believe, is not so much to disclose reality in any definitive sci-entific sense as it is for those engaged in it to become aware of the process by which we refine and deepen our engagement with the world, both individually and together. In that sense, inquiry emphasizes the reflective turn of mind and reflective dimension of experience in general, conceived aesthetically. Hillocks emphasized the tailoring of curriculum to *students'* interests and needs, but much of how individual teachers went about determining that depended equally on their *own* interests, character, and experience—as Bruce observed over and over again in the years he spent as Hillocks's assistant.

In *Strategic Reading* (Wilhelm et al., 2001), Jeff wrote about "teaching in the crosshairs" of the transactional space between students' and teach-ers' experience, artfully moving learners from being novice to becoming more expert. He argued that this kind of "multisided, learning-centered" teaching is far richer and leads to much more engagement and substantive understanding than either teacher-centered and information-driven or student-centered and natural-process teaching, strictly considered. See-ing ourselves as "implied teachers" in devising curriculum may well be the most powerful way we have of "teaching in the crosshairs." The "mi-memic" making of meaning from a created holistic experience is a form of shared life that goes deeper than the supervision of the acquisition of efferent sociocultural memes, even when the latter takes full account of where students are coming from to reach prescribed goals. What the Rus-sian learning theorist Lev Vygotsky called "the zone of proximal develop-ment" (that motivational or cognitive zone where a student can become interested in or learn and perform something with help that could not yet be achieved on her own) is in this case always half-found by the teacher/ author and half-found by the student/reader: creatively envisioned by the former and freely re-created by the latter. Curriculum is, in this case, a gift that is both personally given and personally received. It has what James

Moffett pointed out to be the human reality of the "I-You" relationship that supervenes upon the commodity of the thing that is learned, just as the creative "gift economy" supervenes upon the market economy of known commodities (Hyde, 1979; and Chapter 6, this volume).

Recall Bruce's doctoral student mentioned in the Introduction who said she would always "love and thank" him. If the person who wrote this anonymous evaluation is who Bruce thinks it was, it was someone with whom he had very few direct personal interactions, aside from comments he wrote on papers. "The experiences of the course" that that student found "life-changing" had almost everything to do with the general existential question on which the course centered: What role has wisdom played in my life, and how might my awareness of that help me deepen my teaching? And on the carefully scaffolded activities and writings designed to help students answer that question in their own way and with their own creative endeavors: First, telling the story of their growth in wisdom to this point in time, focusing usually on a single deeply transformative experience. Second, telling the story of a relationship with an important mentor. Third, writing, over several drafts, a dramatic philosophical dialogue about a burning, existential question in their teaching lives. As with implied authors, our love for implied teachers is all the more powerful because we love them through their creations, which we have made part of ourselves. And through those creations, which we have re-created, they remain alive in us, even if we forget almost everything about them as directly experienced persons.

THE IMPLIED TEACHER AND TEACHER RETENTION

Since much of Part II of this book was about the implied teacher personally and artistically constructing inquiry activities, and since more examples of such activities are to come, we are going to move on shortly to our next topic, the philosopher teacher. But like the concept of the good-enough teacher, the concept of the implied teacher can help illuminate ways in which we might transform, not just ourselves but our schools.

Bruce can still remember the thrill of one of his first student teaching lessons that really worked: How powerful an experience it was to see groups of students, with very little need for immediate direction, play off of one another within the activity he'd created, but was now mostly standing apart from. That was a very important moment in his life. Though he still at that point had quite a lot to learn (and still, 20 years later, has experiences of lessons that fail badly), he sensed at that moment that he had become a different kind of person, dedicated to the teaching life. As one of his own students later put it, before that moment, he had chosen teaching as a career; after it, he chose it, and suddenly knew it, as his destiny.

We believe that if there is one single factor that could most improve schools, it would be first teaching teachers to be curricular artists—helping education schools look more like art schools and music conservatories, where technique and subject matter is rigorously taught, but subordinated to the cultivation of individual character, talent, and passion—and then structuring schools so that this artistry can be given rein. The power of "taking one's very life up into [activities], so that others may do the same" (to slightly twist Robert Inchausti's definition of *real teaching*) is what makes teachers, in the end, more like artists than like parents, however "good-enough" they are. The most important and most powerful work they do is usually indirect. The more teachers are able to feel that power—and the life, love, and wisdom it evokes—the more of them, we believe, will stay in the profession. And the more teaching will become a *real* profession.

THE PHILOSOPHER TEACHER, WHO MAKES CONNECTIONS TO A GOOD-ENOUGH WORLD

The first dimension of transactional teaching is about the direct reaching out of teacher to student in "I-You" relationship; the second is about the indirect reaching out of teacher to students through artfully devised curriculum; the third is about connecting students to views of a "good-enough" *world*.[3] Teachers provide love directly, and they offer it through providing a supportive environment. But if they teach students, directly or indirectly, that love can *only* be found in protected environments, then they arc leading their students to form ambivalent attachments to the world and to life as a whole.

Voltaire's *Candide, or Optimism* seems an appropriate source to quote here. We live neither in "the best of all possible worlds," nor in a world that, when seen up close, is filled only with horror, entirely alien to us and our desires—in which there is an "impossibility of reading" except "deconstructively," as we saw another, differently minded Francophone, Paul DeMan, put it in Chapter 2. We live in a world that sometimes responds to us, and sometimes fails to—and insofar as we seek to cultivate the former tendencies and learn from the latter ones, we learn to see the world as neither perfect nor horrifying, but good-enough in its nature to support life and love. Eventually, we learn, as Voltaire put it at the end of *Candide*, "to make our garden grow": to reach out in ways that help make the world a better one, responding to nurture it, as it has often enough responded to nurture us. This is what we saw Angel learn in the first section of this chapter. Winnicott's "True Self" seeks to be true, not just to itself or to others, but to the world in which it lives, which has given it life and to which it can give life back in return.

In Chapter 9 we will sketch out a general transactional worldview: a narrative depiction of the world as a whole as potentially governed by transactional mentality. But we will note here, first, how we ourselves have each been led to such a view of the world by some of our own most important teachers and how we seek to communicate it through our own teaching.

Jeff: Teaching Toward the Great Conversation and Necessary Action

In preparation for writing this section, Jeff listed all his memorable and influential teachers. Though there were a dozen teachers on the list, Jeff thought this list surprisingly short given all of the formal and informal teachers and professors throughout his life. On the plus side, however, just writing each name that did make the list brought an outpouring of gratitude and many powerful memories.

Jeff then wrote about the teachers and their practices individually and found these common themes: (1) Each had leveled an appropriate and personally directed challenge to Jeff; (2) the teaching was suffused with engagement, excitement, and even joy; (3) the substance of the teaching was highlighted as profoundly important; (4) there was a focus on assisting Jeff to be able to *do* something new, on learning the *how* of some kind of process and discipline; (5) intensely personal possibilities and horizons were awakened and roused; and (6) there was a forging of a new connection and conversation with the world—to history, to the environment, to the discipline, and to actual applications and accomplishments in the world.

William Strohm, Jeff's high school teacher for two AP English classes and two novel classes, was the first teacher who really pushed him and introduced him to the debates, drama strategies, small-group discussions, and projects that became such an important part of his own teaching. Bill and Jeff have remained friends to this day and Jeff's abiding love of history, music, and the arts can be traced in large part to his relationship with Bill.

The most stimulating year of Jeff's life was a college year abroad in Saarbrücken, Germany. That year transformed the way he saw the world, most notably through an environmental science class with the aptly named Professor Drastik. What Jeff remembers was the passion he acquired for understanding, appreciating, protecting, and even loving the environment. Every Wednesday, students were sent off with a lab partner to a drainage ditch, a copse of rare trees, or a pond. Jeff and his lab partner had to find their way to each destination and spend 3 hours taking observations, doing identifications, answering application questions. From that year forward, Jeff was indelibly connected to the environment.

At the graduate level, Jeff's great teacher was Michael Smith. Michael's greatest contribution was helping Jeff understand the discipline of English and literacy education as a conversation, and inviting him into this conversation. Michael then introduced Jeff to George Hillocks, Deb Appleman, Peter Smagorinsky, and many other giants of the profession, who have, in turn, become mentors to Jeff. Thus Michael has given Jeff a twofold gift: a personal connection to a mentor and also the connection to a professional community and its conversation.

Remembering all these experiences together reinforced to Jeff that when teachers tell students what they think they should know they deprive them of the great joy, engagement, and learning that is gained from the process of approaching significant problems and figuring them out together with other people. This is why Jeff has devoted the last 20 years of his teaching to developing inquiry methods of designing and delivering instruction.

Throughout this book there are many examples of how Jeff frames instruction as problems to be solved. Here is one more example, a unit framed with the question, Who will survive? Starting close to home, students read about how the local environment, flora, and fauna have changed throughout evolutionary time. Then they read about dinosaurs and Tasmanian tigers, now extinct; about cockroaches and hermit crabs, long-term survivors; and about darter fish and other endangered species. They read about local and global extinction events, involving both flora and fauna. They play Mantle of the Expert, as scientists creating a theory of survivability. Learning groups keep giant Semantic Feature Analyses of every living thing they have studied, and criteria for survivability that explain why this life form either perished or has survived and evolved.

Every time Jeff has taught this unit, the students come to the conclusion, as one boy eloquently maintained, that "Mankind is going down!" or in the words of another, "The hobbits thought *they* had it tough! Middle Earth's got nothing on us in the evil department." Now, Jeff could have told them this was so, as he has been told in lectures by E. O.Wilson, by writers like Jared Diamond, and by his former neighbor George Mazurski, of ice core research fame. But telling them so would have made no impact. When the students figure this out for themselves and understand why this is the case (because we are destroying our habitat, undermining the biodiversity upon which life depends, living in unsustainable ways, losing our soil and salting the earth with farming practices, and so on) and can explain it to themselves and others, they come out on the other end demanding that the class engage in projects like reducing the waste produced in the school, supporting local and organic food movements, charting the carbon emissions from their homes, starting a campaign to walk and bike to school, and many others. The inquiry in which they engaged helped them to forge a new relationship to the subject of science, a far more considered relationship to themselves and each other, and a more wide-awake and responsible relationship to the environment. Their own experience of liveliness, collective inquiry, and collective action has made them want to save life, not just bury their heads in the sand, the most likely effect of knowing the isolated facts. This is nothing short of Voltaire's "make our garden grow" come to global roost, through the most literal kind of existential inquiry, on the question, How can we continue to exist?

Bruce: Teaching Toward Wisdom

As you've probably seen throughout this book, Jeff and Bruce both believe in fully inhabiting both the outer and the inner world, but the main focus of Bruce's life and teaching has been more on the inner world, whereas the main focus of Jeff's has been on the outer one. (And we've found that Jeff's focus on nature and action and Bruce's on culture and thought have transactionally complemented and enriched one another, both in our friendship and in our writing.) Looking back on the whole of *his* education and teaching vocation, Bruce sees its central theme—surprise, surprise—has been the growing understanding of the life of the good-enough world of wisdom. You'll get a fuller grasp of this world in Chapter 9, but this is how it took shape existentially, in the course of his life.

Christine Phillips, Bruce's sixth-grade teacher, was "the one who made the difference" in his life in innumerable ways, The one most pertinent here was her communicating the wealth of imagination and serious inquiry contained in the culture of ancient Greece. (She herself was of Greek extraction.) That year Bruce developed an intense passion for mythology, especially Greek. More important in the long run, he chose Socrates in an assignment that asked students to explain who their greatest hero was, led him eventually to the passion for philosophy that has been central to his life.

A few years later, his 8th-grade religious-school teacher, Eleanor Whitman, introduced him to the wisdom books of the Hebrew Bible, which gave him a sense that his own, Jewish culture also had a philosophical orientation.

Although Bruce was not overly fond of his sophomore English teacher in high school, in that course he encountered a curriculum called Project English, which presented a history of humanistic Western culture from

Gilgamesh to Thomas Hardy, divided into various periods. From this he discerned that there were three distinct periods of Western history—Ancient Greece, the Renaissance, and Romanticism—with which he particularly identified through their extraordinary vitality.

Then as a freshman at the University of Chicago, he took Jerry McGann's humanities class, organized around the question, What is wisdom literature? There he learned to understand and come to like authors such as Thoreau, Montaigne, Jane Austen, and the philosophers Ludwig Wittgenstein and Stanley Cavell, who helped him see how the best human thinking—best because most human and humane—was both deeply personal and organically tied to the language and culture from which it emerged. (Believe it or not, Bruce was, early on, a young math whiz, and his path to the humanities and wisdom was agonizing, wavering, and slow.)

Finally, when Bruce became a teacher educator, he learned to explicitly focus all his classes on the topic of "wisdom," coming full circle from what he had learned from the most important of his own teachers. The syllabus of his philosophy courses starts with this comment:

> This is a course in "philosophy" in the original sense, "the love of wisdom": we will be exploring how even the most ordinary teaching and learning can touch a profound level of experience when we allow ourselves to be open and attentive to life in certain ways, and how that same openness and attentiveness—Teaching, Learning, and Wisdom writ large—can lead us to a healthy, hopeful outlook on life as a whole, no matter what outward circumstances we might find ourselves in. The work of the course will be conducted through dialoguing on several levels—with historic ideas and texts, with current educational policies, with ourselves, with one another, and, centrally, with our own concrete, individual educational situations, past, present, and future.

The highlights of those courses for his students have been books and films that exemplify this kind of teaching: Rachael Kessler's *The Soul of Education: Finding Compassion, Character, and Community in School* (2000); the film *The Hobart Shakespeareans* (Stuart, 2006), depicting a fifth-grade teacher, Rafe Esquith, in the inner city of Los Angeles, who elicits the deep humanity of his students on an intellectual and emotional level that is astonishing to most who watch the film; and the film *To Be and To Have* (Philibert, 2004), which focuses on a teacher exercising deep humanity with his students even while teaching them a limited traditional curriculum. But they also read some of the great wisdom literature from the past that is relevant to their teaching, such as *Socrates's Defense*, Emerson's

"The American Scholar" (1837/1983), Lincoln's Gettysburg Address and Second Inaugural, some of Whitman's *Democratic Vistas* (1871/1972), and Jane Addams's "The Thirst for Righteousness" from *The Spirit of Youth and the City Streets* (1910). Following are excerpts from Stephen Sabovik's journal, showing how knowing something about a good-enough world of wisdom can be a huge support for a meaningful teaching life:

> When I saw the video [*The Hobart Shakespeareans*] of Rafe and his classroom, it was amazing to me. After reading the texts for this week [Emerson, Lincoln, Whitman, Addams], it really helped me put everything into perspective. In accepting the vocation of being a teacher, one of our obligations is to do whatever it takes to pass wisdom on to our students. That means breaking away from stereotypes of what a classroom should be like as dictated by some school districts. We must blaze a path of our own like Socrates did. . . . [Rafe] doesn't see his classroom as a place to prepare students for the next grade. . . . He sees it as a place to prepare students to do good for humanity. This goes along with [Emerson's] concept of the over-soul. . . . It is by the power of everyone together that a massive change will occur. Part of what will be necessary in order to bring everyone together for this cause will be for everyone to practice malice toward none and charity for all. When people truly begin to live that, we will be able to band together and create a true democracy that will take into account the needs of all people. Rafe created this type of environment in his classroom. They united in one cause, creating the *Hamlet* production. Within that common bond of the play, Rafe was able to help students find themselves and to come together as a whole. . . . The students weep at the end of the class, not only because they will miss Rafe, but because they will miss their community that they got to know and love. . . . It is through Rafe's example that I hope to create that close-knit community in which students can see their individual contributions but also feel a part of an important and close community. This sense of We and the larger community is who is going to give birth to a new freedom in our nation. We are all a part of this community and have integral roles. I am ready to take this role as an educator, to take my seat in the great conversation that will contribute to a truly democratic society rooted in the soul.

And he *was* ready. At present, in just his 4th year of teaching, Steve has already been repeatedly nominated for Chicago's Golden Apple Award—very quickly earning his "seat in the great conversation."

EMBRACING AND MOVING TOWARD
TRANSACTIONAL TEACHING

We have been arguing for a reconceptualization of teaching as a transactional and transitional project, a way of moving students toward different forms of love, wisdom, and wisdom-in-caring-action. Obviously, its implementation would be enhanced by certain kinds of teachers, a reformulation of school communities, and changes in teacher training and mentoring. As we have already noted, there are already many teachers doing this kind of work, enacting some version of the vision we have articulated. And all of the teachers with whom Jeff worked most closely this past academic year are teaching for love and wisdom, along with much else of value and substance.

These teachers are very different from one another, yet they share some common features. They know where they begin and where they end. They are willing to compromise, except when that would violate their own core values. They are forthright and say what they think, but are open to other perspectives. They are comfortable with who they are, while always working to improve and address shortcomings. They graciously accept deserved praise, yet welcome critique. And they are very willing to push themselves, push each other, and push back, but in the most collegial ways. They are reflective and work toward transformation in themselves, their students, and the various communities in which they participate. They are also "whole" and integrated people. They are dedicated teachers, but they have a wide variety of other passions and interests. Sarah is involved in various community projects; Andrew is an accomplished skier, outdoorsman, and fly fisherman; Debra is involved in church leadership; Rachel is a highly successful distance runner.

They each have their own individual style, their own unique and inspiring vision for their classrooms and what literary and literacy education can achieve for individuals and the world. But this vision is leavened with a strong sense of reality about the very real challenges facing their students, themselves as people and teachers, and the world. They've each made conscious choices to see the world and its challenges as they are, in a clear-eyed and wide-awake way, and yet at the same time to see all the most positive possibilities and work enthusiastically toward them.

Though each of these teachers embodies the traits of the good-enough teacher, the implied author/curriculum designer, and the philosopher teacher, we've chosen here to highlight one teacher for each dimension of transactional teaching, and then to use Rachel to summarize and integrate all three.

Sarah: Being the Good-Enough Teacher

Sarah Veigel is not only willing to experiment; she is devoted to it. Though eager to succeed, she is also willing to accept and learn from the inevitable failures. "If you don't wipe out once in a while, you ain't skiing hard enough. . . . If you aren't experimenting, you must think you've achieved the pinnacle—and, sweetie, that's just delusional."

Teaching is clearly Sarah's calling. She loves it—and that includes what she learns from continually experimenting, falling short, and seeing that shortcoming as a challenge to keep experimenting. "I'm old enough that I better keep trying new things or I might just totter into the six-foot hole. You have to keep moving to stay alive."

Sarah remains the all-time favorite teacher of Jeff's daughter Jasmine. Jeff can remember that at dinner her freshman year of high school, Jazzy often would say, "Ms. Veigel had us do the craziest thing in English today!" Often it would be a new twist on frontloading, drama, or group work—what Jazzy described made great sense to Jeff. But the point may be that Sarah was always innovating, and with energy and passion. Jazzy (now a university student) still tells stories about Ms. Veigel winking at her (and only at her, Jazzy is still convinced) when Sarah was being particularly ironic—one of her specialties. Sarah is always fully present and alive to her students — always trying to "recognize and call on their best selves." It's amazing how Sarah manages to personally attend to all her students, noticing haircuts and keeping track of extracurricular activities. She even tracks students long after they have left ninth grade. Her room is filled with clippings and photos of former students, and she was continually asking Jeff and Rachel about the seniors that she had taught, where they were going to college, what their writing was like, and so on.

The toughest kids always seemed to be called "sweetie," and they respond to her. Sarah has a great open-mindedness toward her students and their thinking in their current state of adolescent being. "You have to love kids as learners—as who they are right now. And you have to love yourself the same way. Push yourself, sure, but don't try to be perfect. That's a standard that doesn't work for anyone. You can't have absolute standards: you can't say that every ninth grader is going to be six feet tall by the end of the year. That's just not happening. You can't demand that of teachers either!" Sarah laughed; she is a just a smidge above five feet tall. "You need standards of progress—we are going to move from point A to point B. Everybody can achieve that. What you can demand is that everyone keeps moving forward—two steps forward for every step back. That's good enough. Even more, that's fantastic."

Sarah is fairly self-critical but it always comes with a laugh and a shrug and this tough-minded sense that "I'm going to nail this down soon." Sarah is a great example of the good-enough teacher. She is good enough on her own terms, and she makes sure her students are feeling good enough too, celebrating who they are and whatever success they achieve so they can enjoy it and use it as a consolidated base for meeting the next challenge.

How to Promote "Good Enoughness" in Teaching

When Sarah and Jeff discussed cultivating the capacity for good-enough teaching, Sarah's first answer was "learn to listen." Do this by focusing "like a laser" on listening to kids and cultivating this capacity with rituals: lots of surveys, partner interviews, teacher research interviews, and the like. As Sarah effused about noticing students as individuals, listening to them with respect, paying attention to them and their needs in instruction, Jeff was reminded of George Hillocks's famous mantra that "teaching is a transitive verb. It has a direct and indirect object. You teach somebody something, or something to somebody. Ignoring the somebody means you are not teaching."

Part of attending to students is developing discussion strategies like letting kids mediate discussions "and not saying anything during them, just take notes, help them, and then let them ask and answer the questions, teach them how to talk to each other and use each other's ideas." Use small group structures and rituals like literature circle adaptations, "final word," and silent discussion (see Wilhelm, 2007). Cultivate the capacity of listening "by using think-alouds, visualization, and drama/action strategies to elicit what kids think and feel in ways that you can listen in on, getting stuff you can use in your future instruction to show you are listening to them and being responsive to them" (see Wilhelm, 2011a/2002, 2011b/2001).

Sarah's second answer was "provide sustained ongoing teacher professional development in context." Teacher training, in particular, needs to be seen as apprenticeship over time. Sarah very much liked being part of the Boise State Writing Project's initiative to have a master teacher work intensively with a preservice teacher over the course of three semesters. "It's important to be team teaching with the intern from the start, collaborating and sharing in both directions, doing teacher research together" (all of this was required in the initiative Sarah was part of). "We need PLCs (Professional Learning Communities) run by teachers," with deliverables decided upon and valued by the teachers. "Teacher research is a way to listen to kids and to create our own knowledge about good teaching" but it has to be done by teachers in the context of their own teaching. Professional development needs to be run by teachers, for teachers, in the context of teaching in a school community, through teacher research groups and professional reading groups. "And we also need new teacher mentoring—we need to care for the new teachers instead of giving them the hardest teaching load, collaborate with them. We need to assign mentors to the newbies and help them into the profession."

Andrew: Being the Implied Teacher/Curricular Artist

We focus here on Andrew Porter as the artist who orchestrates his students' experiences in the classroom. When asked about how he shapes artful narratives and coherent experiences for students through his own teaching, he had an immediate response:

> This is what inquiry is! It's about shaping the curriculum with a problem and the story of how to address or deal with or maybe even solve that problem in some way. You have to learn the story and history of how people have thought about the problem. The measure of success of an inquiry unit is how far you can help make the story of the unit the students' story. And of course I want the teaching and the learning to be part of a meaningful story for me, too. That's one of the things that keeps me so excited about teaching. . . I also like using drama . . . .
>
> The idea behind my alter ego "Friedrich Mantooth" was, first, to summarize the plot and provide a literary interpretation for a particularly difficult chapter of *To Kill a Mockingbird*, which the students were really struggling to understand at both a literal and symbolic level; and second, to introduce the idea of responding to literature through a lens that might be different from the typical student lens of "here is what _____ is about . . . here is what I thought of it." Mantooth was there to show them that a reader doesn't always need to respond to literature from his own perspective, but has the option of asking himself, "How would someone like _____ see this passage through a gender lens?"—or a power lens, a different cultural or historical lens, that kind of thing. . . .
>
> Good teaching is about having a vision and a thorough plan for its implementation; it's about almost surreptitiously creating a community of possibility within the classroom. I try to bring this vision to fruition *and* use the community of possibility to be flexible and open to useful deviations from this initial map; this combination of planning, leveraging student culture, and flexibility creates a situation in which I look forward to the adventure of seeing what might happen. . . . I often get my best teaching ideas from my students so I am always inviting them to help plan what we will do to learn.

Andrew is locked into many particular texts and curricular activities, but he nonetheless finds nonstandardized ways of getting kids to work collectively and in ways that are differentiated, as we saw with his *Romeo and Juliet* frontloading. His classes—often very diverse in many ways—achieve a great measure of what Dewey calls "complementarity," where people bring their individual interests and strengths and different activities to bear on a common project, which is designed to meet curricular demands, but also provide opportunities for making meaning at both a personal and a community level. Even though he works in a set curriculum, the outcome of the response to the inquiry questions he uses to frame these required texts are not predetermined—this provides the adventure in seeing what will happen—yet he is the artist orchestrating the nurturing of the possible.

On his curriculum planning, Andrew elaborates: "I am an advocate of inquiry, and inquiry as an unfolding human story we are now participating in. There is the beginning —the frontloading where you introduce the students to the drama/trouble/problem/passion underlying the issue. Then there is the body or middle—the substance of the unit—which is about making the conflicts personal and teaching the kids strategies for feeling and thinking and reading and writing their way to come to a new kind of terms with the issue. I like doing drama, think-alouds, and visualization strategies to pursue our inquiries into how to read and write; these strategies require the students to be fully involved and explore their feelings and thinking and give them something to share. It makes the learning communal. The end, of course, is what each student creatively makes out of all this—both their final writing or other project that sums up their learning and their cumulative sense of being in conversation with ideas and other people larger than themselves."

As Andrew speaks, and when he teaches, you sense how he is tuned into the emotional value and valence of this kind of teaching. He is a designer and codesigner of the curriculum, an implied author structuring the experiences of his students toward engagement, the continuing impulse to learn, and deep understanding. And he continuously updates, improves, and tweaks his unit and lesson planning toward these ends.

How to Promote the Artistry of Teaching

Andrew believes that "first and foremost, your planning and your teaching has to be intentional." Andrew does this through his use of inquiry models. In inquiry, you engage in backwards planning—starting with the end in mind. "You have to start by knowing where you want to go, what conceptual and procedural goals you are trying to meet. Then ask what you can do with this group of kids to get after those goals."

Andrew emphasizes, "There has to be lots of attention to sequencing—to making sure kids are prepared for success, that one activity leads to the next one, and layers something new on."

Andrew thinks it is very important to "learn from your students how best to teach them." He's big on teacher research and on using daily formative assessments: think-alouds, visualization, and drama/action strategies "for sure, but also use little daily rituals like muddy/marvy sticky notes [in which students identify something they understand and something they still have questions about], gut-check notecards, graphic organizers about the inquiry. . . . You have to kid-watch and be willing to change a lesson or activity, even in midstream. It's not the lesson that is the thing but the learning, so you have to have a plan but you have to be willing to change the plan to keep progressing toward the real goals."

Andrew is also a proponent of reformed ways of apprenticing teachers into the profession through extended collaborations where they plan and implement units with master teachers "sharing their ways of thinking and their expertise." And he believes in cocreated professional development for all teachers: "dedicate professional development days and faculty meetings to particular areas of instructional design."

Debra: Being the Democratic Philosopher Teacher

For many years, Debra Smith has taught American literature, which she sees as the pursuit to "involve the students in the stories of America, the storying of America, of what it means to be an American, of visions of America and being American that we might want to accept, reject, or adapt. Teaching should be about articulating and testing our values, figuring out how we want to think, believe, and be. The English classroom is very much a crucible of working out a working philosophy."

The Great Gatsby is Debra's favorite novel, and she almost reminds one of a Valley Girl gushing when she talks about it: "The greatest book *evah!*" In regard to her teaching of Gatsby, she explains: "I like going through the back door. I want them [the students] to not know that they are being guided to think really hard about relationships, the role of wealth and power, dreams that are worthy and unworthy—in effect, about America and being American—about what they want to celebrate about America and what they want to work to change."

She knows that the meaning of all stories is not predetermined but is contingent upon personal and interpersonal interpretation. "The stories of our lives and the stories of the history of human culture are constantly being negotiated, reinterpreted, told and retold in varying forms." Debra wants her students to participate in this storytelling tradition, and she works to create curriculum that encourages this to happen. "The narratives constituted by authentic teaching, as opposed to both mere 'instruction' and mere 'diagnosis,' take these larger stories of human meaning into account." Debra summed up this way: "I want my students to see that the most essential meanings are not predetermined but yet to be discovered and decided upon . . . and that the one imperative is that they must be engaged in this process of making meaning."

As a philosopher teacher, Debra is sensitized to the life of students "as evolving beings struggling to become their best possible selves," and of teachers as personal beings involved in an intensely relational pursuit. She loves to think and talk about the issues that this involves. Debra works deliberately "to attune students to their own inner lives" and to the project of "developing their true selves." She regularly and unobtrusively shares snippets of her own inner life to help students develop theirs. During *The Scarlet Letter*, she and her student teacher shared their emotional experiences of divorce and recovery into healthy relationships to challenge the students' judgmental thinking about Hester Prynne.

Debra is enamored of the idea of teaching for democratic living:

> As a species we have continued to enlarge and expand the inclusive circle to encompass more and more of humanity. The trajectory of civil rights is toward more freedom and respect for more marginalized people. Whereas war was once relatively "cheap," a human life rather expendable, and education was expensive . . . .War is now very, very "costly," not only in terms of the expense in treasure, but also because each individual is valued as an individual. At the same time, information—the grossest and yet indispensable precursor to education—is now fairly cheap and incredibly accessible. I think that's progress, and it gives me reason to hope. And it gives my students a profoundly important lifetime mission. When I teach, I try to fit everything into this compelling story: the story of [hu] mankind and what kind of world we want to participate in creating.

How to Promote the Philosophical Dimension of Teaching

Debra and Jeff came up with several ideas for cultivating philosopher teachers. They agreed that teachers should all compose a philosophy of teaching and living and action plans for enacting these. Debra felt that this educational philosophy should "be in your professional file. You should revisit it each year to evaluate your progress, revise the philosophy, and plan the next year with it."

Pedagogically, Debra is another aficionado of inquiry. "Frame curriculum as inquiry—as narratives of struggling to know, value, and act—to philosophize and live out a philosophy—an examined life." She likes the idea of hot-seat dramas with authors (Wilhelm, 2011a/2002)—"I like the idea of personalizing authors, conversing with them, asking them, What are your values? Your philosophies? How is this expressed in your writing? Why should I be compelled by you?"

Debra also is big on students composing autobiographies that explore the questions, Who are you? What do you believe and why? How did you become who you are? Who do you want to become and how will you become this? Jeff and Debra also discussed using Process Analyses or retroactive think-alouds for students "to tell the story of their learning—justifying how they know and have come to know and value certain concepts or ways of doing things—this will awaken you to how you know and value—that's really important."

Debra also desires more focused professional development, "focused on the meaningful: We need to talk about theories, beliefs, values and how to enact them. We need to articulate vision statements and keep revisiting them and use them to guide our practice and decision making at the policy and the pedagogical levels."

Rachel as the All-Round Transactional Teacher

Having worked with Rachel Bear closely through several National Writing Project initiatives and as a coteacher and thinking partner in Rachel's classroom, Jeff knows Rachel and her teaching quite well.

Rachel clearly sets a very high standard for herself, in her own personal life, her academic work (her masters project was the most reflective work Jeff had ever seen from a teacher), and her teaching. Yet she has a ready laugh after a lesson that didn't quite go right. She adopts and often repeats Jeff's mantra "You're only as good as your last bad lesson." She wants to keep improving, and she knows that this requires taking risks and falling down. But she always bounces back off the floor. She knows she has a repertoire of strategies for adapting and for creating new repertoires. At the end of a long hard day, she likes to say: "Tomorrow is a new day." When evaluating a student paper that falls short, she says, "There are possibilities here to work on."

Here is an episode Jeff witnessed: It was spring and the AP English students had several big assignments due in several different AP classes (students tend to take several AP classes). Challis came up to Rachel and said: "Ms. Bear, if I could get a one-day extension on my paper, the paper would be so much better." Rachel readily agreed. Then he said, "Actually, if I could get *two* extra days, it would be even better." Rachel agreed. Then Challis said, "And if I could get until Monday, you would make me so happy and the paper will be *really* good!" Rachel agreed and said, "Let me know if I can be of any help to you over the next few days."

When Jeff asked Rachel about this episode, which left him laughing,

Rachel gave this explanation:

> He can be better and he can do better. And I can do and be better.
> Always. It's our job to help each other be and do better. You can't
> get at that by shutting each other down, or being too rigid, so you
> have to try to open up possibilities and be good with that—even if
> it's not going the way you would have liked.

Rachel is a *good-enough teacher*, who is at peace with being good enough.
And she regards her students as good enough—she believes in them, believes that they face a variety of challenges, and believes that together
they can navigate these challenges.

It was very interesting for Jeff to have his daughter in the class where
he was working with Rachel. Jasmine—used to dinner-table talk of educators—would often comment on Rachel's unit and lesson design, quite
often enthusiastically endorsing the frontloading to prepare students for
success or the routines for group work. But Jeff would have expected this
much, given Jazzy's background.

Interestingly, another student without such a background regularly
made such observations himself. Early in the school year, Renaud turned
to Jeff and said, "I know what is going on here," and proceeded to describe
the unit design to him: how the essential question was designed to invite
students personally into the unit, the frontloading to elicit explicit valuings
and feelings about issues to be explored, how the readings were sequenced
from easier and closer to home to those that were more complex and distant from his experience. Rachel shares a similar story about Renaud:

> Near the end of the year, we were working on how to approach a
> poem. I modeled a think-aloud with the first section of the poem,
> then gave the students a graphic organizer to use in pairs for the
> next section. They did this on their own with the graphic organizer,
> then on their own without one for subsequent sections.

> Renaud came up and said, "I see what you are doing. You start
> by giving us a model and support, then you give us support from a
> graphic organizer and from others with lots of talk, and now we are
> on our own. You figure now we have learned something and are
> prepared to go it alone—but you snuck all that support in there!"

Rachel then comments, "It was almost like a teacher would talk about
gradual release of responsibility, or modeling-mentoring-monitoring. It
was so uncanny!"

Clearly, at least two students recognized Rachel as the *implied teacher* who orchestrated their experiences and supported their success in non-visible ways.

Rachel also fulfills the role of *philosopher teacher*. She sees her role as teaching for democracy. "Democracy, to me, means seeing other perspectives and valuing and respecting these—then making informed decisions and being able to justify them—and realizing that you could have made another decision and had reasons for that, too." She believes that decisions should be based on "evidentiary reasoning" but recognizes the part played by "values and feelings," which must be acknowledged for what they are.

Rachel elaborates how she plans her lessons as a philosopher teacher:

In my unit planning I always start with these big, compelling philosophical and psychological questions. Then I want to embed poetic analysis, and how to write an argument and that kind of work in service of addressing the big questions that are emotionally compelling. I want to explore and converse about philosophical issues through literature and our own speaking and writing. For frontloading I go after preexisting student experiences and values—this is an emotional draw for the kids—it relates what we are doing to their lives. I like the controversial—it gets them to get after the concepts and be willing to learn new procedures for reading and writing. I want them to identify that "this is what I think *now*"—I always emphasize being tentative and challenging what you believe so you can deepen your understanding.

Rachel does a great job incorporating children's books, magazines, paintings, Web sites, YouTube videos, and the like into her teaching, particularly early on in units.

I really like the emotional connections students have to children's books like *The Lorax* or *Where the Wild Things Are*. I like to have them bring them in and read them emotionally, then intellectually—it helps them see the power of story and even children's books have this deep psychological and philosophical depth to them.

What am I trying to get at? I want to put texts in conversation with each other—and us in conversation with texts. That helps us see the various perspectives and engage in democratic conversation. Lots of time new texts are conversations with old ones—new takes on old stories—like we see in *The Odyssey* unit. I want students to think about their version of the hero in the story. What does it say about us and our lives and our culture if this is our hero?

If you forget that democracy is conversation, then you shut the kids down. If you are too explicit in your politics, you cannot have a democratic classroom. It is good to share yourself but not to proselytize. You have to encourage exchange and make the classroom a safe place for trying out ideas. Literature is a safe space—a liminal space. So is drama. Discussion should be, too.

Rachel teaches with a very hopeful view of the world, her students, and the roles her students can play in helping to create a democratic world.

We read a lot of heavy stuff in senior English. That is why I end with comedy—I want to explore the idea of how can we lightheartedly and joyfully improve the world.

At the beginning of the year, we tell the past stories and future stories—past stories are most often about obstacles, but the future stories are mostly about hope and optimism and the ideal world. Literature is like that; it tells stories about problems but also about the ideal world we want—and the possibilities for getting there— sometimes in the same story.

At the end of the year, I do a bulletin board about where the kids are going next and what they will do next. We return to future stories: What new things do you want for yourself based on what you have experienced and learned this year? I want them to be telling themselves and each other hopeful stories about their roles in the world—right now and in the future.

On Integrating the Dimensions of Transactional Teaching

Rachel believes that to meet the challenges of the future "we have to learn to work together." She is big on collaborations with other teachers, with National Writing Project initiatives, and with university professors. "We need more of them in school, collaborating, coteaching, working with us where education happens—and universities need to encourage and reward this."

She also emphasizes that "Teachers need to create and share their own knowledge" through reflective teaching and teacher research. "We let others speak for us and tell us what to do. As a profession, we need to speak for ourselves and justify what we say in ways others can understand."

Interestingly, each of the teachers echo an important finding of Tharp and Gallimore's landmark study *Rousing Minds to Life* (1988) that teachers need exactly what students need to achieve transformative kinds of growth: a clear vision and powerful assistance to meet that vision provided continually over sustained time periods.

TEACHERS *MATTER,* MORE THAN ANYTHING

Undeniably, the challenges facing teachers are considerable, particularly at the present moment. But the challenges facing the human species are also considerable. It will take many, many courageous and visionary teachers like the ones described here to undertake the transactional and transitional project to establish new ways of thinking and interacting, of living and being. This project can be abetted by new visions, policies, and professional practices, but it can only be brought to life by people like these.

All of these teachers express a wide-awake hope in the future and have a vision and procedures for actualizing that hope. It fills us with hope to hear their stories, and even more to see them in action, relating to their students and working with colleagues, helping themselves and others outgrow their current selves in the most substantive ways. This is the fundamental groundwork for the *collective* outgrowing of beliefs and behaviors that are no longer serving us well—as a democratic people and as a species—that we'll be looking at over the next two chapters and in our conclusion.

CHAPTER 8

Aesthetic Democracy
Government of People by People for the Shared Life of People, Writ Small and Writ Large

I've never been in a classroom that was a real community before!

When one of Bruce's students made this comment halfway through the first undergraduate Philosophy of Education class he taught, he felt he had reached a new level of his practice as a teacher, one he'd been seeking for some time but never fully achieved. A few weeks earlier, he had made a critical decision with this class, cutting John Dewey's *Democracy and Education* from the syllabus, because he realized that it would be far too difficult for these students, and moving up another work, Rachael Kessler's *The Soul of Education*. This was a book he'd used in some of the graduate-level Philosophy of Education classes he'd taught earlier, but only at the end, as it was not a traditional work in the field. What he can see now, looking back on this decision, was that it enabled this and future classes to *center* on the experience of transaction, which Kessler called simply "deep connection"—a term she got from the many students she researched in the course of writing the book, who told her that this phrase, more than any other, captured what "soul" in education meant to them. Contrary to both the more intellectual, text-centered approach and the more *efferently* practical approach that such courses tend to focus on, Bruce's courses became newly focused on *aesthetic* practice, by engaging regularly and directly in it.

The key day in the establishment of this classroom community came when Bruce did for the first time the "mystery question" activity described in the introduction to this book. As students heard one another's deep questions about life, read anonymously one after another, detached from association with any particular person and the automatic fixed judgments we are accustomed to make about particular people we see and hear, what John Dewey said about the special kind of communication that can happen through art suddenly happened in real life: "The gulfs and walls that limit community of experience" suddenly shrank away. And from that moment on, this was a different *kind* of class than Bruce had taught before.

What had happened? Well, just what happens *psychologically* in the transactional experience of art: The normal boundaries between self and world fell away, and a "third space" was created in which the students took in one another's life. The questions became group transitional objects, belonging to all. Not every class Bruce taught from that point on was able to sustain this sense of community, but it became a new central goal for him, in whatever he taught, to seek to create it.

MOVING THIRD SPACE FROM THE INWARD TO THE OUTWARD WORLD

Jeff pushed Bruce to use the term *third space* to think about this kind of community. His article, "Creating 'Third Spaces': Promoting Learning Through Dialogue" (Wilhelm, 2010), draws on how this concept has been used in learning theory. In what follows, we draw together Jeff's ideas about third spaces in classrooms with the understanding of psychological third space evoked by transitional objects that we have been drawing on since Chapter 4. Bruce actually latched onto the idea of psychological third space in Winnicott *because* Jeff encouraged him to use this term in its more social ramifications.

Those social ramifications are hardly confined to classrooms, though in many ways they need to begin there. The temporary suspension of the boundaries between self and world that art induces in us can also be employed in a temporary suspension of the customary boundaries that exist between selves, to form a certain kind of intentional community: psychological third space can be made the underpinning for social third space, as happened in Bruce's class. But the immediate social level is not the final level of third space. The intentional formation of social third spaces in classrooms and other places like them is also a form of grassroots, microcosmic community organizing that can give us a stunning view of what a large-scale democracy would look like in which *political* third space is intentionally and regularly created: in which diverse selves habitually seek aesthetically shared stories, shared life, and shared possibilities with one another in public as well as in private life.

The democracy that Abraham Lincoln first clearly called for—"a new birth of freedom" in which we seek "malice toward none, and charity for all"—already occurs on a small scale, whenever, as happened in Bruce's class, the members of any group learn to become implied authors and responsive readers of one another. Such groups seek to become self-governing organisms whose central purpose is the search for personal communion: They literally *are* "government of, by, and (above all) *for*" shared personhood. And as we learn to organize our social and political institutions around the formation of such groups—in particular our schools, which are the evocative "gateway activity" for democratic life—so does democracy writ large become more than an expedient arrangement for mutual benefit and begins to approach the ideal of true friendship, the social and political "marriage of true minds" seeking to "be true to one another."

As Chapter 5 was for Part II, this is the critical, central chapter of Part III. It shows how the social and political world becomes authentically peopled as it grows transactionally self-aware. As Chapter 5 showed how the experience of art peoples the world of the *past* for us with the implied authors we choose as friends, this chapter shows how the creation of social and political third spaces can come to people our *present* world with new friends. The experience of Bruce's student whose comment opened the chapter—and the experience of all those who felt the community in that room—was that of being members of a social group that formed an organic whole; an experience of "multeity in unity" of real, not imagined people, whose coming together was a work of art they all helped create, maintain, and grow. This is what we've been seeking to understand since Chapter 1, when we saw the disparity between the "personal growth" and "democracy through language" agendas that the discipline of English has adopted, and started to look for a new basis of "growing together," synthesizing the two, upon which to found a new discipline. An understanding of the formation of aesthetic social and political spaces on the basis of aesthetic psychological space *is* that new basis of "growing together."

Recall Emerson's comment quoted earlier in Chapter 2, the last sentence of his great essay "The American Scholar": Through a new, democratic "study of letters . . . [a] nation of [human beings] will for the first time exist, because each believes [themselves] inspired by the . . . Soul which inspires all." Understanding how the aesthetic loosening of the boundary between self and world allows us to make deep connections *among* selves *in* the world will provide the road map for how to make Emerson's new, authentically democratic nation come into real existence. "Of Experience," another great essay by Emerson (1844/1983), put it like this: "Let us treat [the people] as if they were real . . . perhaps they are."[1] Taking in and responding to one another's questions, stories, and other life processes *makes* us real for one another. Seeing how small-scale communities of existential inquiry, aesthetic collaboration, and just social action are formed, maintained, and enlarged turns out to be the essential question that unlocks the mystery of what a mature large-scale democracy would look like.

THIRD PLACES AND THIRD SPACES:
COMMUNITY AND LEARNING

The first time Jeff became familiar with the notion of "third spaces" was in Ray Oldenburg's *The Great Good Place: Cafes, Coffee Shops, Bookstores, Bars, Hair Salons, and Other Hangouts at the Heart of a Community* (1989). The "third place" is a term used in that book to describe social settings separate from the two usual social environments of home and the workplace/school. Oldenburg argues that third places are essential to civil society, civic engagement, a sense of belonging, and localized empowerment, even democracy itself. They are "anchors" of community life, facilitating and fostering broad and creative interactions and social projects that go beyond as well as integrate the concerns of home and work/school. All societies have informal social spaces, but for Oldenburg what is new in modern times is the need to intentionally create them to address vital, current social needs—just as Dissanayake claimed we need to refind the cultural attachment we're now missing through intentionally cultivating the arts.

The third places already in most schools are called "extracurriculur activities": the sports and clubs that students belong to usually because they choose to. A high school principal Bruce worked under was fond of quoting research showing that the best measure of student success in life (at least in terms of their earnings and social status) had nothing to do with their grades or test scores, but with the amount and kind of involvement they had in such activities. Can it be surprising that how well students learn to play with others is more important for their futures than how well they learn to work in isolation? Yet, if this is indeed so, why are we making them suffer through so much pointless work, in the name of "success" it doesn't really lead to?

It's not that we should turn school into what we now call extracurricular activities. (And, of course, not all third places are totally benign: Racist and sexist talk often gets an easier pass in hair salons and locker rooms than it does in more critical spaces.) School still needs to be a place for the acquisition of knowledge and skills, and for encounters with persons and things one would not necessarily choose on one's own. But we can import the structure and sensibility of what Oldenburg called "third places" to make classrooms and schools into what Elizabeth Moje and her colleagues (2004) call "third spaces," in this case meaning places where traditions and disciplines of various kinds are brought by educators to meet students at places they already are in their lives, so that learning becomes playful dialogue among True Selves rather than the meaningless compliance of False Selves. This process is described as a "transformative pedagogy of literacy fusion" by Millard (2003), who suggests that students' out-of-school interests and knowledge should be fused with school literacy in classroom practices that attend to what happens when the two worlds meet, particularly when that meeting results in palpable human connections and the visible solution of real-world problems.

Jeff's collaborative research in national demonstration sites for adolescent literacy found that the following factors were most important to the success of dialogic, inquiry-oriented learning and projects:

1. Start with the interests of kids.
2. Frame curriculum as a problem that engages student interests.
3. Fuse the personal aspects of inquiry with disciplinary concerns and knowledge.
4. Involve multiple parties—disciplinary experts, parents, critical friends, faculty—as speakers, coinquirers, and audiences for authentic products and presentations.
5. Sustain the learning over time.
6. Promote learning that leads to sharing and/or social action and actually engage in this sharing and social action.
7. Use various modes and media—popular culture, primary disciplinary materials, and student-generated data—brought into conversation with one another (adapted from Wilhelm, 2010).

Generalizing from these seven factors, we want to suggest here that learning takes place in third space when those belonging to a learning community both are brought by their teachers and consent to bring one another to in some way introduce an element of aesthetic *copoiesis*—a cocreative fashioning of life together—into the learning process. This is what takes learning itself to a new existential level; it is not just mental mastery of material or purely inward personal growth but an active combining of minds. Sometimes this has a common outward, efferent goal: understanding a text, resolving a problem through joint inquiry, making something together, or accomplishing some conjoint action in the world. But at other times the aesthetic appreciation of the sharing of minds itself is the central goal—as it was in that critical classroom moment of the sharing of "mystery questions." And the tacit awareness of this sharing of minds and the way it lifts us to a new level of being in shared third space is present in all forms of dialogic inquiry. It is key to what makes inquiry both deeply pleasurable and deeply meaningful, in the very same way we found the tacit awareness of conjoint mental experience with an implied author is key to the pleasure and meaning we experience through art.[2]

MODES AND RESOURCES FOR THE CREATION
OF SOCIAL THIRD SPACES IN CLASSROOMS

We could easily write another book, or several of them, on the topic of how to create social third spaces. But since there is already quite a large amount of writing about teaching that reflectively creates social third space, though mostly without using this term for it, we are going to confine this "how" section of the chapter to an overview of the main ways we have found to do this, referring you to some of the best practitioners we know who have written on each topic.

1. *Dialogue about texts.* The classic mode of creating social third space among English teachers—and the ancient mode of humanistic discourse generally, including some religious discourse such as Bible study—is to read and respond to a text together. Even when the discussion is confined to the question of the author's meaning, the various processes through which readers construct that meaning allow for the various readings to richly nourish one another. We have already referred to Gordon Pradl's *Literature for Democracy* (1996) and Sheridan Blau's *The Literature Workshop* (2003) as fine works promoting third space within the transactional tradition. We have also learned quite a bit from the works of Sophie Haroutunian-Gordon (1991, 2010). Sophie has spent a lifetime studying the intricate processes of "interpretive discussion" to "turn the soul" toward intent listening both to texts and to other readers. She has deep insights and deep experience of how to create complex classroom communities through such discussions. And, just as important, she has deep insights and deep experience of how to teach teachers from all disciplines to elicit such discussions, which are the centerpiece of the Master of Science in Teaching Program at Northwestern University she directs. Another work Bruce has found helpful— and which he has used to teach these skills in his own teacher education classrooms—is Chapter 5, on "focused discussion," of *Exploring the Moral Heart of Teaching* (2001) by Sophie's student David Hansen.

2. *Make something together.* Bruce's strongest single memory of Christine Phillips's sixth-grade classroom is of the classroom mural that her students planned and created together, using the entire back wall, at the end of the year. Later, when he became a teacher himself, a centrally transformative experience came through his involvement with CAPE (Chicago Arts Partnerships in Education), which pioneered arts-integrated curriculum in

the Chicago Public Schools. Three language arts and three art teachers collaborated on a yearlong humanities curriculum, a version of which Bruce found still in place at the school after many years. The way the teachers' thoughts came to flow together as we built the curriculum together mirrored the way the students' lives were brought together as they cocreated the various projects built into that curriculum throughout the next year. Much of our and other schools' curriculum, and resources for other arts-integrated curriculum projects from around the world, can be found on the CAPE Web site, as well as the Web site for the national program named Arts Education Partnership. Two inspiring, though more theoretical works on this topic, are Maxine Greene's *Variations on a Blue Guitar: The Lincoln Center Institute Lectures on Aesthetic Education* (2001) and Eliot Eisner's *The Arts and the Creation of Mind* (2002). In addition, many activities specifically designed for the English classroom can be found in Jeff and Brian Edmiston's *Imagining to Learn* (1998), Jeff's *Action Strategies for Deepening Comprehension* (2011a/2002) and *Engaging Readers and Writers with Inquiry* (2007).

3. *Take action together.* Social action can take many forms (Wilhelm, 2007). The simplest is sharing through presentations, public service announcements, infomercials, and the like. Jeff typically asks his students in both school and university to present the results of their inquiry work to the community at Nights of Inquiry each semester. Andrew and Sarah likewise sponsor Nights of Writing where student writing about their projects is shared. The continuum of social action can extend to sustained social action in the community, such as the work described earlier for promoting good relationships through antibullying campaigns and peer mediation, helping Special Olympians, refugee families or other groups through ongoing programming and events, promoting a zero waste and carbon-neutral school. Such work requires substantive conceptual knowledge, procedural knowledge, deep understanding, and the capacity to translate understanding into action by decomposing tasks, working collaboratively, monitoring progress, and much more.

4. *Celebrate one another.* This is the direct, unmediated, and fully conscious way of creating social third space. We practice it whenever we ask students to share of themselves and appreciate that sharing. Jeff's Nights of Inquiry are for the purpose of sharing and celebrating each other's work and growing understanding. So are his daily rituals of Author Chair and Appreciation and formative assessments such as Marvy/Muddy,

celebrating what is understood and naming challenges to be
undertaken (see Wilhelm, Wilhelm, & Boas, 2009). Here Bruce
would like to mention an extraordinary school—he calls it his
"educational Shangri-La" and it is the wisest and most loving
educational community he has ever observed anywhere—in
which this sharing is made central to the educational process.
The Center for Inquiry in Columbia, South Carolina, is a public
elementary school founded by Heidi Mills and Amy Donnelly,
two professors at the University of South Carolina, along with a
number of their former graduate students and Heidi's husband
and colleague Tim O'Keefe, as a place where collaborative inquiry could be securely made the centerpiece of the education
of young children (see Mills & Donnelly, 2001). You can read
about the collaborative processes through which the school was
founded in partnership with leaders from the school district in
their edited volume *From the Ground Up* (2001), to which all the
founding teachers and many of the first students at the school
contributed. The title refers both to how they built the school
and to how they see the inquiry process itself needs to integrated into formal education from its very onset. One of the most
important decisions they made was to have each day in each
room begin and end with a "friendship circle" in which students simply share what has been most meaningful in their daily lives, both in and out of school. One very perceptive kinder-
gartner observed this to be the most important work they did:
"to take each other into our hearts and become friends" (quoted in Shamlin, 1997). Those of you who teach at the secondary
level are probably familiar with Erin Gruwell's *Freedom Writers
Diary* (1999): a stunning depiction of how personal reflection
can help turn a classroom community dominated by hatred and
fear into one filled with love, wisdom, and mutual transformation. The key, according to Gruwell (2010), is to see everyone
around you as a story "whose beginnings can't be changed, but
whose endings can be freewritten" once those stories are truly
heard and responded to in a supportive community. At the
level of higher education, philosopher Martha Nussbaum's *Cultivating Humanity* (1997) is a study of liberal education programs
and classrooms around the country that lead toward the values
of "narrative imagination" and "world citizenship" through
"self-reflection" and the appreciation of diverse others.[3]

THE PLAYROOM FOR TRUE SELVES:
THIRD SPACE AND THE DEMOCRATIZATION OF CULTURE

Since we left behind the history of English in Part I, we have for the most part put aside the current thinking and research being done in our field to focus fully on the deep psychology of aesthetic, transactional literacy we have been presenting. At this point, though, we return to tie that deep psychology back into the teaching of "sociocultural literacy" that has been the focus of much of our field (and much of Jeff's prior work), roughly since Vygotsky's *Mind in Society* was published in translation in 1978 and Shirley Brice Heath's *Ways with Words: Language, Life, and Work in Communities and Classrooms* was published in 1983.[4]

Earlier in this chapter we referred to the work of Elizabeth Moje and her colleagues (2004), who took the idea of "third space" to bring into play the intersection of student interests and knowledge and the academic disciplines that we use as discourses of social power. Moje refers to postcolonial theorist Homi Bhabha's use of this term in *The Location of Culture* (1994) as "a space in which colonial authority is challenged by those being colonized and where hybrid identities are created" (cited in Wilhelm, 2010, p. 56). Bhabha himself, though, is pretty clearly drawing on the work of Winnicott. Winnicott's essay "The Location of Cultural Experience" (Chapter 7 of *Playing and Reality*, 1971) whose epigraph is the Tagore quote we used to begin this section, is almost certainly the source of the title of Bhabha's book. And the essay in which Bhabha introduces the term *third space* ends with an observation both political and psychological: "[B]y exploring this Third Space, we may elude the politics of polarity and emerge as the others of our selves" (1994, p. 39).[5]

What we would like to suggest here is that there is an extremely important connection that needs to be made between what Winnicott calls the "False Self," induced by anxious, ambivalent, fear-inducing parenting and schooling, and what we, informed by Moje and Bhabha, might call false, colonizing, social and political relations. What Bhabha calls "the politics of polarity"—political nonrecognition and misrecognition—is largely brought about by the *relational* polarities of parents' and teachers' nonrecognition and misrecognition of their children and students. These dysfunctional relationships produce False Selves, inwardly polarized by *self*-nonrecognition and misrecognition—the repression and marginalization of *feelings*. So the more we are awake to becoming good-enough, implied, and philosopher teachers, working to reach out to elicit the True Selves of our students—selves able to loosen the boundaries of their egos and their social and cultural identities enough to come into play with the possibilities offered by art, one another, and the world—the more likely it is that our overall social and political relations can become healthier and freer than they have long been! You can't have a democracy of False Selves—only a society that pretends democracy, as we and our schools have long been doing. Third Space is the space democracy needs to live and breathe.

According to Stevenson and Deasy's *Third Space: When Learning Matters* (2005), a study of 10 arts-integrated schools nationwide serving extremely disadvantaged students, the deliberate creation of third space in those schools changed the very idea of "what school was about" for the students, teachers, and families involved in them. It became less about learning inert material—and in important ways also being treated *as just such material* by a colonizing education system—than about being actively taken up into an enlivening human community in which they did real and substantive kinds of personal and social work and became engaged in personal and social as well as factual, practical, and intellectual knowledge. The authors chose this title for their book because they found "this set of stories [of the creation of these spaces in these disadvantaged and in many ways dysfunctional communities] had profound implications for the way we in the United States think about and define the purposes of school."

Homi Bhabha's writing is notoriously difficult to understand. But these words are not, in the context of the operations of transactional mentality we have laid out up to this point:

> [I]t is . . . the inbetween space that carries the burden of the meaning of culture . . . . [A] willingness to . . . begin envisaging national, anti-nationalist histories of the "people" . . . may open the way to conceptualizing an international culture, based not on the exoticism of multiculturalism or the diversity of cultures, but on the articulation of culture's hybridity. (pp. 38–39)[6]

We begin here to get a picture of transactional social relations and a transactional democratic politics that can eventually emerge from the aesthetic reflection of individuals. As we learn, by going out of ourselves in aesthetic experience to "become the others *of* ourselves," we also learn to be at home in various kinds of social and political spaces with others *different from* ourselves. As the epigraph to Toni Morrison's *Beloved* out it, we learn, though often in fiery trials of our souls, "to call them my people who were not my people, and her beloved which was not beloved," and so what Martin Luther King called "the Beloved Community" comes into being.

THE DEMOCRATIZATION OF DEMOCRACY:
SEEING THE STORY OF DEMOCRACY AS THE
GROWTH OVER TIME OF TRANSACTIONAL THIRD SPACE

We come here to the largest question of this book, How might transactional mentality actually be used to do what Dewey said it could do:
save the modern world from the chaos into which it has been plunged?
Up to this point, we've seen what transactional mentality is: its psychological roots, how it works through literature and art, and how we can
help it come to flourish in the small-scale communities of classrooms and
schools. But how might it be spread much farther than these small-scale
communities, as Dewey so passionately believed it needed to be? Clearly,
we need to come to a lucid transactional view of large-scale democracy
and eventually somehow make it the prevailing view of what democracy
is. How might that ever happen?

We've just laid out a model for how aesthetically reflective persons
organize themselves into aesthetically reflective communities: through
the process we've called *copoiesis* (cocreation among moral partners) in
which people share life with one another in real space the way authors
and readers do in the imaginary space of literature and art. But it is an entirely different problem to see how those communities can combine with
one another to share life on a broad scale. They can't do so directly—in
present, face-to-face ways—in anything like the way the people in small-
scale communities like third space classrooms and schools can. At the end
of the last section, we saw Homi Bhabha envision a coming-into-being
of "international" third space through a certain general understanding of
the "inbetweenness" of cultural life. But we're pretty sure he would be at
a loss to articulate how to convey the meaning of this to the democratic
masses or to embody it in real-life national and international politics.

What we need above all is a new large-scale *story* we can tell about
democracy: a story that people (and democratic peoples) will want to play
a meaningful part in, a story growing out of the other, older stories that
aren't working well these days. That story will be what people can live
and grow together within, even if they can't directly see all the characters
involved in it. But what might that story be?

As we write this, there are two, often violently competing, stories
about democracy that dominate the political scene in this country, neither
of which is fully satisfying. One looks more to the past, the other more to
the future, but neither is big enough or moving and compelling enough
to bring people effectively together at this point in time when political democracy itself seems very much at an impasse—and at the very historical
moment in which people most need to come together, to change both the
way we live together and the way we inhabit the earth.

The first is the *libertarian* story: the tale of a sudden, historic liberation from tyranny and the subsequent governmental protection of individual rights required to maintain the condition of liberty. The second story, an *egalitarian* one, complicates the first one: seeing the moment of liberation not as final and definitive, but as a starting point of a movement toward social equality, with the force of government and social movements required to bring that progress about. If you're reading this book, you're probably more interested in the second story than in the first one, perplexed as to why so many people are satisfied with the first one, and suspicious that those who are dedicated to it might be so for selfish reasons, protecting not their rights but their social status. Let us take them at their word, though. Because maybe what we most need to do is integrate these two contrasting stories in a way that will make a new story, more complete and more satisfying than either of the two currently prevailing ones. It's pretty easy to see that this new story has to have something to do with people's learning to value *both* liberty and equality in a spirit of fraternity—but simply saying we need to form a "beloved community" doesn't show us how to get from the two conflicting stories to a third one. Put in aesthetic terms, it gives us the ending of the story but not its plot, not the aesthetically seen, personally involving process (in the sense of moral *trial*, not just of mechanical *procedure*) by which the other two stories can both be taken up into this new one.

That plot, we think, is the story of the development of individual gifts and the interweaving of those gifts in all realms of life for evocative pleasure, mutual benefit, and, most important, expansive friendship. This is a story that puts education, and the cultivation of transactional mentality, at the heart of democracy. And it combines the liberty to write one's own narrative with the vision to see that the stories of our lives are better ones—not just more ethical, but more aesthetically pleasing and more humanly satisfying—as they become interwoven. This is another way of putting what Einstein said about *how* we now need to change the way our species thinks to ensure our survival: Education needs to focus on individual development toward serving communities larger than oneself with one's personal gifts. It does for the masses of humanity what Einstein did for mass itself: revealing and allowing us to harness and connect our inner energy and inner light (Bellow, 1967).[7]

We are going to tell you a brief version of this story—which also is the story of the discovery and development of the understanding of the importance of personal wisdom in social, political, and historical life—in Chapter 9. But before we do that we are going to show you that we are not inventing this story out of whole cloth—that others have told it before us, and all we will be doing is contextualizing and fleshing it out a bit more than has been done before: by showing in large-scale historical terms how it is more than a story of the moral development of democracy, and showing in intimate classroom terms how the seeds of wisdom can be deliberately germinated.

A TALE OF THREE PRESIDENT-TEACHERS
WITH POETIC VISIONS OF TRANSACTIONAL DEMOCRACY

The first version of this story that we can trace is over 230 years old. John Adams—who is becoming generally recognized as the wisest of America's founders since the publication of David McCullough's 2001 biography (the source of all the Adams quotes below)—said this in a letter to his wife Abigail in 1780, in the midst of the Revolutionary War: "I must study . . . war, that my sons have the liberty to study commerce, in order to give their children the right to study [art]" (pp. 236–237). Though Adams was referring to traditionally considered works of "fine art," not to what we have called "aesthetic transactions" in general, this is an early, elemental vision of the coming into maturity of democratic life, first through the outward liberty militarily won to make free material transactions, then through the inward freedom aesthetically won to make free human transactions in the intellectual and moral commerce of a gift economy, open—we feel quite meaningfully—not just to "sons" but to "children" of both genders. And though this is Adams's only complete depiction of the historical progress of democracy toward a gift economy, it had been developed over time. It was preceded by a 1760 diary entry asking, "How can any man judge unless his mind has been opened and enlarged by reading?" (p. 223). His 1776 *Thoughts on Government* made the observation that "Laws for the liberal education of youth, especially for the lower classes of people, are so extremely wise and useful that to a humane and generous mind no expense for this purpose would be thought extravagant" (p. 103). And Section II, Chapter 6, of the first Massachusetts Constitution, of which Adams supervised the writing in 1779, was titled "The Encouragement of Literature, Etc.," which McCullough observes "was like no declaration to be found in any constitution ever written until then, or since" (p. 222).

Less than a century later came another such vision, both far more elaborate and far clearer: that of Walt Whitman in his 1871 *Democratic Vistas,*[8] which can be thought of as the literary *conceiving* of his idol Lincoln's "new birth of freedom." Whitman's outline of the past, present, and future of American democracy has the same three stages as Adams's: political, commercial, and aesthetic.

For the New World, indeed, after two grand stages of preparation-strata, I perceive now a third stage, being ready for, (and without which the other two were useless,) with unmistakable signs appears. The First stage was the planning and putting on record the political foundation rights of immense masses of people—indeed all people—in the organization of Republican National, State, and municipal governments. . . . The Second stage relates to material prosperity, wealth, produce, labor-saving machines, . . . intercommunication and trade with all lands, . . . cheap appliances for comfort, numberless technical schools, . . . &c. The Third stage, rising out of the previous ones, to make them and all illustrious, . . . a native expression-spirit, . . . adult, and through mentality, . . . more expansive, more rich and free, to be evidenced by . . . personalities, plenty of them, . . . and by a sublime and serious Religious Democracy sternly taking command, . . . and from its own interior and vital principles, reconstructing, democratizing society. (Whitman, 1871/1982, pp. 976–977)

Whitman, though, was unsure whether we would ever get from the material exchange of commerce to the full, human exchange that would fully embody democracy. At the very beginning of the age when even American political affairs were dominated by entirely materialistic commercialism, he had this to say:

Democracy, however great a success in uplifting the masses out of their sloughs, in materialistic development, . . . and in a certain highly deceptive superficial . . . intellectuality, is, so far, an almost complete failure in its social aspects, and in really grand religious, moral, literary, and esthetic results. In vain do we march with unprecedented strides to empire. . . . It is as if we were somehow being endow'd with a vast and more and more thoroughly appointed body, and then left with little or no soul. (1871/1982, p. 938)

This dilemma remains. How do we convince the people of far and away the most powerful military and economic empire the world has ever known that they need to acquire a new soul? To value transactional deep connection in third space even more highly than they value material wealth and power?

Well, the very first thing we need to do is simply to note the absolutely astonishing political and historical fact that the man who at this writing is the most powerful single person in the most powerful nation in history acquired that very power precisely through his asking us to do just that! And also to note that even if we think he himself hasn't done it since acquiring power, *we* still may . . . and can. "*We* are the ones we've been waiting for!" and "the change we need" were the two central slogans of the presidential campaign of Barack Obama, the announcement of which in early 2007 prompted Bruce to begin work on the full-time research into education for wisdom that led up to this book.[9] "If we indeed are 'the ones we've been waiting for,'" Bruce thought, "the change we most truly need is for us to be able to find one another, and ourselves, and we're going to have to have a pretty convincing rationale for a system of education that will enable us to do that."

You'll find some of the results of that research—a history of the hopeful story of wisdom-centered education within the more compromised story of world history—in the next chapter. For now, we will simply point out, first, that Obama is the *product* of such education and, second, that some, though certainly not all, of his leadership to this point has in fact pointed national consciousness toward the development of transactional mentality.

"You gave me my start in life," Obama wrote to Roger Boesche, the Tocquevillian scholar who was his teacher at Occidental College in Los Angeles.[10] Bruce learned this in a visit he made to Boesche shortly after he began his research, and later visits to Boesche's classes revealed a master of the art of evincing deep reflection within and probing dialogue among his students. That educational "start" that eventually gave our nation a collective political "start" developed organically over the next several years of Obama's life: first through a period of intense, monastic personal reflection after Obama transferred to Columbia, then to a time of equally intense person-to-person dialogue in the well-known period he spent as a community organizer in Chicago (Mendell, 2008; see also Novak, 2010b).

Since becoming President, Obama's mode has certainly so far (in very early 2011) been more wonkishly "interactional" than visionary and "transactional"—as was so much of his campaign, which for a short time around the election effectively united a long- divided nation.[11] And certainly Race to the Top, his infamous education program is, if anything, only a slightly more efficient way of accomplishing the superficial, entirely efferent goals set by *A Nation at Risk* (1983) and by his predecessor in the No Child Left Behind Act of 2002.

Yet regardless of how you regard the accomplishments of Obama's administration, witness these words, spoken at various moments throughout his political career, showing that this is someone who beyond a shadow of a doubt has the development of transactional mentality at the heart of his political mission (all the quotes below are taken from Remnick's *The Bridge*, 2010):

> The most pervasive malady of . . . the American experience generally is that elaborate patterns of knowledge and theory have been disembodied from individual choices. . . . What [we need] . . . to do is . . . bring the words of . . .

names like Thoreau, Jefferson, and Whitman to bear on the twisted logic of which we are today a part.

—1983 (age 21)

What if a politician were to see his job as that of an organizer, as part teacher and part advocate, one who does not sell voters short but who educates them about the real choices before them? . . . The right wing, the Christian right, has done a good job of building these organizations of accountability, much better than the left or progressive forces have. But it's always easier to organize around intolerance, narrow-mindedness, and false nostalgia. And they also have hijacked the higher moral ground with this language of family values and moral responsibility.

Now we have to take this same language—these same values that are encouraged within our families—of looking out for one another, of sharing, of sacrificing for each other—and apply them to the larger society. Let's talk about creating a society, not just individual families, based on these values. Right now we have a society that talks about the irresponsibility of teens getting pregnant, not the irresponsibility of a society that fails to educate them to aspire for more.

—1995, from his first campaign for political office

By itself that single moment of recognition between that young white girl and that old black man is not enough to change a country. By itself, it is not enough to give health care to the sick, or jobs to the jobless, or education to our children. But it is where we begin. It is why I believe that the walls in that room began to crack and shake at that moment. . . . [I]f enough of our voices join together, if we see each other in each other's eyes, we can bring those walls tumbling down. The walls of Jericho can finally come tumbling down.

—2008, from the presidential campaign

This book, and particularly this chapter, have been about the aesthetic process of *learning* "to see each other in each other's eyes." What you will see in the next chapter is how this process has, in fact, been central not just to the history of democracy, but to human history as an aesthetic whole. Once we can get a convincing version of *that* story across, we may be able to learn, in Erin Gruwell's (2010) words, to "freewrite the ending" of the history of democracy, so we can all finally see just who it is we've been waiting for. And a very large part of our coming to tell and enact that story will take place through our replacing our inhumane and antidemocratic education policy of No Child Left Behind in the Race to Nowhere with a humane, authentically democratic policy of Each Person Drawn Forward to a Life of Responsiveness and Responsibility[12]—centering on a new discipline called "Personal Studies" that will help us all *regularly* see each other in each other's eyes, by first helping us reflectively become the others of our selves.

Whether or not the Obama Administration ever comes to formulate such a policy, it would clearly be the fulfillment both of the education Obama said "gave him his start in life" and of the campaign that gave us as a nation a similar start. And in a way it seems only right for it to be up to *us*—the "ones we've been waiting for" to freewrite the ending to that start.

CHAPTER 9

Aesthetic Humanity
The History, and Possible Future, of Wisdom

As [humanity] advances . . . , and small tribes are united into larger communities, the simplest reason would tell each . . . to extend . . . social instincts . . . to all the members of the same nation, though personally unknown. . . . This point being once reached, there is only an artificial barrier to prevent [our] sympathies extending . . . to all nations and races.
—Charles Darwin, *The Descent of Man*
(the epigraph to Robert Wright's
Nonzero: The Logic of Human Destiny)

Her full nature . . . spent itself in channels which had no great name on the earth. But the effect of her being on those around her was incalculably diffusive, for the growing good of the world is partly dependent on unhistoric acts, and that things are not so ill with you and me as they might have been is half owing to the number who lived faithfully a hidden life and rest in unvisited tombs.

—George Eliot, *Middlemarch*

I hear from Dion that you are now one of his closest companions and that you have been so throughout, exhibiting the wisest habit among those that constitute philosophy. Steadfast personal dedication, magnanimous trust and trustworthiness, and sincere speech—that, say I, is the genuine manifestion of philosophy. Other kinds of cleverness that lead to results other than these are just fancy parlor-tricks. Fare well and hold on to those habits to which you are now holding!

—Plato, Letter X

To be a philosopher is not, or not merely, to have greater or subtler thoughts than other men, or to found a school, but so to love wisdom as to live a life according to its dictates: a life of independence, simplicity, magnanimity, and trust.

—Henry David Thoreau, *Walden*

Ordinary people can make meaningful change through the practices of
everyday life.
> — Asef Bayat, *Life as Politics: How Ordinary People Change
> the Middle East*

In Parts II and III of this book we have been gradually enlarging our
understanding of aesthetic experience: from an immediate feeling of living in the third space of a created story world (Chapter 4); to implied
connection, through the gift of the transitional object, to the creators of
the experiences that have enabled us to feel and live anew (Chapter 5);
to reflection on the new meaningful possibilities these new, implicitly
shared feelings, experiences, and connections reveal in our individual
lives (Chapter 6); to the responsibility to givingly create and responsively
receive in the authorship and readership of transactional teaching and
learning (Chapter 7); to the responsibility to enter into and help create
ever larger and more integrated communities of "copoetic" democratic
fellowship (Chapter 8). It is now time to examine the largest personal,
historical, and indeed cosmic horizons of these phenomena, in the responsibility we cultivate in ourselves and one another for life itself, on Tagore
and Winnicott's "seashore of endless worlds [where] children play."

The ultimate third space is that where we sense that we live in a
good-enough world and that the care we come to have for the world is
a living, creative force of the world working within us (Lear, 1990). We
often feel this force most clearly and purely in the experience of art and
literature, which evolved precisely to help us feel it. But, as Lisa Ruddick
observed, literature is basically a listening device to the creative force of
the world as a whole. And as John Dewey and Louise Rosenblatt showed
us, "aesthetic" experiences are all experiences and aspects of experience
in which we are aware of living life for life's sake rather than for external, efferent ends.

It is only when we are able to see ourselves as playing an integral,
integrative part in this largest of all stories—the story of what George Eliot, at the end of her novel *Middlemarch*, called the potentially "growing
good of the world"—that we can truly be said to find meaning *in life*. Not
just a meaningful "secure base" for our own lives—and maybe those of
a few good friends, or of a single, small or large community—but in life
itself. This is where the notion of "wisdom" fully enters in. And where we
move from the *copoiesis* of democratic fellowship to *cosmopoiesis*: the sense
that we are acting as responsive and responsible citizens of the world, co-
creating the world through the life force that is the best part of each one
of us. Here the three virtues Martha Nussbaum found to be integral to
"cultivating humanity"—"self-reflection," "narrative imagination," and
"cosmopolitan citizenship"—are integrated into a compelling worldview,

the full worldview of transactional mentality: a narrative of the potential integration of the lives of persons with life as a whole.

The transactional aesthetic psychology developed in Chapters 4–7 together with the transactional sociality developed in Chapter 8 lead us to an understanding of transactional gift *ecology*. The experience of inward third space, where the temporary fusion of self and world is imaginatively evoked by authors and readers, and teachers and students, together with the experience of outward third space in mutually evoked real-life community, lead us to a vision of universal cosmopolitan citizenship: the real, active integration of our own and all other selves not just with one another, as in the "gift economy"—but with the world as a whole.

At this point in the history of the world, when cumulative human actions are rapidly making the world unfit for the life of our own and millions of other species (see Russell, 1998; McKibben, 2010; Wilson, 2006), making "the next forty years [at this writing] the most important in [all of human] history," according to Stanford historian Ian Morris (2010), it is achingly clear that we now very badly need to spread this understanding. But how do we deliberately communicate this worldview to the masses of world citizens? How do we institute it within democratic education and democratic life?

THE TRANSACTIONAL WAY OF THE WORLD: THE POSSIBILITY FOR THE GROWTH OF DEMOCRATIC CONSCIOUSNESS AT THE END OF THE AMERICAN EMPIRE

"America Can Do It!"

No, this is not a quote from the Obama campaign. It comes from the end of the 1983 government report *A Nation at Risk*, the document that inspired the national educational standards movement and eventually the No Child Left Behind Act (NCLB). What was the "It" that America could "Do" if it only summoned up all of its "self-actional" national educational will? "We can have unchallenged preeminence in commerce, industry, science, and technological innovation."

By the early 1870s, less than a century after its founding, the United States was already the richest country on earth. Seventy years later, by the 1940s, it quickly also became the country with the most military power. In the second decade of the twenty-first century, another seventy years down the road, America's material standard of living lags behind that of many developed nations; its educational attainments still lag way behind most of them, despite NCLB; and though its military might is still unchallenged, the economic preeminence that funds that might seems destined to be eclipsed in the very near future.

It is high time to remember that the gifts of our nation are not limited to the wealth and power we have come to pride ourselves on. The fact that our traditional powers appear to be unsustainable over the long term could even become a blessing, if we can come to see that there are other, better parts of our national culture than the drive for "preeminence" that NCLB and its successor, Race to the Top, have attempted, so far futilely, to spur. For Lincoln and Whitman, what characterized America most fundamentally was not being preeminent in wealth and power among nations but being "the last, best hope of earth," a *humanizing* power, whose true calling is to effect the humanization of the human spirit. What might it mean to gear the way we educate our children so that we might better answer that calling? Though our powers of dominating the earth may be waning, we may well be at the dawn of realizing our power to help the world reauthor itself[1]: through the soft power of the transactional mentality and ensuing gift economy that are latent in democratic life.

The Way of the World: A Story of Truth and Hope in an Age of Extremism, the 2008 book by Ron Suskind, is in a way the follow-up to his 1999 book *A Hope in the Unseen*, the book Bruce taught in his recent community college communications class, described in Chapters 5 and 6. The earlier book was an account of an individual "American odyssey"; the more recent one is an account "of how America [itself] lost its way" in emotional storms after the 9/11 attacks, and of how it can find its way again by reclaiming "the moral authority upon which its survival depends" (back cover). Bruce, in fact, was led to the book he taught through first reading *The Way of the World*, which tells the stories of numbers of people seeking to spread democratic consciousness in a newly combustible world, in which "we struggle to leap forward, to reshape instinct enough to reach across the divides" (p. 1): in our terms, the stories of people who seek to grow together with others within a world that in many ways seeks to drive them apart. The book starts with a "fundamental two-part question: Can disparate people ever truly understand one another, and is such understanding necessary for them to coexist?" (p. 1). By the end, the stories it tells answer those questions in the affirmative. But this answer leads to another question: Can those many stories of people living in "truth and hope in an age of extremism" add up to a cumulative story, one that can help redefine the way *most* people live?

Suskind calls this story "the American story," and ends his book with a call for us all to tell it:

> In its report about the September 11 attacks, the 9/11 Commission blamed U.S. leaders . . . for a "failure of imagination". . . . Now it's a lack of imagination again that is America's greatest vulnerability—a lack of imagination about what the nation might yet become. . . .

> The American story is . . . not about the privileged defending what they have with mighty armies or earnest self-regard. It's about common people coming to the shores of a vast, challenging place, discovering their truest potential, and re-creating, over and over, a new world.
>
> That's why people across the erupting planet want us to tell that story and help them tell it too.

Bruce didn't teach Suskind's newer book in his class, but the part of the class that most students found most valuable involved his students' *living* what Suskind calls "the American story" through a curriculum called "The Personal Creed Project"—designed to help students articulate how their highest values have come to be shaped over the course of their lives and how they can best live those values through the continuing stories of those lives. This curriculum was developed by John Creger, who teaches English at American High School (yes, that *is* its *real* name) in Fremont, California. It is detailed in *The Personal Creed Project and a New Vision of Learning* (2004).

John designed this curriculum as an educational rite-of-passage for high school sophomores—taking literally the idea that this age is when we can and should pass from youthful "foolishness" to mature "wisdom." The book's subtitle is significant in this regard: *"Teaching the Universe of Meaning In & Beyond the Classroom."* (There is, of course, an allusion here to James Moffett's *Teaching the Universe of Discourse,* which we discussed in Chapter 2. And John received the 2001 NCTE James Moffett Award for this project.) The message here is that by learning to take oneself and one's fellows seriously, a whole universe of meaning is opened—centering on one's own life, but unselfishly so—as the development of meaning depends on how well we are able to share our own stories and take others' in.

Over the week of Creed presentations that took place in Bruce's class, the students, one by one, became real to one another in ways many of them never suspected they could before. By hearing, not just one another's opinions or feelings, but one another's life journeys—coherent accounts of both struggles and hopes—they were able to take in one another's lives as living aesthetic wholes. Cedric Jennings's "American Odyssey" (from Suskind's *A Hope in the Unseen,* 1999) served as the initial model for someone who successfully underwent an important personal metamorphosis. But seeing one another in the midst of their own metamorphoses took what they had experienced through the book to another level. They became witnesses to one another's humanity, in the midst of the search for wholeness.

"This project totally opened up my eyes to myself and everyone in my class," said one of John Creger's sophomores. This is a theme that has arisen repeatedly over the course of this book: from John Dewey's assertion that the spread of transactional mentality was about "nothing less than the right to open one's eyes to see" in the introduction; to Brian Fischer's student Angel in Chapter 7, who ended his posttest on his philosophy of life with the comment: "It's all up to me and the others who have opened up their eyes"; to Emerson's prayer, "Let us treat the men and women as if they were real, perhaps they are" and Obama's prophecy, "If we see each other in each other's eyes . . . the walls of Jericho can finally come tumbling down" in the last chapter. What we want to suggest here is that this witnessing of emerging life stories of both "truth and hope" opens up "the universe of meaning" in definitive ways. These ways help us understand both what Suskind called "the American story" and also the human story as a collection of coexisting and potentially converging odysseys that it is our central task as human beings to bring into convergence. "The way of the world" as a whole is of either the fruitful convergence or the destructive collision of these odysseys. And its "last best hope" may be of our learning how to teach people to bring their separate odysseys into fruitful convergence before they collide in iliads that now have the potential to take the world as we know it down with them.

HOMO VIATOR: SEEING THE HUMAN BEING AS ESSENTIALLY AN EXISTENTIAL JOURNEYER

It will be helpful to bring in an official philosopher here. Gabriel Marcel's *Homo Viator: Introduction to a Metaphysic of Hope* (1951) is a series of essays written in Paris when it was under German occupation during World War II. "Homo viator" means "the human being as journeyer." Stop and think about the implications of that for a moment, particularly the implications for schools. The current biological designation of the human species is, of course, *homo sapiens.* But the Latin *sapiens* can be translated either as "knowing" or as "growing wise." The latter translation would in many ways be the equivalent of *homo viator,* but we know very well that currently our schools are organized almost entirely on the premise of the former one.

Marcel's book begins with the following observation: "Perhaps a stable order can only be established on earth if human beings always remain acutely conscious that their condition is that of travellers." Some of the parameters of the narrative philosophy of Paul Ricoeur,[2] and of the connection between meaningful friendship and meaningful reflection on the future that has been woven into this book, can already be observed: "We recall those who bore us company, that is to say who did such and such a part of the journey with us. . . . This is precisely where hope comes into its own. . . . Hope is only possible on the level of the *us*" (pp. 9–10).[3] In addition, the education of the soul, Rachael Kessler's central concern, is here given philosophical definition, in the context of seeing our essential nature as travellers:

> I spoke of the soul. This word, so long discredited, should here be given its priority once more. We cannot help seeing that there is the closest of connections between the soul and hope. I almost think that hope is for the soul what breathing is for the living organism. Where hope is lacking the soul dries up and withers. . . . It is precisely the soul that is the traveler; it is of the soul and of the soul alone that we can say with supreme truth that "being" necessarily means "being on the way" (*en route*). (pp. 10–11)

These are not just philosophical observations that are interesting and relevant here. They also have deep historical influence and importance. Marcel's book appears to have been the source of the definition of hope that was central to the speech that launched Obama's national political career, to his book *The Audacity of Hope* (2006), and, of course, to his presidential campaign as a whole. Though we have no idea whether Obama himself has ever read Marcel, it's pretty clear that one of Obama's central mentors on questions of hope and faith, Jim Wallis—whose motto, "We are the ones we've been waiting for" was also made central to the campaign—*has*.

Here is Marcel:

> It is not difficult to see that hope . . . involves a fundamental relationship of consciousness to time. . . . [I]f time is in its essence a separation and as it were a perpetual splitting up of the self in relation to itself, hope on the contrary aims at reunion, at recollection, at reconciliation: in that way . . . it might be called a memory of the future. . . . [T]he intellectual core of hope . . . is the very movement by which it challenges the evidence. (pp. 52–53, 67)

Here is Wallis, from the end of *The Soul of Politics* (1994):

> With the eyes of hope, we can see the door through which we too can walk, through which we are all invited. . . . With this hope, we can know our lives made whole. We can look into the faces of our children and believe there is a future for them. . . . With this hope, we can together build a new community. . . . With this hope, we can envision an America finally able to live without racism and oppression, but no longer able to live without justice and compassion. . . . And with this hope we can find the faith and courage to bear the cost of such possibilities. Hope is believing in spite of the evidence and watching the evidence change. And hope is a sign of transformation. (p. 240)

And here is Obama, from the end of his keynote speech to the Democratic National Convention in 2004:

> Do we participate in a politics of cynicism, or do we participate in a politics of hope? I'm not talking about blind optimism here. . . . I'm talking about something more substantial. It's the hope of slaves sitting around a fire singing freedom songs. The hope of immigrants setting out for distant shores. . . . The hope of a skinny kid with a funny name who believes that America has a place for him, too.
>
> Hope in the face of difficulty. Hope in the face of uncertainty.
>
> The audacity of hope! In the end that is God's greatest gift to us, the bedrock of this nation. A belief in things not seen. A belief that there are better days ahead. . . .
>
> I believe that we can . . . reclaim young people . . . across America from violence and despair. I believe that we have a righteous wind at our backs and that as we stand on the crossroads of history, we can make the right choices and meet the challenges that face us. (2004, p. 452)

Why is hope so important, more than *just* a fantasy? (Though, like the fusion of "self" and "world" in the experience of art, it *is* that in part.) Using Ricoeur's matrix of human, narrative time, we can see how it is built into our nature as narrating beings who live in story time: It is the beneficent mimesis$_3$ (the "present-future") *toward* which responsibility points us, a necessary extrapolation of poetic logic from our feeling response in the evoked, living present to beneficent creations of all kinds given to us from the past.

As we have been nurtured, so do we wish to nurture. If we have been nurtured securely, it becomes our wish to in turn actively nurture the world. We see "the evidence" of the world's imperfections, and desire, through the life that has been given us, to perfect them. And when we see that desire reflected in others around us, we draw on that mutually reinforced energy to act against even the most seemingly overwhelming seas of troubles. As Marcel did in writing his book in Nazi-occupied Paris. As Wallis did in daring to proclaim that "soul" should be the heart of politics in the world's greatest empire. As Obama did in acting (even though imperfectly) to make "hope" the *actual* heart of American politics. And as we now all can and must do in acting to forestall military, social, and environmental devastation in the coming years.

Hope is the ultimate expression of human life force, and the ultimate, historical and spiritual third space. It is the vision of the perfect "inbetweenness" of the universal "us" toward which all our strivings within the present world lead. The unobtainable, but nonetheless very real horizon that lives in collective human imagination, beyond what Dewey, in *Art as Experience*, called "the world of gaps and walls that limit community of experience." Hope is the belief that we can *find* "the ones we've been waiting for"—that the temporary experience of this in art, in wise teaching, and in democratic community can come to be more and more regularized within the human community, as our separate odysseys are gradually brought into convergence. It is the belief that, beyond all the meaninglessness and conflicting meanings we find in our present circumstances, our separate journeys have a single end—growing together toward a universe of coherent meanings, "multeity in *cosmic* unity," through the enactment in each one of us of cosmopolitan citizenship.[4]

AND WHAT *IF* EDUCATION IS NOT A RACE TO PREEMINENCE BUT A JOURNEY TOWARD HOPEFUL RESPONSIBILITY?: FROM NO CHILD LEFT BEHIND TO EACH PERSON DRAWN FORWARD

Unfortunately, we can't say an education program called Race to the Top begins in any way to be an adequate expression of a philosophy of hope (see Novak, 2010b). We'd like to continue this chapter, though, first, by leading you to a number of educational programs already in existence that do this—that work to help young people see that being a member of the species *homo sapiens* is more about "growing wise" than it is about "knowing" pure and simple. Then, finally, by sketching out a narrative of a factual history of the development of hope and wisdom lying within the mostly dismaying facts of human history to date: that, once we are aware of it as an ongoing story, can be extended through our educational work to become the prevailing story of the human future. The combination of these two things—the means of embodying hope and wisdom in our current educational institutions and the story of how we can see this as representing nothing less than the collective reauthoring of human history, the definitive emergence of the highest potentials latent in our species, our "last best hope"—are the means and end of the Wisdom Revolution to which we referred in the introduction, and to which we shall return at the very end of the chapter.

GROUPS AND PROGRAMS ALREADY PROMOTING LOVING WISDOM IN TEACHING AND LEARNING

1. *The Courage to Teach*. In 1983, the same year *A Nation at Risk* started to tilt American education toward treating children as measurable commodities, Parker Palmer published a book called *To*

Know As We Are Known: Education as a Spiritual Journey. Over time this evolved into a "teacher formation" program, "The Courage to Teach," based on Palmer's 1998 book *The Courage to Teach: Exploring the Inner Landscape of a Teacher's Life*—recently put forward by the editors of *The Journal of Teacher Education* as the model toward which all teacher education should tend (Whitcomb, Borko, & Liston, 2008). Kessler's *The Soul of Education* (2000), upon which Bruce centers his Philosophy of Education classes, is very much a product of the movement initiated by Palmer's book, and Palmer wrote the foreword to Kessler's book. A landmark 1997 conference on "Spirituality and Education" sponsored by Naropa University brought Palmer and other educators into dialogue with the Dalai Lama and other spiritual leaders (for the proceedings, see Glazer, 1999). This in turn spawned the growth of many groups such as the Spirituality and Education Network, the Holistic Education Special Interest Group of the American Educational Research Association, and the biannual Holistic Learning Conference of the Ontario Institute for Studies in Education. There is a great wealth of thought, research, and practice available to those who seek it out, as well as many communities devoted to teachers' mutual exploration of "education as a spiritual journey."

2. *The Assembly for Expanded Perspectives on Learning* (AEPL). One very special such group can be found within the National Council of Teachers of English. Founded in 1993 with the help of educators like James Moffett, Peter Elbow, and Gabriele Rico, it publishes an award-winning scholarly journal and sponsors sessions at NCTE events. But for many, as for Bruce, its main function is to provide a sense of warm-hearted educative community unparalleled elsewhere in people's lives, through its annual summer conferences taking place in bucolic settings. Jane Tompkins, author of *A Life in School* (1997), who helped lead the conferences of 1997 and 2000, said at the latter, "AEPL is like Brigadoon. It vanishes into the mists, then once again all of a sudden pops up into vibrant life." To start to give you an idea of how, here are titles of some of those conferences: "Fostering Transformations in Teachers and Learners," "Building a Culture of Partnership through Education," "Building a Culture of Listening in Our Institutions of Learning," "Keeping the Flame Alive: Celebrating the Life and Work of James Moffett," "The Emotional Life of Teachers," "Reclaiming the Wisdom Tradition for Education," "The Believing Game as a Model for Thinking," and "Literacy for Love and Wisdom." (Yes, this very book is to

be launched at the 2011 conference!) Much more about the
group, its history, and its activities can be found at aepl.org.

3. *The National Writing Project* (NWP). This is a network of educators that does not endorse any particular philosophy or method
of teaching. It does organize its work around central tenets: that
expertise and wisdom about teaching resides with teachers; that
teachers can be the wisest teachers of other teachers; that teachers must learn to listen to and converse with each other—not
to mention students and other stakeholders—about the whats,
the hows, and the whys of teaching; that teachers must practice
what they teach others to do; that teaching is a science, an art,
and in many ways a religious vocation. Together these show
how NWP helps its teachers develop a transactional mentality
leading the profession into a wiser future.

4. *The National Network for Educational Renewal.* Currently a nona-
genarian, John Goodlad was a student of John Dewey's student
Ralph Tyler and is as close to a living embodiment of Dewey as
we have. Many educators have read his landmark study of the
seemingly permanent stagnation of American public education,
A Place Called School (1984). Since that study, he has spent his life
dedicated to the NNER, a consortium of K–16 schools and institutions of teacher education who together work to transform
the cultures of individual schools from dead, ever-unchanging
places into living, self-renewing organisms (see Goodlad, et.
al., 2004, 2008). This book is in certain ways a long-delayed
response to an assignment John gave to Bruce, to describe the
inner renewal of the soul needed to germinate educational and
democratic renewal.

5. *Nonviolent Communication, Felt Sense, and Focusing.* The psychologist Carl Rogers specialized in empathic listening. Two of Rogers's students, Marshall Rosenberg and Eugene Gendlin, have
extended Rogers's work into education and other fields. Bruce
and Jeff both regularly incorporate Rosenberg's *Nonviolent Communication: A Language of Life* (2003) into the classes they teach,
and many of their students have found it an invaluable re-
source, not just in their teaching but in their living. The work
of both Rosenberg and Gendlin could easily be understood as
the incorporation of transactional responsiveness and aesthetic
reflection into everyday life. Gendlin's work, a method of inner
awareness called "focusing," first laid out in a bestselling 1978
book of the same title, has been translated into a writing pedagogy called "felt sense" (Gendlin's term) by Sondra Perl, also the
title of a book and accompanying CD that can be used in writing
classrooms at almost any level (2004).[5]

6. *Facing History and Ourselves.* This program is a model for the cultivation of personal responsibility and cosmopolitan citizenship by directly facing the many elements of what James Joyce called "the nightmare of human history" with the knowledge that history has been made by human beings, and as human beings develop a sense of personal responsibility the tenor and tone of history can change. Twenty million students have benefited from their programs in eight countries. According to an email from them: "For over 30 years, FHAO has taught young people to make small choices that can change the big picture. What if [more] people were capable of making better choices? Could we change the course of history? We think so." And we agree.

We started this book with portraits of individual teachers who sought to do far more with their students than was strictly expected of them by their schools or by the state. The fact is, teachers like these, and probably like you, are not alone. There are vast support networks out there that have already created what Václav Havel has called a "parallel polis" in democratic education: social networks existing beneath, outside, or alongside the state apparatus, like those that existed behind the Iron Curtain before its fall, and helped bring it down, through the spread of the perception of the emptiness of the social and political life endorsed and propagated by the state by contrast with the life that could be created outside it. Beneath and alongside No Child Left Behind and Race to the Top, there already exists a very strong movement (and what we've covered here is barely the tip of the iceberg) toward a democratic educational program that could very well be called Each Person Drawn Forward—focusing on the cultivation of joy, connection, wisdom, and personal responsibility in whatever is taught, at whatever level—where human beings are treated fundamentally as those who grow wise together, not as inert knowers of inert things.

What remains to be done is to connect those separate networks into a coherent program that can stand against the dehumanizing programs put forward by the State. And that coherent program will come about when we find a better story for ourselves. Against the nightmare-story of A Nation at Risk—which began with the pronouncement "History is not kind to idlers"—and the many dehumanizations that have followed upon it, we need another story of human history. That story will not call us to push one another to run faster, and to put standardized blinders over our eyes to shut us off from seeing anything but preset, entirely efferent, "I-It" goals. It will call us to call one another to exercise what Dewey called our collective "right to see": to remove the barriers that keep us from seeing ourselves and one another as fellow-journeyers, "to know as we are known" by our moral equals and existential fellows, in "I-You" copoetic relationship.

TELLING THE STORY OF WISDOM

When Bruce teaches philosophy of education, his first goal is to get students to see the relational wisdom in their own lives. But he also tries to get them to see how wisdom is a force, not just in their own lives, but in life itself: grounded in the functioning of the human brain; transcending the differences among our religious traditions, or lack thereof; and having itself a history that can be concretely traced. That history can be conveyed as a coherent story that embraces and unites disparate traditions in an encompassing narrative "container."

The religious scholar Huston Smith (1991/1958) and the philosopher (and Gandhi scholar) Michael Nagler (2005) have pointed to the existence of a "wisdom tradition"; and many current works in education point to the need to focus our educational institutions on the cultivation of wisdom rather than knowledge and skills (e.g., Miller, 2006; Lin, 2006; Fox, 2007). But for the wisdom tradition as a whole to enter effectively into human life, we need to be able to *see* it as a whole: how it arose and whither it tends. As we have seen wise teachers providing "containers" for the anxieties and aggressions of their students, as Brian Fischer did for Angel in Chapter 7, so the truth- and soul-force of wisdom itself can be seen as eventually coming to largely contain the violent forces that now seem to prevail in human life, once we are able to find a convincing narrative through which we can collectively envision its doing so.

If a Wisdom Revolution stands any chance, it had better be grounded in coherent historical facts, facts that can establish widespread understanding of a potentially cohering drama in which we can now collectively come to act. The overwhelming evidence is that wisdom and the love for it have been quite rare in the recorded history of our species. What seeds can we see in that history, though, that we can now germinate and proliferate, so that we can see the whole of history as an aesthetic thing, a megatransitional object, a coherent space for the meaningful interplay of our species that can amount to something more than an endlessly protracted "nightmare from which [we] are trying to awake"?

THE HISTORY OF THE WORLD OF WISDOM, PART ONE: PARTNERSHIP CULTURE (9000-1000 B.C.E.), WHEN WISDOM WAS NATURAL AND SOCIAL

Riane Eisler, in her landmark 1987 book *The Chalice and the Blade: Our History, Our Future* compiled the archaeological evidence that our species lived for thousands of years, just before the beginning of recorded history, in agriculturally based "partnership cultures" characterized by peaceful cooperation, enormous artistic and technological invention, and religious experience connected with natural and human fertility.[6] In Eisler's account, what Joyce called "the nightmare of history" began around 3500 B.C.E., when alien "dominator cultures"—characterized by strict, patriarchal, hierarchical, top-down ranking rather than the partnership linking of aesthetic "inbetweenness"—first violently conquered and then culturally co-opted these peaceful partnership cultures, using their great wealth and knowledge to build successions of powerful empires that vied with one another over the course of time over which of them would be the most powerful and preeminent, at the top of the hierarchical heap.

David Korten, a former Harvard economist, now publisher of *Yes! Magazine* and director of the Positive Futures Network, in his 2006 work *The Great Turning: From Empire to Earth Community* envisions a way for us to permanently dismantle the succession of dominator empires—the latest being the corporate capitalist system he first exposed as the continuation of such empires in his bestselling *When Corporations Rule the World* (1995). This can happen, he believes, through our turning the growing world awareness of the emergency of the unsustainability of current economic practices into growing consciousness of the potential for the emergence, or reemergence, in our species of the ability to live in partnership with one another and the Earth, in "transition from a corporate-led global economy to a planetary system of community-led local living economies," which he calls "Earth Community." In our terms, Eisler found that we once lived in what might be called "transactional, aesthetic societies" fundamentally characterized by the cultivation of partnership with life. Korten charts a way for us to rebuild a global society and economy with those same characteristics.

Eisler and Korten know one another well, and Korten attributes much of his own vision of the human past and future to what he has taken from Eisler. Yet we find it essential to supplement what they have to say about refinding our long-lost "partnership culture" in "Earth Community" with what we know about earlier semicoherent efforts to do something similar, which have persisted within the "dominator cultures" under the yoke of which most of humanity has lived for about the last 5,000 years. Here we need to bring in a work of philosophy, as the reflective bridge between the naturally arising assortment of Neolithic partnership cultures that gradually spread over most of the earth starting 10,000 years or so ago and the single Earth Community we now need to consciously build—both in a far shorter span of time and in the face of the prevalence of the dominator mentality that now governs us—to assure the health both of our species and of the planet.

THE HISTORY OF THE WORLD OF WISDOM, PART TWO: THE GREAT LEAP OF BEING IN THE AXIAL AGE (900-200 B.C.E.), THE MULTICULTURAL SEEDS OF PERSONAL WISDOM

"Where shall wisdom be found?"

This question was the title of a book published a few years ago by the Yale literary critic Harold Bloom (2004) in the wake of the new Age of Terror that gripped America after 9/11. "In great literature" was Bloom's answer to that question. Bloom was not the first person in history to ask that question, though. It is a question that naturally arises in us when we seek to respond sanely and humanly to trauma, often in the midst of a world we see responding insanely and inhumanly to it. Many seek wisdom, as Bloom seems to have done, as a form of loving solace in what they see as an irredeemably violent world: If we can't truly live in our day-to-day life, we can, again and again, temporarily, come to truly *be* by living aesthetically, by "being the book." Yet there are others who lovingly seek wisdom because, in addition to finding temporary solace and bliss within it, they have managed to remain so full of the love of life, and of the living world, as to retain the conviction that the world cannot be necessarily violent in nature, and so seek actively to redeem it from what they see as the abnormal violence into which it has been temporarily plunged.

Bruce knew of Karl Jaspers as one of the central existential philosophers of the twentieth century, and as the teacher and lifelong mentor of his personal favorite among modern thinkers, Hannah Arendt. But he didn't come to see Jaspers's enormous importance as a thinker in his own right until he became engaged in research in the history of the idea of wisdom that led to the 2008 AEPL conference "Reclaiming the Wisdom Tradition for Education," and, eventually, to the book you are now reading. In the course of that research he happened upon a book called *The Great Transformation: The Origin of Our Religious Traditions* by the well-known religious scholar Karen Armstrong (2006). That book, begun not long after the crisis of 2001 struck, started out with the following claim:

"Unless there is some kind of spiritual revolution that can keep abreast of our technological genius, it is unlikely that we will save our planet. A purely rational education will not suffice." Armstrong's book revisits the thesis first advanced by Jaspers (1953/1949) in a work written a few years after the unprecedented human devastation caused by World War II—*The Origin and Goal of History*—which found an Axial Age, a broad spiritual revolution occurring across several very different cultures in an era beginning around 900 B.C.E. and ending at about 200 B.C.E.[7]

In that first Wisdom Revolution—Jaspers called it "the Axial Age" because it appeared as the original "axis" upon which all further meaningful history came to turn—there was a contemporaneous arising of pedagogies of disciplined wisdom in cultures across Eurasia in response to the tyrannous, dehumanizing powers of new empires, which decimated the aesthetic partnership relations that had long characterized human social life: the mystical Hinduism of the *Bhagavad Gita*, and then Buddhism in India; Confucianism and Taoism in China; prophetic Judaism in Palestine; and tragedy and philosophy in Greece. What Huston Smith, Michael Nagler, Bruce, and others have called "the wisdom tradition," in other words, reflected the efforts of several different cultures to preserve and cultivate within the individual the aesthetic sensitivity and presence to life that had for thousands of years prior to that characterized social life. This is how Jaspers described what historian Eric Voegelin (1952/1987) later called the "Great Leap of Being" that occurred across these various cultures in the Axial Age:

> What is new about this age . . . is that human beings become conscious of "Being" as a whole, of themselves and their limitations. They experience the terror of the world and their own powerlessness. They ask radical questions. Face to face with the void they strive for liberation and redemption. By consciously recognizing their limits they set themselves the highest goals. They experience absoluteness in the depths of selfhood and in the lucidity of transcendence. (p. 2)

Armstrong's *The Great Transformation* goes into far more depth than Jaspers regarding the parallel development across China, India, Palestine, and Greece of ethical communities who together practiced cathartic self-surrender, wise insight, compassion for suffering, and the recognition of the ultimate oneness of the universe. And she draws on the far greater historical knowledge that has been developed in the more-than-half century since Jaspers wrote, confirming the common economic and technological phenomena, such as the horse-drawn chariot, that gave dominator empires new power both to wage war and to exploit those they conquered. Most important though, she also goes into far more depth about the educational implications of the Axial Age, of what we have to learn from it:

> We must continually remind ourselves that the Axial sages developed their compassionate ethic in horrible and terrifying circumstances. They were not meditating in ivory towers but were living in frightening, war-torn societies, where the old values were disappearing. Like us, they were conscious of the void and the abyss. The sages were not utopian dreamers, but practical men; many were preoccupied with politics and government. They were convinced that empathy did not just sound edifying but actually worked. Compassion and concern for everybody was the best policy. We should take their insights seriously because they were the experts. They devoted a great deal of time and energy to thinking about the nature of goodness. They spent as much creative energy seeking a cure for the spiritual malaise of humanity as scientists today spend trying to find a cure for cancer. We have different preoccupations. The Axial Age was a time of spiritual genius; we live in an age of scientific and technological genius, and our spiritual education is often undeveloped. (p. 397)

Vital to our concerns here, the Axial Age invented spiritual *politics* as the antidote to the brute power politics of corrupt empires. As Armstrong puts it, "What they created was a spiritual technology that utilized natural human energies to counter . . . aggression." As democracy in the West became the political counterweight to tyranny, wisdom became the personal and political counterweight to it throughout the empires of both West and East. Deprived of the reassurance of natural social community, people learned to become citizens of the cosmos; to attune themselves to life in general, finding their immediate life circumstances deeply out of joint. Though the word *kosmopolites* was coined by Diogenes, one of Socrates's followers,[8] the notion of individuals' belonging to, seeking to attune themselves with, and to act on the world as a whole was an integral part of all Axial Age cultures. Some retreated from their societies to regroup and eventually reemerge, like the original practitioners of yoga in India. Others deeply criticized their corrupt societies from the sidelines in jeremiads, a genre named, of course, for an Axial Age prophet. Still others—like Confucius, Buddha, Socrates, and, later, Jesus and Mohammed—sought to spread educational reform and personal renewal within existing society.[9] But all placed hope in ultimate world transformation, based on the power of the transformed human soul they witnessed every day, both in themselves and in those with whom they sought diligently to live in fellowship.

The Axial Age originated a new notion of meaningful, redemptive history—most explicit in prophetic Judasim, but implicit in all four Axial cultures. Neolithic partnership cultures did not live in three-dimensional history. They had no reason to; they created myths of the origin of life, but saw life itself as largely cyclical in nature, paralleling the cycle of the agricultural life upon which they were based. Empires have self-glorifying histories, usually projecting a future greater than the past. But their stories are exclusively linear and self-referential ones of their own ever-more-triumphant power, which, like that of Macbeth, lose all positive meaning and become empty tales "told by idiots, signifying nothing" as soon as they lose their power to dominate. By contrast—both to the original, Neolithic partnership cultures and to the dominator cultures of the empires that conquered first them and then one another—reflective wisdom, once it enters the world, endlessly concatenates. It seeks fellowship with others who diversely reflect, and lives both in that collective reflection and in the beneficent actions that arise from it, forming a culture of itself, a culture of all those who—in diverse times and places—love and seek to propagate reflective, loving wisdom.

THE HISTORY OF THE WORLD OF WISDOM, PART TWO-AND-A-HALF: THE AFTERLIFE OF AXIAL CULTURES

Aspects of wisdom culture can be extinguished. The original Axial Age cultures were all eventually wiped out by the new powers of new empires. On the surface, the same thing now seems to be happening to our own long-standing humanistic culture—descended from the Axial Age—in the face both of the colonizing educational standards movement and much of the critical theory that seeks to intellectually undermine dominator culture instead of transforming or breathing life into it. But the fact that wisdom can be found in writing—the tool invented for the administration of empires, but that can then be used for aesthetic, transactional purposes, in wisdom *literature*—enables it to concatenate and spread over long distances of space and time.

First, wisdom cultures can be brought to life again, as Buddhism took root in East Asia after being extinguished in South Asia where it was born, and as Christianity and Islam, each in its own way, brought prophetic Judaism to newly vibrant life. Although Axial cultures are susceptible to corruption and cooptation by empires, as both Christianity and Islam—the two largest living religions, comprising together half the world's current population—have often been, they can also find recourse within that cooptation to renew themselves, as Franciscanism and Sufism exhibit.

But second, and more important for our own time, these cultures can be brought together in the lives of individuals. And because their goal is not domination but integration, the life of those cultures has great potential to grow and integrate—to enliveningly "hybridize," to use Bhabha's term—through those individuals' lives. Thoreau, for instance, kept copies of Homer, the Bible, the *Bhagavad Gita*, and the Confucian *Analects* in his hut at Walden Pond, effectively bringing the heritage of all four Axial cultures to coalesce in that tiny third space. And what deeply beneficent effects that short coalescence came to have! *Walden*, the reflective product of that cultural coalescence, as well as of Thoreau's reflective experiences of nature, became one of the central influences on Gandhi, across half a century and half the globe. Gandhi became the central influence on Martin Luther King, back across the globe again. And all three have come richly into play in the thought and life of Barack Obama.

The ready road, we believe, from Neolithic partnership culture through our current, deeply entrenched, empire-driven dominator culture toward the horizon of what Korten has called "Earth Community" is the way of wisdom: the cultivation of cosmopolitan consciousness in individuals, which can sustain and aid them in the search for meaningful life even in deeply inhospitable social and cultural surroundings. Like the mythical life in paradise, once partnership culture is overtaken by dominator culture, it is extremely difficult to get it to appear again in pure, lasting form; the most we can do is to create third spaces within and among ourselves in the hope that the joy and understanding that are generated within those spaces will come to spread. The key now, as the Axial Age saw, is to help each person find and broaden *inner* third space, to learn to come into play with oneself in reflective personhood. This is the only generally reliable source of our learning to come into play with others and the world, particularly with those large segments of our world that have been consumed by dominator culture.[10]

The Axial Age as a whole had a clear educational policy, directly opposed to the uniform educational policy of empires. Empires all seek in various ways to "leave no child behind" in mobilizing their collective triumphal march across the world. Axial cultures all seek in various ways to facilitate and inspire an inner revolution that will "draw each person forward" to cosmic consciousness and the responsible cosmopolitan action that ensues from the understanding that you and your fellows all have integral parts to play in the world's unfolding. The first seeks a totally regulated, top-down, in-step military march. The second promotes an integrated, personally facilitated and nurtured, individual, cultural, and universal "Great Leap of Being" (Voegelin's phrase for the Axial Age as a whole).

Plato, in his Seventh Letter, described this "great leap" as a consciousness that "after long-continued intercourse between teacher and pupil in pursuit of philosophy, suddenly, like light flashing forth when a fire is kindled, . . . is born in the soul and straightway nourishes itself." Buddhism, similarly, is simply the belief, based on reflective and pedagogical experience, that we all have the potential to become awake to life. In *Inner Revolution: Life, Liberty, and the Pursuit of Real Happiness* (1998), Robert Thurman, the Columbia scholar of Buddhism who was also the first American ordained by the Dalai Lama, declares: "'Buddha' is not a personal name. It is a title, a state we can attain. It means 'awakened,' 'blossomed,' 'enlightened.' It is the blossoming of all happiness and positive powers. It is perfect freedom. . . . A social buddhaverse is a place where everything is geared toward enlightenment, where every lifetime is made meaningful by optimal evolutionary development" (pp. 87, 32).

There are, in other words, major historical precedents for the call to exercise what Dewey, Brian Fischer's student Angel (see Chapter 7), and many others we have seen in the course of this book have called our right "to open up our eyes to see." And the course of history may come to turn on how we call one another—on the base of these precedents as well as on our own highest experience—to do just that. As Angel said, "It's all up to [us] and the others who have opened their eyes." We think he is probably right.

THE HISTORY OF THE WORLD OF WISDOM, PART THREE: THE WISDOM REVOLUTION, WHAT WE CAN HOPE FOR AND MUST ACT TOWARD

The physicist Peter Russell, in *Waking Up in Time* (1998), has said what we need is a "Wisdom Revolution" to succeed the Agricultural, Industrial, and Information revolutions, and to clean up the ecological, sociological, and psychological messes the last two have made. Ironically, just as many educational systems of industrial nations around the world have become almost exclusively focused on subjecting their younger generations to ever new batteries of tests, barren of human meaning, our species has found itself faced with what Russell calls "an evolutionary exam, a cosmic intelligence test" that the tests *we're* making up are actually serving as blinders to the need for. "We have prodigious powers at our disposal," declares Russell, "enough to harm a planet—and before we can continue our evolutionary journey we must prove we have the wisdom to use these powers for the benefit of all" (pp. 185–186).

We live in times that are literally trying both our souls and our material existence on the earth. So in our conclusion we will share with you some of the small and large ways that we English teachers can help our students, our schools, our nation, and our species learn how to pass the mother of all tests, which we are now being given in, and by, the real world. Precisely by working for a Wisdom Revolution.

What Can "English" Become?

Ordinary people can make meaningful change through the practices of everyday life.

—Asef Bayat, *Life as Politics: How Ordinary People Change Life in the Middle East*

Now we come to the truly challenging part: how to bring the ideas and practices of this book into the real world; how to literally realize Whitman's and Dewey's and Rosenblatt's transactional democratic vistas, developing a new core discipline of the curriculum we propose calling "Personal Studies," dedicated to fostering the growth and sharing of wisdom.

To connect and recenter everything now going under the names of "English," "Literacy," "Language Arts," "Reading," "Writing," "Cultural Studies," "Postmodern Theory," and so on under this new name is—no question about it—a daunting task. But such a renaming or, more important, the attendant reconstrual and unification of our subject would emphasize that here is a discipline explicitly designed to foster the democratic growing together of human beings through the cultivation of aesthetic responsiveness, existential inquiry, and a resultant sense of personal responsibility to the world.

And we need to remember that we have quite a bit of support for this task. This book has been largely about the intellectual—scientific, philosophical, and historical—support for it, which we will review briefly below. But that intellectual support is already undergirded by broad, deep human support that needs only to be fully awakened and organized to work the transformation that Whitman, Dewey, Rosenblatt, and so many others foresaw. In many ways the main thing we need to keep in mind is that this new name simply seeks to explicitly call forth an understanding that is already there, lying just beneath the surface of our educational practices and institutions.

THE HUMAN ELEMENT: SOME OF THE
NOT-SO-BURIED SOURCES OF LIFE WE CAN DRAW ON

First and foremost, there is the support of educators like you. The majority of English teachers already believe—no matter what they are told by government or administrative policies or the hierarchically designated leaders of their profession—that the most important thing they do through "English" is to foster the personal growth of their students (Goodwyn, 2005; Grossman & Stodolsky, 1996). What this means is that most of us deeply value and may already be teaching "Personal Studies," just without naming it as such. The name, if we can just make it publicly acceptable, will encourage and guide us to do far more effectively what most of us are already seeking to do.

Furthermore, English teachers are hardly alone in recognizing the centrality of the personal dimension of education. As Bruce has seen over and over again in the many wisdom-centered Foundations of Education classes he has taught, most everyone who enters the field of education has come to do so mainly because at least one of their teachers—in or out of school—was able to touch them in a deeply human way, bringing them eventually to choose to devote their lives to extending the reach of that touch. In Jeff's research on the literate lives of boys, he likewise found that his informants held an "implied social contract with teachers" demonstrating how they regarded teaching and learning as intensely relational interpersonal pursuits. However "high-tech" our world gets, education, as long as it is education, will remain a "high-touch" field (Palmer & Zajonc, 2010). Having a "touch-centered" discipline at the center of our educational endeavors—that is, one that is not merely sentimentally "touchy-feely," but is deliberately connected to substantive thought and warranted action—will serve to recenter all teaching on the connective dimension that is at the core of the profession as a whole. Because most teachers are "high-touch" folk, who have chosen to make a difference in the world by making meaningful connections with young people, our profession is filled with natural allies to this cause.

Second, there is the support of our students, most of whom have a strong sense of their own liveliness and of their capacities for deep love and wisdom. Students have a desire for challenge and a need for edgy and substantive work that leads to applications in the world, to their own personal growth and evolving competence, and to encountering others both like and unlike themselves. And they have souls, desiring not just what is good for themselves, but what is good for the world. Our work is simply to tap into and develop the tendencies inhering in most students' own deep desires: first to become more responsively feeling and thinking individuals; then to become responsible, active members of larger and larger social groups; eventually to become responsible citizens of the world, both the political world and the natural one.

To see the "real" world transactionally is to see that one's own being is an integral part of the world's being and that one's individual actions—especially now, on a planet whose life support systems collective human actions have made newly fragile—affect the very nature of the world for better or worse. It is comforting as well as stirring to see that we are not alone in the universe, either as individuals or as a species. Throughout this book we have seen many images of students and classrooms—from the first grade with Laura and her classmates, through the doctoral level with Bruce's middle-aged student who said, "This [one] class has totally changed my life and my perspective and outlook on life"—who have been brought into new awakeness to life through ways of teaching and learning that deliberately seek to evoke that awakeness and channel it into the flow of the whole of life. Certainly, there always have been and always will be students who will resist this awakening process. But we have no doubt but that if we are able to make the evocation and cultivation of this awakeness to the flow of life the clearly articulated central goal of education, it will be broadly and heartily embraced by the vast majority of students, certainly by far more of them than now embrace the current testing regime, organized around the inculcation of inert knowledge and skills.[1]

Starting with the second Foundations of Education class he taught, Bruce has begun every class with a discussion of the difference between "knowledge" and "wisdom." Most students immediately see which of these our schools tend to value most and which the best teachers—in and out of schools—tend to value and seek to spread. One student, on being asked which of his teachers was the wisest, mused unforgettably, "I've never thought of this before, but it's really strange they don't let anyone teach like that any more."

Imagine what our schools could be like if the norm was not just letting some remarkable teachers teach like that, but deliberately helping all teachers do so. In the previous chapter, we saw Plato describing the love of wisdom as being like a wick buried deep in the soul—difficult to light, but inextinguishable once it *is* lit. Imagine what the world would be like if the central effort of schools around the world was to awaken students to the light of their own and one another's life. What if we stopped treating our young primarily as tools for economic ends and started treating them primarily as ends in themselves? It would not be nearly as hard as Socrates, Plato, and others found it to bring that inner wick of the love of wisdom to light.[2]

For those doubting the feasibility of such a project, think of the teacher or teachers who most influenced you. A single teacher can plant and light the wick. If few teachers do so, then it is all the more important that you work for this end. And unless some few teachers do, the necessary models and mentors for a wider adoption of this work will not exist.

It's not *just* teachers and students, though. While many of the powers-that-be in our world may powerfully resist a wisdom-centered curriculum, there are also forces that can be brought to heartily embrace it.

The strongest of those forces is the love of parents for the good of their children. Most parents want their children to be successful and to work hard, but they also want them even more to be good, to be wise, and to be happy. So far, they just don't see school as a central way we can learn to be these things—and so far, they've been largely right. Many schools are currently being moved to de-stress testing through the action of concerned parents who have seen the film *The Race to Nowhere*, according to the *New York Times* (Gabriel, 2010). Imagine how schools could also be moved—even transformed—in positive ways were we to put clearly before the eyes of parents the possibilities of real schools like The Center for Inquiry, Bruce's "educational Shangri-La," which thrives in Columbia, South Carolina (see Chapter 8).

Next, there is the force of democratic culture. We saw this directly at work in Bruce's teaching of Suskind's *A Hope in the Unseen* in Chapter 6, and, of course, in Chapter 8, but it has been indirectly at work throughout. "Democracy demands wisdom" is the new slogan of the National Endowment for the Humanities. We could say as well that wisdom is *internalized* democracy—the responsible self-government of selves for themselves—which is *why* democracy itself demands it. A people as a whole cannot become self-governing unless the individuals composing it are. In his 1996 article "Democracy's Forgotten Dimension," Václav Havel (1997) said democracy would only truly be able to spread through the world through "a process of internalization." A curriculum of "Personal Studies" is precisely this process.

Last, but hardly least, there is the force of the wisdom tradition itself, which inheres not just in philosophy and art, but in all the major religious traditions that are alive today, which at root have far more in common than they differ. As we saw in the previous chapter, the major Wisdom Revolution occurred over 2,000 years ago, when Socrates, Confucius, Buddha, and others discovered and taught, in various ways, how to subvert and soften the dehumanizing power of empires with the force of personal truth. In some ways, all teachers need to do is link together these deeply embedded cultural teachings, which already constitute a firmly historically established "Personal Studies" curriculum. In Bruce's experience, it's not hard to show many deeply believing Fundamentalist Christians that in today's world one of their main allies is Gandhian non-violence, which is a fusion of Tolstoyan Christianity and the philosophy of the *Bhagavad Gita*. Often all that's necessary is for people to know what else is out there and to explore how and why this does or might resonate with them.

REASONS TO RETHINK: A REVIEW OF THE SUBSTANTIAL INTELLECTUAL SUPPORT WE CAN DRAW ON

Now that we understand the human support that already exists for the establishment of a "Personal Studies" curriculum, let's review the substantial number of ideas supporting it that we have encountered throughout this book

1. *Language.* Because, as James Moffett so clearly pointed out, the center of the universe of discourse lies in personhood, in the "I-You" relationship, there is no inherent conflict between language study and the study of connected personhood. We have, up to now, improperly centered language study on grammar rather than on personhood, in a way that has made the teaching of language dehumanizing rather than humanizing, and made it far more difficult than it needs to be.
2. *Biology.* Art is not cheesecake in the diet of our species. It is mother's milk: the central evolutionary process attaching us in educative ways to personal and cultural experience. Through art we live in the purest form of "I-You" relationship that exists, through a shared holistic experience of life with an implied author to whom we meaningfully, re-creatively respond.
3. *Psychology.* Besides being an evolved form of alloparenting, art is a form of the secure parenting. Art provides us with an environment in which we can safely explore life, where we can engage in pure existential inquiry without worry for our immediate existence. As such, it provides each of us with a kind of liminal space of possibility, an inner psychic womb for the creation of new life.
4. *Anthropology/Sociology/Economics.* Art, and aesthetic experience generally, thus form the basis of a transactional "gift economy," an economy of persons and peoples that supervenes upon the economy of the interactive and self-actional market of commodities and is humanly, not just materially productive.
5. *Philosophy.* Human time is story time. And narrative knowledge is connected knowledge. The deep experience of the present, the past, and the future is as a story that leads to and from each one of us. All human "e-duc-ation"—education that treats humans

as ends in a gift economy rather than as means in a market economy—is a transactional "drawing out" of human personhood toward livelier participation in the human story and the larger story of life. The personal presence of the teacher, eliciting transaction through the forging of personal, curricular, and philosophical relationship, "taking one's very life up into speech so that others may do the same" (Inchausti, 1993, p. 141), is therefore essential.

6. *History.* In response to the dehumanizations of the first great expansionist empires that sprang up across Eurasia in the first millennium B.C.E., the various groups of Axial sages initiated humanizing wisdom revolutions that have left permanent residues in the world's major religions and philosophical and humanistic traditions. Later, much of the movement called Romanticism was an attempt to recapture—in a way that could cut across the separate cultures of those traditions—the rehumanizing reverence for life within dehumanizing culture that was first cultivated in the Axial Age. The curricular discipline that came to be called "English" served to spread the democratic humanism—liberal education for the masses of humanity—arrived at by the Romantics, but because it needed to do so under the cover of utilitarian "literacy" its humanizing potential was easily obscured by hierarchical systems of education seeking primarily to economically exploit rather than to humanly educate the masses. That democratic humanism is reclaimed in the designation "Personal Studies."

7. *Politics/Ecology.* Economic globalization has produced "supercapitalism" (Reich, 2007), the hegemony of the market economy over all spheres of life. This can be conceived as the ultimate, final form of empire—which, in maximizing the exploitation of global natural and human resources, is currently exhausting and dehumanizing them in unprecedented, life-threatening ways that are making it subject to sudden collapse. Whether to prevent that collapse or to cope with it after it arrives, the only way to definitively overcome the dehumanizing market forces of supercapitalism is by cultivating the humanizing truth force of "superdemocracy." "Personal Studies" does this. Its goal is to cultivate both the responsiveness and the responsibility of each human being, to Draw Each Person Forward to responsibility for the world as a whole, as part of a transactional gift economy, rather than to Leave No Child Behind in The Race to Nowhere of an interactive market economy that has conferred radically unequal material benefits, savagely unjust human ones, and has

catastrophically ignored the integration of human and natural life. What Dewey claimed in 1949 is far clearer now: The cultivation of transactional mentality may well be the only force that can save the modern world from chaos. We are now literally witnessing what Einstein said in 1945: Everything, *now the whole of nature*, is changing, due to human actions, except the way we human beings think. It is therefore high time for *all* of us to "be the change" in human thought. The times we have collectively created are now trying all of our souls. And how we, and much of the rest of nature, emerge from that trial is up to us.

GETTING PEOPLE TO TRANSACT: CHANGING "THE WAY WE THINK," ONE PERSON AT A TIME

Given all this, one would think everyone would readily embrace "Personal Studies." But we know they won't. We know that if the educational change we need is going to happen, it is going to involve some major struggles on the policy level, and many daily ones on the practical and interactional level as well. So we'd like to anticipate what some of those struggles will be. First, we'd like to provide you with two handy conceptual distinctions: between "wisdom" and "knowledge" and between "the personal" and "the private." Next, we'd like to offer three brief pieces of practical advice. Finally, and most importantly, in the rest of this section we'll let Jeff's teachers speak directly to you about how they work change in their schools. Obviously, many, many structural changes in the educational system will be called for as well, but we'll leave those for another book.

Distinction 1: Wisdom Includes *Knowledge.* An unforgettable moment in Bruce's teaching occurred when one student objected to wisdom-centered education: "I'd rather teach *robots* than incompetent *people*!" Bruce answered back, "What on earth makes you think those are your only two choices?" He's pretty sure he didn't change this one student's mind. On the other hand, he thinks many of his other students could clearly see from this exchange the delusional structure of current education. No one with any degree of wisdom would think one could have wisdom without knowledge. But we have constructed a whole system of education that fantasizes that decontextualized information and skills are of the highest human use, and that the only efficient way to structure education is toward a series of totally impersonal, totally measurable objectives regarding factual and procedural knowledge—*whats*, and sometimes *hows*, with no *whys* at all. The search for wisdom by the all-important *whos*—also entirely neglected by this system—will not make people incompetent. It will help them become *responsibly* competent, competent because of their love for the world that leads them to cultivate wisdom in order to care for it.

Distinction 2: There Is a Difference Between "the Personal" and "the Private." We each have private family and fantasy lives that affect who we are in public, but need not necessarily be disclosed. Yet public life is life that is shared between persons who learn to become present to one another. As Karl Jaspers (1947/1952) said in his essay "On the Conditions and Possibilities of a New Humanism":

> It is only on the ground of personal reality that I can join in the collective life of a whole that would remain imaginary otherwise—of the smallest community, or of the state, or of humankind. . . . The future lies in the presentness of each individual. . . . The moral power of the seemingly infinitesimal individual is the sole substance and the real instrumentality of humanity's future. (p. 98)

Piece of Advice 1: Let Students Speak to Other Students About Their Experiences. The expression of personal truth, as Gandhi discovered, has enormous power. When we see it in others, most of us can't help seeing it in ourselves, even when we are reluctant to express it in public. Not all of Bruce's Philosophy of Education classes have been as successful as communities as the one he described at the beginning of Chapter 8. But most (though not all) of the students who are either generally silent or publicly resistant to his personal, wisdom-centered methods of teaching teachers are regularly reflective and show enormous personal insight and growth in their journals. Most students gravitate strongly toward the authenticity they see, even in classes that never on the outside overcome the "Mean Girl" (Fey, 2006) syndrome of the tyranny of cliques that tends to prevail in unreflective democratic mores (Tocqueville, 1835/2000). (This is explored more thoroughly in Novak, 2009.)

Piece of Advice 2: Be Patient with Resistant Students and Colleagues. This is often the hardest and the biggest part of seeking to be wise. For Thoreau, the highest and most important parts of leading a life of the love of wisdom were "magnanimity"—largeness of soul—and "trust"—faith and hope that acts undertaken in good faith will have good effects in the long term, even when we can't see those effects in the short term. One of George Hillocks's mottos was, "*Never, ever give up on your students.*" Jeff trusted in Dan Feight, his most resistant student, and through that he became Dan's favorite teacher. The same thing goes for our colleagues and higher-ups.

Piece of Advice 3: Take Standardized Measures Seriously; Just Don't Center Your Teaching Around Them. When Bruce's students have to take important tests, as they always did when he taught in public secondary schools and again when he recently taught at a community college, he totally centers his classes on those tests, but only for a few weeks right before them, and the vast majority of his students—many coming up from extremely low levels of "achievement"—do well and feel better about themselves for having done so. In his recent community college class, he adapted an old unit he used to use effectively in his high school classes: "Writing Meaningful Essays for Tests." One piece of advice: If a topic doesn't interest you, take it as a joke—the grader won't care as long as you follow the format, and you'll have some intrinsically rewarding fun to send you on your way to the extrinsic reward of your test score.

THE TEACHERS LET THEIR LIVES SPEAK

As Bruce and Jeff were in the final throes of revising this book, Jeff had lunch with the teachers featured earlier in this book. He asked them first how they would define their "story" as a teacher.

> *Sarah:* My story is about cultivating hope and possibility. Always asking: How do we cultivate hope and meaning in the midst of fear and questions about meaning? This struggle is the essence of my teaching and of the human journey and particularly important today. What do I want for my legacy? Teaching is about doing what needs to be done. It's about focusing on the needs of my students as literate human beings, and not neglecting what needs to be done administratively at the school level to make it happen. And not letting myself off the hook to keep pushing to meet those needs. Constantly reminding myself: Sarah, you are one of the ones who *just has to do it*.
>
> *Rachel:* My story, right now anyway, is about decelerating for democratic teaching. Everybody has something to learn and it must be taught. I'm trying to do less to do more. To make sure every day is energizing and meaningful. Making sure that what really needs to be learned really gets taught and that time is given to it. I've learned to provide the same opportunities, albeit in different ways, to all my students. Even AP kids need modeling, mentoring, and monitoring. Everybody needs and deserves motivating and meaningful contexts—we forget [AP students'] needs because they will do what you ask them. Regular-track kids, English Language Learner kids, and AP kids need the same things [both] as students and human beings.

Andrew: I think my current story would have the theme of "keep getting better; keep moving forward!" That's true for me and for my kids. I try to celebrate where they are and how far they have come and where they are going next instead of applying some arbitrary set of standards that might not motivate them or help them grow. I try to think about what I've achieved as a teacher with some measure of satisfaction while at the same time trying to keep moving forward and getting better, and I'm trying to get better at promoting forms of competence that lead to savoring literature and life and each other.

Sharon: My story is about promoting care for each other and the world through reading and composing. It's about telling our stories of our lives, and also imagining the kinds of stories we want to be telling about ourselves and about our future and making these stories come true.

Debra: My teaching is about promoting community and civic life in thoughtful ways that benefit everybody. It's about both/and instead of either/or thinking. It's about creative problem solving and tenacity. At least I hope it is. That's my goal.

Jeff next asked them about the role of helping students relate to and love authors, the critical first step of consciously connecting to the transactional "gift economy." They all agreed this was a major part of their classroom project.

Sarah: My kids think about a novel as something that just appeared. It came onto the planet on a rocket ship. That's how they've experienced it: let's read this fabulous piece of literature. So I focus on the writing as a craft that is meant to communicate to a reader. Looking at the author as someone who has worked hard to communicate to you—it's not hard for ninth graders, but it is new to them. I do it mostly through think-alouds of the texts we read, helping kids think of themselves as authors, and doing think-alouds on their work, focusing on their purposes and rhetorical choices.

Andrew: I like my students to write author and artist statements for all their work so they think consciously of themselves as an author making choices to communicate. And I do lots of drama work where the kids play the role of the author we are reading. The focus of my teaching centers on creating a classroom climate that fosters and honors student voices. I'm trying to engage students in ways that promote feelings not only of enjoyment, but of ownership in the process of both making and sharing the meaning they glean from the material.

Rachel: I explore relationships with authors through drama, and by promoting the many ways students are authors of many different texts, including multimedia ones. I cast a wide net around what we consider texts, ways of composing, ways of authoring texts and our very lives. I like to name and celebrate those things.

Debra: The work has to be real. Kids will go all the way to the wall if they get to do work that expresses who they are and who they can be (really) and how they can become that—and I mean that the work has to be real right now about real issues and real problems that are important and pressing because they smell the fake stuff ten miles away (really). I want them to see authors as people who are doing really important inquiry around the most important issues, and I want them to see themselves as part of that work. And I try to remember this quote from Lillian Smith: "I soon realized that no journey carries one far unless, as it extends into the world around us, it goes an equal distance into the world within."

Sharon: I focus on how authors explore the human condition and focus on how we have to do the same thing. Once we understand the human condition, we can begin to act on what we come to understand to live meaningful lives.

Jeff then asked the teachers how they dialogue with parents, other teachers, and administrators about this kind of work.

Sharon: I am proactive in communicating with my students and their parents, focusing on what we do as being vitally important right now to our real lives.

Andrew: I think that is key, as well as doing the same with colleagues. I try to let them all know how all the preset goals are being met, but how we are doing so much more. I name the big stuff and I tell them how excited I am by the big stuff we are doing that meets the requirements and then goes so far beyond them. I also am respectful to colleagues in letting them know I will listen to them, but that there are some things too important to compromise on.

Sarah: You have to step up to the plate. I tell students and parents up front what I value. And then, for other teachers, I just don't hold back. I am not shy. If they disagree with me, I say: Convince me. Let's listen to each other. You have to be vocal, then jump for the foxhole if you have to. If you don't speak, then it is the kids and the future getting silenced. It is too important!

There are some things that cannot go unsaid. You have to take it to the administrative level. Get some credibility and then talk; tell people what you are doing and why. I have to be critical to teach kids to be critical. I have to offer positive alternatives instead of just complaining. I am not subversive. I say what I have to say—no one is surprised about what I believe. And I show them how I make what I value happen. Sometimes I say—just let me show you how I can do this. You don't have to do it, but let me show you how I can live out my values as a teacher.

Rachel: Proactivity and communication, always. I have to know why I am doing what I am doing and I involve the kids in defining and justifying what they are doing in class. For example, what is my answer if someone asks why is your AP student working on a Facebook page? I have to know the moves she is making and why I value them and how this project motivates her and moves her to do things she wouldn't have otherwise done. And I have to help her to name those things too and be willing to justify them. I also try to improvise. In doing research, I do lots of activities so kids can induce that research is something you are wondering about, not something you have already decided about or know about. It's about something that intrigues you and that you want to create knowledge around. I also think it is important to have regular rituals for talking with colleagues. Making time to talk in department meetings can really work.

Sharon: Be honest. Be yourself. Say what is on your heart and be willing to converse. Democracy is conversation. Truth cannot be bested by a bad argument so say what you have to say and be willing to listen, to students first and foremost, but also to parents and colleagues and administrators. Be willing to volunteer and to lead the way sometimes.

Debra: With Monk (my student teacher) we keep going back to "What's the value in literary criticism for a 16-year-old?" How do we communicate this to them, and to their parents and other stakeholders? I guess it comes down to this central theme: *listening.* Close reading is close listening. Oh, hark! We're going to explore how Edith Wharton and her surrogate, Ethan Frome, have a cautionary tale to share with us about crucial moments of decision making (or not). We have to listen carefully to the story *and* the way Edith and Ethan tell it. We're listening to her use of symbols—the vessels that contain our dreams. And just as we listen to authors and characters, we have to listen to parents and business people—we have to dialogue with them in their terms. We have to communicate and be willing to make meaning together for the good of our children and the world. You have to find a starting point and see what you have in common, despite differences. Listening is the key. And the starting point for everything. Then responsive conversation where you don't hold back. "Truth was never bested by a bad argument unless the arguments were not made."

THE TRANSACTIONAL PARADIGM SHIFT: TOWARD MATURE, WISE, AND LOVING SELF-GOVERNMENT

In seeing democracy as conversation, these teachers are doing what Shakespeare, Emerson, and Arnold asked: not admitting impediments to the marriage of true minds; treating the people as if they were real; seeking always to be true both to others and to themselves. This is the essential existential work. As Emerson (1844/1983) put it in "Of Experience," just after his injunction "to treat [the people] as if they were real":

> Without any shadow of doubt, amidst this vertigo of shows and politics, I settle myself ever firmer in the creed, that we should not postpone and refer and wish, but do broad justice where we are, by whomsoever we deal with, accepting our actual companions and circumstances, however humble or odious, as the mystic officials to whom the universe has delegated its whole pleasure to us. (p. 479)

Yet these teachers also see, as we must too, in the words of Karl Jaspers (1947/1952), that "in the presentness of each individual" a new future opens. We have spoken throughout of the opening of eyes—to the gifts of the past, to others present before us, and to the new possibilities of life that they and we can cocreate. As Erin Gruwell (2010) sought to see both the realities and the possibilities in the lives of her students, and helped them see the way to "freewrite the endings of their stories" no matter how they had gone to that point, so can we all freewrite our *collective* ending. We have to keep our eyes open both to those immediately around us and to the new world we can cocreate as more eyes are opened. To "keep our eyes on the prize" as well as on what and who is right there. "[I]f enough of our voices join together, if we see each other in each other's eyes, we can bring those walls tumbling down. The walls of Jericho can finally come tumbling down," said Barack Obama during his presidential campaign.

Those walls are in part the walls of the American empire that Walt Whitman (1871/1982), at its outset nearly a century and a half ago, saw had "endow'd [us] with a vast and more and more thoroughly appointed body, and then left [us] with little or no soul." John Dewey, in his 1932 *Ethics*, called ours a democracy of spoiled children, and spoke of creating democracy anew through *wise* self-government:

> A spoiled child . . . is encouraged to yield to every desire that arises. . . . What is true on this personal scale is true on a wide social scale. The general social order may be such as to put a premium upon the kind of satisfaction which is coarse, gross, "materialistic," and on attitudes which are in impatient haste to grab any seeming near-by good. This state of affairs is characteristic of many phases of American life today. Goods that are more ideal, esthetic, intellectual values, those of friendship which is more than a superficial comradeship, are forced into subordination. The need of fostering the reflective and con-templative attitudes of character is therefore the greater. Above all, there is the need to remake social conditions so that they will almost automatically support fuller and more enduring values and will reduce those social habits which form the free play of impulse unordered by thought, or which make [people] satisfied to fall into mere routine or convention. The great bulwark of wisdom in judging values is a just and noble social order. Said Santayana: ". . .There is a . . . capacity in [people] to live nobly if they would give one an-other a chance. The ideal of political perfection . . . is . . . approachable, . . . as definite and constant as human nature." (Dewey & Tufts, 1932, pp. 211–212)

The prize we seek is a democracy of True Selves living in a good-enough moral world, who know "they're the ones they've been waiting for," and so seek constantly to find themselves and one another. To reach out, just as the good-enough parent does toward her child—to "give one another a chance," as Santayana said. We all need to learn—as Sarah, Sharon, Andrew, Debra, and Rachel have learned, and seek to get their students to learn—to reach out to that good-enough world. If we can just get people to see that wisdom lies at the heart of education, it is not far at all from getting them to see that the heart of democracy is love: Lincoln's "govern-ment . . . for people . . . with malice toward none, with charity for all," a large and ongoing marriage of true minds seeking to be true to—and so to become real for—one another.

Notes

Introduction

1. Bruce's suggestion to Appleman, after this presentation, about how the "transaction" could be seen as the fundamental literary experience, around which other "theory" should be centered (echoing Booth, 1995) was in some ways the origin of the theoretical stance of this book.

Chapter 1

1. Even social studies teachers agree that their subject matter derives from the various social sciences, whether they teach that subject matter from a more conservative or a more progressive bent. There is no such agreement about the basic subject matter of English.

2. Starting in 2007 the Conference on English Education nobly, on its own, initiated a third such effort, in which Bruce has participated. But so far this effort has attracted only a sliver of the profession as a whole, and has not even attempted to arrive at a unifying catchphrase for the public, as did the other two.

3. We follow Elbow's usage in naming this group in these two ways, with "Joy" capitalized to capture the sense of poetic personification. When referring to "holistic education" ourselves, on the other hand, we follow the usage both of J. C. Smuts, who invented the term *holism* in his 1926 work *Holism and Evolution*, and the Holistic Education Special Interest Group of the American Educational Research Association, which took the *w* from its name in accordance with the original spelling of this term (Clarken, 2006).

Chapter 2

1. Throughout, Bruce has retranslated passages from Plato, based on the Hamilton and Cairns 1961 edition and his consulting the original Greek. Readers who have been prejudiced against Plato for his surface-level stances against democracy should consult Sara Monoson's *Plato's Democratic Entanglements* (2000) for a thorough and well-reasoned alternative view. Readers who have been prejudiced against him by "postmodern" readings of him as the first representative of "phallo-logocentrism" (e.g., Derrida, 1976, 1982, 1987) would do well to consult Catherine Zuckert's *Postmodern Platos* (1996) and *Plato's Philosophers* (2009), which present thoroughly considered and well-reasoned views that Plato was both al-

ready a "postmodern" thinker—*vis a vis* the rationalistic "sophists" and natural scientists of his day—and also much more than that.

2. Just as Moffett distinguished between "I-You" and "I-It" discourse, Noddings (1998) and Valenzuela (1999) differentiate "caring about" ideas and things from "caring for" persons, and find the latter both to be far more important and much neglected in our current educational institutions—particularly, for Valenzuela, when members of dominant classes educate disadvantaged minorities.

3. We need to note here that *inquiry*, a key term in many of Jeff's earlier works, as well as this one, can be used for either purely "issue-centered" interaction or for growing together through aesthetic transaction, as we referred to in the distinction between essential and existential inquiry we made in the introduction. What the latter entails will be seen in our last four chapters, once the topic of "reflection" is introduced. We also need to note that we don't mean to outlaw any particular kind of literacy here, but do think we can clearly show that there are more and less humane forms of it, and that we sorely need to better understand, better teach, and better integrate the most humane ones. Issues, of course, need to arise before people can genuinely and lastingly grow together. It is not raising issues in the curriculum that we are at odds with, but an issue-*centered* curriculum that presupposes that generating issues, no matter how divisive this becomes, is the best and most important thing we can do, reflecting the noxious assumptions of what linguist Deborah Tannen calls our "argument culture" through which America has become engaged in an unending war of words with itself (1998).

We also recognize that "softness" without reflection has its own limitations and poses real dangers. Many past and current controversies in English have come about because some of its teachers have been drawn to its "softer" parts, others to its "harder" ones [pun intended]—and there has been insufficient effort to bridge the gaps between those two camps. This book is in many ways an effort to bring the opposing camps of "Venus" and "Mars" of our field together on common ground they can meaningfully share—in large part through the *inquiry* into "the power of softness" we take up in the next chapter, and through our general emphasis on the combination of love and wisdom.

Chapter 3

1. These two terms were invented by Jacques Derrida, the Frenchman whose 1967 *Of Grammatology* spawned the takeover of university English departments by "postmodern critical theory" soon after the appearance of its 1976 translation by Gayatri Chakravorty Spivak.

2. Richards (2003) documents how deeply and richly Darwin's thought was influenced by the tradition of "natural supernaturalism" we referred to in the last chapter, particularly by the aesthetic natural philosophy of Kant.

3. Derrida served as Ricoeur's teaching assistant in the early 1960s. And for those who are interested in a direct comparison of the Derridean deconstructive worldview with the Ricoeurean worldview of narrative renewal, there is a wonderfully illuminating and wonderfully accessible transcript of a dialogue between

them in 1971, which can be found in *Imagination and Chance: The Difference Between the Thought of Paul Ricoeur and Jacques Derrida* (Lawlor, 1992).

4. Those philosophically inclined will notice that these two different centers for human life are reflected in Kant's Second and Third Critiques, in the two parts of Ludwig Wittgenstein's *Philosophical Investigations* (1953) and in Heidegger's distinction between "common sense" ("das man") and "authenticity" or "ownness" ("Eigentlichkeit") in *Being and Time* (1927/1996).

Chapter 4

1. Noted educational psychologist Carol Dweck (1998) differentiates "the learning mindset" which tends to see life as presenting constant opportunities to grow and change from "the fixed mindset" which tends to see life as either a positive or negative reflection of one's own fixed ego. The habit of aesthetic immersion, precisely by *un*-fixing the ego, thus may be key to the learning process as a whole.

Chapter 5

1. We take the term *transpersonal* from the field of transpersonal psychology, which empirically investigates spiritual phenomena. We are going to confine the use of the term here to consciously shared aesthetic experience, though at the end of the chapter and through the end of the book, we will show how widely—by far more than just two people—aesthetic experience can be shared.

2. This is not what literary critics call "the intentional fallacy," because of the accompanying tacit recognition that we are actively constructing an image of the author, as we do a therapist. Without that accompanying self-awareness, we *can* succumb both to the "intentional fallacy" and to the blind idolization of the authors we love.

3. When Bruce spoke to him in private about the ideas of this chapter, though, he said they made sense.

4. See Kerr, 1996, for a poignant contrast between "avoidant" and "nurturant" conceptions of democracy, conceived in educational terms.

5. Readers who are sceptical or cynical about the morality of upward social mobility are urged to read the works of Dierdre McCloskey on the "bourgeois virtues" (2006, 2010) and their critical function of lifting the poor out of poverty wherever they have been adopted around the globe, as in China from the 1980s and India from the 1990s.

Chapter 6

1. The philosophical importance of givenness in human life is laid out by Jean-Luc Marion, Ricoeur's successor at the University of Chicago, in *Being Given: Toward a Phenomenology of Givenness* (2002).

Chapter 7

1. As Mark Schwehn notes in the introduction to his collection *Everyone a Teacher* (2000), "Good thinking by citizens about the everyday practice of good teaching begins with the recognition that teaching is a basic human activity whose excellence depends upon the exercise of certain intellectual, moral, and spiritual virtues."

2. The complete prompt went like this: What is your philosophy on life? In other words, how do you see the world and how do make the choices that determine what your life will be like? Write an essay in which you help me understand your philosophy on life. In order to help me fully understand what you mean, you may use examples from your life, situations that you have thought of, and stories, books, and movies that you have read or seen.

3. This is a term Bruce learned from one of his own teachers, the philosopher/psychoanalyst Jonathan Lear, one of the teachers with whom he first studied the works of Winnicott. It is found in *Love and Its Place in Nature* (Lear, 1990).

Chapter 8

1. This clearly is a prayer historically intermediate between Shakespeare's "Let me not to the marriage of true minds / Admit impediments" and Arnold's "Ah, love, let us be true / To one another!"

2. We need to note here that learning in transactional third space goes beyond most versions of constructivism or the social construction of knowledge, which, though cooperative and interactional, are not necessarily aesthetic and transactional. To put this concretely, and in the terms of this book, those who enter into aesthetic dialogue with present others in social third space do so as a way of extending the processes of aesthetic reflection—self-and-world integration—that occur in protected, nurtured psychological third space. Aesthetically self-integrating individuals naturally also seek integration with directly present others. But the acquired habit of personal reflection is a precondition for democratic relations that are not at constant risk of devolving into socially constructed tyrannies, as is powerfully illustrated in Thucydides's *History of the Peloponnesian Wars*, in Plato's *Gorgias*, and in Tina Fey's *Mean Girls*—the last being the text Bruce uses in his Philosophy of Education classes to illustrate the perils of unreflective social construction. In functional democratic life, aesthetic, environmental teaching in families and schools precedes, conditions, and reinforces moral life: The learning of personal self-government precedes, conditions, and reinforces the processes of mutual self-government. And doesn't it make sense that a self-regulating community or people can only be composed of self-regulating persons? (See also Jane Roland Martin's "Democracy Writ Small" in Goodlad et. al., 2008.)

3. Nussbaum's magnum opus, *Upheavals of Thought: The Intelligence of Emotions* (2001), is a thoroughly thought through philosophy of what we have called "aesthetic reflection" that relies heavily on Winnicott. And her more recent *Not for Profit* (2010) is a philosophical justification for a humanistic educational "gift economy" (though she does not employ that term for it).

4. This too is a topic that needs a book, or several of them. We hope here simply to point to ways that transactional and sociocultural literacy might in the future come to be thoroughly integrated. The ready theoretical bridge for that lies in the work of Mikhail Bakhtin (1981, 1990), whose thought, like the thinkers we examined in Chapter 2—Moffett, Schiller, Coleridge, Emerson, Carlyle, and Arnold—is grounded in the Kantian/Buberian ethics and aesthetics of transcendental personhood and democratic partnership (Emerson, 2000; Bazerman, 2004), rather than in Marxist materialism and relativistic readings of Nietzsche, whose intellectual substrate is the self-actional and interactional "will-to-power," not the deliberate cultivation of the transactional will to responsive and responsible multeity in unity we have been examining throughout. But to make this bridge a sturdy one we will have to engage with those aspects of current Bakhtinian scholarship that seek to downplay or decenter the role of the relational and the personal, such as Dressman (2004), which seeks to undercut Rosenblatt's "efferent/aesthetic" distinction as un-Deweyan. Dressman fails to notice either that this is directly derived from Dewey's consistent distinction between "instrumental" and "consummatory" experience, or that for at least the late Dewey, who sharply distinguished "interactional" from "transactional" mentality, "personalization" is *not* the equivalent of "trivialization" (as Dressman contends), rather, in certain cases, the opposite: "individuals with democratic habits of thought and action are the sole final warrant" for democracy itself. [This comes in Dewey (1939/1988), where he announced the decisive "change in emphasis" toward the individual in his philosophy that eventually led to the "interaction"/"transaction" distinction, 10 years down the road.] More positively, Knoeller (2004), Bazerman (2004), Ball & Freedman (2004), and Halasek (1999) have perspectives on Bakhtin that are thoroughly in line with our own: as a philosophy and practice of "how *people* can and do communicate across . . . divides and the role such communication plays in teaching and learning" (Ball & Freedman, 2004, emphasis ours) in which "dialogism is a moral imperative rather than a fact of social development" (Bazerman, 2004).

5. The book Paul Ricoeur published directly after his *Time and Narrative* was entitled *Oneself as Another* (1992).

6. We need to note here that "hybridity" is about the coming into being of new wholes from old ones and is, as Bhabha notes, very different from versions of multiculturalism and intellectual perspectivism emphasizing static diversity and variety rather than the "growing together" that both he and we stress. Another way of seeing "cultural hybridity" is as "the marriage of true minds" and True Selves across social, cultural, and political "impediments."

7. Another way of understanding what Bhabha has called "becoming the others of ourselves"—and what we have called "aesthetic reflection" from the standpoint of an inner "beyond me," or benign conscience—is as an inward splitting that facilitates outward connection, converting the energy of passionate self-will into that of *em*pathic *good* will. This understanding of democracy represents in some ways a simple updating of the concept of "mass" to bring it in line with the understandings of contemporary physics: helping us see we can be connected through deeper forces than the mere gravitation of self-will assumed by most of

the eighteenth-century founders of American democracy. [Here see also Naoko Saito's *The Gleam of Light* (2005) and Palmer & Zajonc, (2010).]

8. Dewey (1927) called Whitman "the seer of democracy," and Rosenblatt closed *The Reader, the Text, and the Poem* with a quote from *Democratic Vistas*. And Whitman knew his Emerson, Carlyle, and Arnold—the tradition of "natural supernaturalism" we discussed in Chapter 2.

9. Bruce had known Obama since 1996, when his friend Sam Ackerman, who helped launch his political career (he'd *just* been elected State Senator), invited him to speak at the Foundation for Ethics and Meaning conference "Re-Awakening Hope in a Time of Cynicism" just before the DNC in Chicago that year (also featuring Cornel West, Tom Hayden, Michael Lerner, and many other speakers, including a figure with whom Obama would later become closely associated in the public mind, William Ayers). Bruce served as Program Director for the conference and the title was of his devising—one reason he felt *so* personally invested in Obama's presidential campaign centered on the theme of "hope."

10. Tocqueville's *Democracy in America* was a central influence on Matthew Arnold, as can be seen in Bruce's "Humanizing Democracy" (Novak, 2002b).

11. A penetrating history of the story of how those divisions were intentionally forged by "conservative" political forces, then played into by "liberal" ones, from 1965 to the present can be found in Rick Pearlstein's *Nixonland: The Rise of a President and the Fracturing of America* (2008).

12. The original formulation of this name came from Bruce's student Rob Tesmond, now an English teacher in Lake Isabella, California.

Chapter 9

1. Perhaps the major reason why we still study the culture of Ancient Greece is that there was a determined effort by its philosophers and rhetoricians to spread that culture through the world in the wake of the loss of the Athenian Empire, because they saw the culture as more valuable than the empire in the first place (Bloom, 1955).

2. Gabriel Marcel and Karl Jaspers (who will figure greatly later in this chapter) were two of Ricoeur's most important teachers. Marcel also has a connection to Dewey and America, as his dissertation was on the democratic philosopher Josiah Royce, whose notion of "the beloved community" was first adopted by Martin Luther King, then implicitly adopted within the title of Toni Morrison's *Beloved*.

3. A beautiful comparison of Dewey's and Marcel's visions of educational hope can be found in Fishman & McCarthy (2007).

4. See Dauenhauer's *The Politics of Hope* (1986) (Foreword by Paul Ricoeur) for a thoroughly practical philosophical working out of these ideas.

5. For the theoretically inclined, there is also a stunning tribute to Gendlin by over a dozen of the foremost contemporary philosophers: *Language Beyond Postmodernism* (Levin, 1997).

6. Eisler found the last extant partnership culture was ancient Crete, which died out around 1000 B.C.E., but left much artistic evidence of a social life in which joy was the prevailing emotion. Eisler also has a wonderful book on educa-

tion, *Tomorrow's Children* (2000), with a foreword by Nel Noddings. On a related note, English teachers may be interested to know that there is a series of terrific historical novels depicting the transition between "partnership" and "dominator" culture in the decline of a single community: Mary Mackey's *The Earthsong Trilogy*.

7. Ian Morris's (2010) recent synoptic view of human social development places a similar stress on Jaspers's Axial Age, though his reading of the Neolithic archaeological record is quite different from Eisler's.

8. Our understanding of the "beauty" in "cosmopolitan" education comes from David Hansen's extensive work on this topic (esp. 2007b, 2010), and from a 2008 AERA session at which Hansen and Molly Quinn gave moving papers on both the beautiful and sublime sides, respectively, of modern cosmopolitan education.

9. In the light of Bruce's studies of Islam—informed in part by his (and James Moffett's) friend the Islamist Tom Gage, who has worked extensively with the Islamic humanist Gülen Foundation—we have added a fifth to Jaspers's (1957/ 1962) list of four "exemplary individuals" who grounded and exemplified the genuine philosophical worldview based on the practice of moral and existential inquiry.

10. David Hansen has compiled a series of gorgeous essays, *Ethical Visions of Education* (2007a)—on putting into practice a variety of Axial-inspired modern philosophies of education—that is well worth reading.

Conclusion

1. One of the most depressing findings for Jeff—in his various studies that involve shadowing students through school—is the astoundingly low quality of their lived-through experience during the school day. This is a finding echoed by other seminal studies including Csikszentmihalyi's famous beeper studies (see especially Smith & Wilhelm, 2002; Csikszentmihalyi, Rathunde, & Whalen, 1993).

2. Those worried about our falling behind through this new emphasis may well be surprised to find that having a well-functioning gift economy seems also to improve the operations of the market economy, in making economic actors more responsible than they now tend to be. As Eisler (2007) has found, the nations that have most instituted "caring economics" also tend to prosper materially from this.

References

Abeles, V. (Producer). (2010). *The race to nowhere: The dark side of America's achievement culture* [Motion picture]. Lafayette, CA: Reel Link Films.

Abrams, M. H. (1971). *Natural supernaturalism: Tradition and revolution in romantic literature*. New York: Norton.

Addams, J. (1910). *The spirit of youth and the city streets*. New York: Macmillan.

aepl.org/2008conf. (2008, June). Reclaiming the wisdom tradition for education. Summer conference of the National Council of Teachers of English Assembly for Expanded Perspectives on Learning, Watsonville, CA.

Alexander, T. M. (1987). *John Dewey's theory of art, experience, and nature: The horizons of feeling*. Albany, NY: SUNY Press.

Alter, J. (2007). *The defining moment: FDR's hundred days and the triumph of hope*. New York: Simon & Schuster.

Appiah, A. (2010). *The honor code: How moral revolutions happen*. New York: Norton.

Applebee, A. N. (1974). *Tradition and reform in the teaching of English: A history*. Urbana, IL: National Council of Teachers of English.

Appleman, D. (2006, April). Literary theory as pedagogical content knowledge. Paper presented at the annual meeting of the American Educational Research Association, San Francisco, CA, March.

Appleman, D. (2009). *Critical encounters in high school English: Teaching literary theory to adolescents*. New York: Teachers College Press.

Armstrong, K. (2006). *The great transformation: The origin of our religious traditions*. New York: Knopf.

Arnold, M. (1993). *Culture and anarchy and other writings*. New York: Cambridge University Press. (Original work published 1869)

Arnold, M. (1994). *Selected poems*. New York: Penguin.

Bacon, A. (Ed.). (1998). *The nineteenth-century history of English studies*. Brookfield, VT: Ashgate.

Bakhtin, M.M. (1981). *The dialogic imagination: Four essays*. Austin: University of Texas Press.

Bakhtin, M.M. (1990). *Art and answerability*. Austin: University of Texas Press.

Ball, A., & Freedman, S.W. (Eds.) (2004). *Bakhtinian perspectives on language, literacy, and learning*. New York: Cambridge University Press.

Baumgarten, A. (2007). *Ästhetik*. Hamburg: Felix Meiner Verlag. (Original work published 1750, 1758)

Bayat, A. (2010). *Life as politics: How ordinary people change the Middle East*. Palo Alto, CA: Stanford University Press.

Bazerman, C. (2004). Intertextualities: Volosinov, Bakhtin, literary theory, and literacy studies. In A. Ball & S. W. Freedman (Eds.), *Bakhtinian perspectives on language, literacy, and learning*. New York: Cambridge University Press.

Beck, I. L., & McKeown, M. G. (2006). *QtA: A fresh and expanded view of a powerful approach*. New York: Scholastic

Bellow, S. (1970). *Mr. Sammler's Planet*. New York: Viking.

Berlin, J. (1982). Contemporary composition: The major pedagogical theories. *College English, 44*(8), 765–777.

Bhabha, H. K. (1994). *The location of culture*. New York: Routledge.

Blau, S. (2003). *The literature workshop: Teaching texts and their readers*. Portsmouth, NH: Heinemann.

Bloom, A. D. (1955). *The political philosophy of Isocrates*. Unpublished dissertation, University of Chicago, Chicago.

Bloom, H. (2004). *Where shall wisdom be found?* New York: Riverhead Books.

Bollas, C. (1987). *The shadow of the object: Psychoanalysis and the unthought known*. New York: Columbia University Press.

Booth, S. (1977). *Shakespeare's sonnets*. New Haven, CT: Yale University Press.

Booth, W. C. (1961). *The rhetoric of fiction*. Chicago: University of Chicago Press.

Booth, W. C. (1974). *Modern dogma and the rhetoric of assent*. Chicago: University of Chicago Press.

Booth, W. C. (1988). *The company we keep: An ethics of fiction*. Berkeley: University of California Press.

Booth, W. C. (1995). Foreword. In L. M. Rosenblatt, *Literature as exploration* (5th ed., pp. vii–xiv). New York: Modern Language Association.

Botstein, L. (1997). The development of talent and the reforming of secondary education: A university president's perspective. Meeting of the American Educational Research Association, Chicago, March.

Bowlby, J. (1969). *Attachment and loss. Volume 1: Attachment*. New York: Basic Books.

Brazelton, T. B. (1983). *Infants and mothers: Differences in development* (Rev. ed.). New York: Delta.

Brown, S. (2009). *Play: How it shapes the brain, opens the imagination, and invigorates the soul*. New York: Avery.

Bruner, J. (1996). The narrative construal of reality. In *The culture of education* (pp. 130–149). Cambridge, MA: Harvard University Press.

Bruns, C. (2011). *Why literature? The value of literary reading and its implications for pedagogy*. New York: Continuum.

Carlyle, T. (1999). *Sartor resartus*. New York: Oxford University Press. (Original work published 1834)

Christenbury, L (2007). *Retracing the journey: Teaching and learning in an American high school*. New York: Teachers College Press.

Clarken, R. H. (2006, April). Wholistic education: Toward a definition and description of the field. Paper presented at the annual meeting of the American Educational Research Association, San Francisco.

Creger, J. (2004). *The personal creed project and a new vision of learning: Teaching the universe of meaning in and beyond the classroom*. Portsmouth, NH: Heinemann.

Csikszentmihalyi, M. (1990). *Flow: The psychology of optimal experience*. New York: Harper.

Csikszentmihalyi, M., Rathunde, K., & Whalen, S. (1993). *Talented teenagers: The roots of success and failure.* Cambridge: Cambridge University Press.

Damasio, A. (1999). *The feeling for what happens: Body and emotion in the making of consciousness.* New York: Harcourt.

Darwin, C. (1871). *The descent of man and selection in relation to sex.* New York: Appleton & Company.

Dauenhauer, B. P. (1986). *The politics of hope.* New York: Routledge & Kegan Paul.

DeMan, P. (1979). *Allegories of reading: Figural language in Rousseau, Nietzsche, Rilke, and Proust.* New Haven, CT: Yale University Press.

Derrida, J. (1976). *Of grammatology.* Baltimore: Johns Hopkins University Press.

Derrida, J. (1982). *Dissemination.* Chicago: University of Chicago Press.

Derrida, J. (1987). *The post card: From Socrates to Freud and beyond.* Chicago: University of Chicago Press.

Derrida, J. (2001). The future of the profession, or the university without condition (thanks to the "Humanities," what could take place tomorrow). In *Jacques Derrida and the humanities: A critical reader* (pp. 24–57). New York: Continuum.

Dewey, J. (1910). *How we think.* New York: D. C. Heath.

Dewey, J. (1916). *Democracy and education.* New York: Macmillan.

Dewey, J. (1925). *Experience and nature.* New York: Open Court.

Dewey, J. (1927). *The public and its problems.* New York: Henry Holt.

Dewey, J. (1934). *Art as experience.* New York: Minton, Balch.

Dewey, J. (1988). I believe. In Jo Ann Boydson (Ed.), *John Dewey: The Later Works, Vol. 14* (pp. 91–97). Carbondale: Southern Illinois University Press. (Original work published 1939)

Dewey, J., & Bentley, A. (1949). *Knowing and the known.* Boston: Beacon Press.

Dewey, J., & Tufts, J. H. (1932). *Ethics.* New York: Henry Holt.

Dickstein, M. (2009). *Dancing in the dark: A cultural history of the Great Depression.* New York: Norton.

Dissanayake, E. (1988). *What is art for?* Seattle: University of Washington Press.

Dissanayake, E. (1992). *Homo aestheticus: Where art comes from and why.* Seattle: University of Washington Press.

Dissanayake, E. (2000). *Art and intimacy: How the arts began.* Seattle: University of Washington Press.

Dixon, J. (1967). *Growth through English.* Reading, UK: National Association for the Teaching of English.

Dressman, M. (2004). Dewey and Bakhtin in dialogue: From Rosenblatt to a pedagogy of literature as social, aesthetic practice. In A. Ball & S. W. Freedman (Eds.), *Bakhtinian perspectives on language, literacy, and learning.* New York: Cambridge University Press.

Dweck, C. (1998). *Self-theories: Their role in motivation, personality, and development.* Philadelphia: Psychology Press.

Edelsky, C. (1994). Education for democracy. *Language Arts, 71*(4), 252–257.

Edmundson, M. (2002). *Teacher: The one who made the difference.* New York: Vintage.

Eisler, R. (1987). *The chalice and the blade: Our history, our future.* New York: HarperCollins.

Eisler, R. (2000). *Tomorrow's children: A blueprint for partnership education in the twenty-first century.* Boulder, CO: Westview Press.

Eisler, R. (2007). *The real wealth of nations: Creating a caring economics.* San Francisco: Berrett-Koehler.

Eisner, E. W. (2002). *The arts and the creation of mind.* New Haven: Yale University Press.

Elbow, P. (1973). The doubting game and the believing game. In *Writing without teachers* (pp. 147–192). New York: Oxford University Press.

Elbow, P. (1990). *What is English?* New York: Modern Language Association.

Elbow, P. (2009a). *The believing game as a mode of thinking.* Summer conference of the NCTE Assembly for Expanded Perspectives on Learning, Estes Park, CO.

Elbow, P. (Ed.) (2009b). Pictures of the believing game. *Journal of the Assembly for Expanded Perspectives on Learning, 15.*

Emerson, C. (2000). Keynote at the Bakhtin and Vygotskyan Studies SIG, Conference for College Composition and Communication, Minneapolis, MN.

Emerson, R. W. (1983). The American scholar ([1837]; Of experience [1844]. In Ralph Waldo Emerson: *Essays and lectures* (J. Porte, Ed.). NewYork: Library of America.

Ferguson, C. (Director). (2010). *Inside job* (Motion picture). United States: Sony Pictures Classics.

Fey, T. (2006). *Mean girls* (screenplay). Paramount.

Fishman, S. M., & McCarthy, L. (2007). *John Dewey and the philosophy and practice of hope.* Urbana: University of Illinois.

Fox, M. (2007). *The A.W.E. project: Reinventing education, reinventing the human.* Kelowna, BC, Canada: CopperHouse.

Gabriel, T. (2010, December 9). Parents embrace documentary on pressures of school. *The New York Times.* Retrieved May 18, 2011, from http://www.nytimes.com/2010/12/09/education/09nowhere.html

Gallagher, K. (2009). *Readicide.* Portland, ME: Stenhouse.

Gardner, H. (1983). *Frames of mind: The theory of multiple intelligences.* New York: Basic Books.

Gardner, H. (1999). *Intelligence reframed.* Cambridge, MA: Harvard University Press.

Gendlin, E. (1978). *Focusing.* New York: Bantam.

Gibney, R. (2005). *Enron: The smartest guys in the room.* [film]. Jigsaw Productions.

Glazer, S. (Ed.). (1999). *The heart of learning: Spirituality in education.* New York: Tarcher/Putnam.

Goodlad, J. I. (2004). *A place called school.* New York: McGraw-Hill. (Original work published 1984)

Goodlad, J. I., Mantle-Bromley, C., & Goodlad, S. J. (2004). *Education for everyone: Agenda for education in a democracy.* San Francisco: Jossey-Bass.

Goodlad, J. I., Soder, R., & McDaniel, B. (2008). *Education and the making of a democratic people.* Boulder, CO: Paradigm.

Goodwyn, A. (2005). *Teaching English: A handbook for primary and secondary school teachers.* New York: Routledge/Falmer.

Gould, S. J. (1980). *The panda's thumb.* New York: Norton.

Graff, G. (1987). *Professing literature: An institutional history.* Chicago: University of Chicago Press.

Greene, M. (2001). *Variations on a blue guitar: The Lincoln Center Institute lectures on aesthetic education.* New York: Teachers College Press.

Grossman, P., & Stodolsky, S. (1996, November). Research on teacher knowledge. Paper given at the annual meeting of the National Council of Teachers of English, Chicago.

Gruwell, E. (2010, November). Presentation given at the annual meeting of the National Council of Teachers of English, Orlando, FL.

Gruwell, E. (Ed.). (1999). *The freedom writers diary.* New York: Broadway Books.

Gunderson, L. H. & Holling, C. S. (2002). *Panarchy: Understanding transformations in human and natural systems.* Washington, D.C.: Island Press.

Halasek, K. (1999). *A pedagogy of possibility: Bakhtinian perspectives on composition studies.* Carbondale: Southern Illinois University Press.

Hansen, D. T. (2001). *Exploring the moral heart of teaching: Toward a teacher's creed.* New York: Teachers College Press.

Hansen, D. T. (Ed.). (2007a). *Ethical visions of education: Philosophies in practice.* New York: Teachers College Press.

Hansen, D. T. (2007b). Presidential address. *Proceedings of the Philosophy of Education Society.* Urbana, IL: Philosophy of Education Society.

Hansen, D. T. (2008, March) Curriculum as cosmopolitan inheritance. Paper given at the annual meeting of the American Educational Research Association, New York, March.

Hansen, D. T. (2010). Cosmopolitanism and education: A view from the ground. *Teachers College Record, 112* (1).

Haroutunian-Gordon, S. (1991). *Turning the soul: Teaching through conversation in the high school.* Chicago: University of Chicago Press.

Haroutunian-Gordon, S. (2010). *Learning to teach through discussion: The art of turning the soul.* New Haven: Yale University Press.

Havel, V. (1997). *The art of the impossible: Politics as morality in practice: Speeches and writings, 1990–1996.* New York: Knopf.

Hawken, P. (2007) *Blessed unrest: How the largest movement in the world came into being and why no one saw it coming.* New York: Viking.

Heath, S. B. (1983). *Ways with words: Language, life, and work in communities and classrooms.* New York: Cambridge University Press.

Heidegger, M. (1996). *Being and time.* Albany: State University of New York Press. (Original work published 1927)

Hillocks, G., Jr. (1986). *Research on written composition: New directions for teaching.* Urbana, IL: National Conference on Research in English/ERIC Clearinghouse on Reading and Communication Skills.

Hillocks, G., Jr. (1996). *Teaching writing as reflective practice.* New York: Teachers College Press.

Hillocks, G., Jr. (1999). *Ways of thinking, ways of teaching.* New York: Teachers College Press.

Hrdy, S. B. (1999). *Mother nature: A history of mothers, infants, and natural selection.* New York: Pantheon.

Hyde, L. (1979). *The gift: Imagination and the erotic life of property.* New York: Vintage.

Hynds, S., & Appleman, D. (1997). Walking our talk: Between response and responsibility in the literature classroom. *English Education, 29* (4), 272–294.

Inchausti, R. (1993). *Spitwad sutras: Classroom teaching as sublime vocation.* Westport, CT: Bergin & Garvey.

Isaacson, W. (2007). *Einstein: A life.* New York: Simon & Schuster.

Jaspers, K. (1952). On the conditions and possibilities of a new humanism. In *Existentialism and humanism: Three essays* (pp. 81–98). New York: R. F. Moore. (Original essay published 1947)

Jaspers, K. (1953). *The origin and goal of history*. London: Routledge & K. Paul. (Original work published 1949)

Jaspers, K. (1962). *Socrates, Buddha, Confucius, Jesus: The paradigmatic individuals. The great philosophers, Vol. 1*. New York: Harcourt, Brace.

Jensen, J. M. (Ed.). (1989). *Stories to grow on: Demonstrations of language learning in K–8 classrooms*. Portsmouth, NH: Heinemann.

Kant, I. (1952). *The critique of judgment*. New York: Oxford University Press. (Original work 1790. Also known as the Third Critique.)

Kant, I. (1956). *The critique of practical reason*. Indianapolis: Bobbs-Merrill. (Original work published 1788. Also known as the Second Critique.)

Karen, R. (1994). *Becoming attached: First relationships and how they shape our capacity to love*. New York: Oxford University Press.

Kerr, D. (1996). Democracy, nurturance, and community. In R. Soder (Ed.), *Democracy, education, and the schools* (pp. 37–68). San Francisco: Jossey-Bass.

Kessler, R. (2000). *The soul of education: Helping Students Find Connection, Compassion, and Character at School*. Alexandria, VA: Association for Supervision and Curriculum Development.

Kliebard, H. (1995). *The struggle for the American curriculum 1893–1958*. New York: Routledge.

Knoeller, C.P. (2004). Narratives of rethinking: The inner dialogue of classroom discourse and student writing. In A. Ball, & S. W. Freedman, (Eds.), *Bakhtinian perspectives on language, literacy, and learning*. New York: Cambridge University Press.

Korten, D. (1995). *When corporations rule the world*. Bloomfield, CT: Kumarian.

Korten, D. (2006). *The great turning: From empire to Earth community*. San Francisco: Berrett-Koehler.

Lakoff, G. (1996). *Moral politics: What conservatives know that liberals don't*. Chicago: University of Chicago Press.

Lawlor, L. (1992). *Imagination and chance: The difference between the thought of Paul Ricoeur and Jacques Derrida*. Albany: State University of New York Press.

Lear, J. (1990). *Love and its place in nature: A philosophical interpretation of Freudian psychoanalysis*. New York: Farrar, Straus, & Giroux.

Levertov, D. (1982). Writing in the dark. In *Candles in Babylon*. New York: New Directions.

Levin, D. M. (1997). *Language beyond postmodernism: Saying and thinking in Gendlin's philosophy*. Evanston, IL: Northwestern University Press.

Lin, J. (2006). *Love, peace, and wisdom in education: A vision for education in the 21st century*. Lanham, MD: Roman & Littlefield Education.

Lloyd-Jones, R., & Lunsford, A. A. (Eds.). (1989). *The English Coalition Conference: Democracy through language*. New York: Modern Language Association.

Loye, D. (Ed.). (2004). *The great adventure: Toward a fully human theory of evolution*. Albany: State University of New York Press.

Marcel, G. (1951). *Homo viator: Introduction to a metaphysic of hope* (E. Crauford, Trans.). New York: H. Regnery.

Marion, J-L. (2002). *Being given: Toward a phenomenology of givenness*. (J.L. Kosky,

Trans.). Stanford, CA: Stanford University Press.

Martin, J. R. (2008). Education writ large. In J. I. Goodlad, R. Soder, B. McDaniel, *Education and the making of a democratic people* (pp. 47–64). Boulder, CO: Paradigm.

McCloskey, D. (2006). *The bourgeois virtues: Ethics for an age of commerce*. Chicago: University of Chicago Press.

McCloskey, D. (2010). *Bourgeois dignity: Why economics can't explain the modern world*. Chicago: University of Chicago Press.

McCullough, D. (2001). *John Adams*. New York: Simon & Schuster.

McKibben, B. (2010). *Eaarth: Making a life on a tough new planet*. New York: Times Books.

Mendell, D. (2008). *Obama: From promise to power*. New York: Amistad.

Millard, E. (2003). Transformative pedagogy: Towards a literacy of fusion. *Reading: Literacy and Language, 37*(1), 3–9.

Miller, J. H. (2002). *On literature*. New York: Routledge.

Miller, J. P. (2006). *Educating for wisdom and compassion: Creating conditions for timeless learning*. Thousand Oaks, CA: Corwin Press.

Mills, H., & Donnelly, A. (Eds.). (2001). *From the ground up: Creating a culture of inquiry*. Portsmouth, NH: Heinemann.

Moffett, J. (1968). *Teaching the universe of discourse*. New York: Houghton Mifflin.

Moffett, J. (1988). *Storm in the mountains: A case study of censorship, conflict, and consciousness*. Carbondale: University of Southern Illinois Press.

Moje, E. B., Ciechanowski, K. M., Kramer, K., Ellis, L., Carillo, R., & Collazo, T. (2004). Working toward third space in content area literacy: An examination of everyday funds of knowledge and discourse. *Reading Research Quarterly, 39*, 38–70.

Monoson, S. (2000). *Plato's democratic entanglements*. Princeton, NJ: Princeton University Press.

Morris, I. (2010). *Why the West rules—for now: The patterns of history and what they reveal about the future*. New York: Farrar, Straus, & Giroux.

Morrison, T. (1987). *Beloved*. New York: Knopf.

Morrison, T. (2008). The future of time. In *What moves at the margin: Selected nonfiction* (pp. 170–186). Jackson: University Press of Mississippi. (Original essay published 1996)

Muller, H. J. (1967). *The uses of English*. New York: Holt, Rinehart, & Winston.

Nagler, M. N. (2005). *Our spiritual crisis: Recovering human wisdom in a time of violence*. Chicago: Open Court.

National Commission on Excellence in Education. (1983). *A nation at risk: The imperative for educational reform*. Washington, DC: United States Department of Education.

Newkirk, T. (2009). *Holding onto good ideas in a time of bad ones: Six literacy principles worth fighting for*. Portsmouth, NH: Heinemann.

Noddings, N. (1998). "Caring about" is not enough. Keynote address for the Summer Conference of the NCTE Assembly for Expanded Perspectives on Learning of the National Council of Teachers of English, "Fostering Transformations in Teachers and Learners," June, Estes Park, CO.

Novak, B. (2002a). *Humanism and freedom: Matthew Arnold's call for the founding of a great-souled, educative democracy, and its bearing on the crises of our time.* Unpublished dissertation, University of Chicago, Chicago.

Novak, B. (2002b). Humanizing democracy: Matthew Arnold's nineteenth-century call for a higher, educative pursuit of happiness, and its relevance to twenty-first century democratic life. *Journal of the American Educational Research Association, 39*(3), 593–637.

Novak, B. (2003). "National standards" vs the free standards of culture: Matthew Arnold's *Culture and Anarchy* and contemporary educational philistinism. In *Philosophy of Education 2003* (pp. 376–383). Urbana, IL: Philosophy of Education Society.

Novak, B. (2008, November). Beyond "English" and "literacy": Envisioning a wisdom-centered discipline of democratic humanism named "Personal Studies." Paper presented at the annual convention of the National Council of Teachers of English, San Antonio, TX.

Novak, B. (2009). The audacity of thought: Seeing thinking as the moral virtue pivotal to the refounding of democracy on a moral basis. *Philosophical Studies in Education, 40*, 83–93.

Novak, B. (2010a). No Child Left Behind or Each Human Person Drawn Forward?: Arendt, Jaspers, and the thinking-through of a new, universalizable existential-cosmopolitan humanism. *Philosophy of Education 2010.* Urbana, IL: Philosophy of Education Society.

Novak, B. (2010b). What if education is not a race? The need within democratic life of seeing education as a personal, interpersonal, and transpersonal journey, and the present possibilities of helping the people to see this. *Philosophical Studies in Education, 41*, 38–47.

Novak, B. (in press). Reverence for things not seen: Implied authors in works of art and implied teachers in experiential pedagogy, and the instituting of a democratic gift economy. In A. G. Rud & J. Garrison (Eds.), *Reverence and teaching.* New York: Palgrave Macmillan.

Novak, B., & Bruns, C. (2010, November). Teachers, students, and authors together: How literature renews us, and how we can teach to help it do so. Paper presented at the annual meeting of the National Council of Teachers of English, Orlando, FL.

Novak, B., & Fischer, B. (1998). Seeing student/teacher relationships as hidden dramas of personal development. *Child and Adolescent Social Work Journal, 15*(6), 479–496.

Nussbaum, M. C. (1997). *Cultivating humanity: A classical defense of reform in liberal education.* Cambridge, MA: Harvard University Press.

Nussbaum, M. C. (2001). *Upheavals of thought: The intelligence of emotions.* New York: Cambridge University Press.

Nussbaum, M. C. (2010). *Not for profit: Why democracy needs the humanities.* Princeton, NJ: Princeton University Press.

Nystrand, M. (1997). *Opening dialogue: Understanding the dynamics of language and learning in the English classroom.* New York: Teachers College Press.

Obama, B. (2004). *Dreams from my father.* New York: Three Rivers Press.

Obama, B. (2006). *The audacity of hope: Thoughts on reclaiming the American dream.* New York: Crown.

Oldenburg, R. (1989) *The great good place: Cafes, coffee shops, bookstores, bars, hair salons, and other hangouts at the heart of a community.* New York: Paragon House.

O'Reilley, M. R. (1993). *The peaceable classroom.* Portsmouth, NH: Heinemann.

O'Reilley, M. R. (1998). *Radical presence.* Portsmouth, NH: Boynton/Cook.

Palmer, P. J. (1983). *To know as we are known: Education as a spiritual journey.* San Francisco: Harper.

Palmer, P. J. (1998). *The courage to teach: Exploring the inner landscape of a teacher's life.* San Francisco: Jossey-Bass.

Palmer, P. J., & Zajonc, A. (2010). *The heart of higher education: A call to renewal.* San Francisco: Jossey-Bass.

Pearlstein, R. (2008). *Nixonland: The rise of a president and the fracturing of America.* New York: Scribner.

Perl, S. (2004). *Felt sense: Writing with the body.* Portsmouth, NH: Heinemann.

Perls, F. (1969). Gestalt prayer. *Fritz Perls.* Retrieved February 9, 2011, from http://www.fritzperls.com/gestalt-prayer

Philibert, N. (2002). *To be and to have.* [Motion picture]

Pinker, S. (1997). *How the mind works.* New York: Norton.

Plato. (1961). *Dialogues* (E. Hamilton & H. Cairns, Eds.). Princeton, NJ: Bollingen.

Pradl, G. M. (1996). *Literature for democracy: Reading as a social act.* Portsmouth, NH: Heinemann.

Probst, R. (2010, November). Contribution to the "Engaging non-fiction texts" roundtable at the annual meeting of the National Council of Teachers of English, Orlando, FL.

Quinn, M. E. (2008). "Ex and the city": On cosmopolitanism, community, and the "curriculum of refuge." Paper presented at the annual meeting of the American Educational Research Association, New York, March.

Rabinowitz, P. (1987). *Before reading.* Ithaca: Cornell University Press.

Rabinowitz, P. J., & Smith, M. W. (1998). *Authorizing readers: Resistance and respect in the teaching of literature.* New York: Teachers College Press.

Ravitch, D. (2010). *The death and life of the great American school system: How testing and choice are undermining education.* New York: Basic Books.

Reich, R. (2007). *Supercapitalism: The transformation of business, democracy, and everyday life.* New York: Knopf.

Remen, R. (1996). *Kitchen table wisdom: Stories that heal.* New York: Riverhead Books.

Remnick, D. (2010). *The bridge: The life and rise of Barack Obama.* New York: Knopf.

Richards, R. J. (2003). *The romantic conception of life: Science and philosophy in the age of Goethe.* Chicago: University of Chicago Press.

Rico, G. L. (2000a). *Re-Creations: Inspiration from the source.* Spring, TX: Absey.

Rico, G. L. (2000b). *Writing the natural way.* New York: Tarcher/Putnam. (Original work published 1985)

Ricoeur, P. (1984, 1985, 1988). *Time and narrative, Vol. 1–3.* Chicago: The University of Chicago Press.

Ricoeur, P. (1992). *Oneself as another.* Chicago: University of Chicago Press.

Roosevelt, F. D. (1945). Speech draft, composed in the month of his death. Cited in Alter, J. (2007). *The defining moment: FDR's hundred days and the triumph of hope.* New York: Simon & Schuster.

Rosenberg, M. (2003). *Nonviolent communication: A language of life.* Encinitas, CA:

Puddle Dancer Press.

Rosenblatt, L. M. (1931). *L'art pour l'art dans la literature anglaise pendant la periode victorienne.* Paris: H. Champion.

Rosenblatt, L. M. (1978). *The reader, the text, and the poem: The transactional theory of the literary work.* Carbondale: University of Southern Illinois Press.

Rosenblatt, L. M. (1995). *Literature as exploration* (5th ed.). New York: Modern Language Association. (Original work published 1938)

Rud, A. G. (2010). *Albert Schweitzer's legacy for education: Reverence for life.* New York: Macmillan.

Rud, A. G., & Garrison, J. (Eds.). (in press). *Reverence and teaching.* New York: Palgrave Macmillan.

Ruddick, L. (2001, November 23). The near enemy of the humanities is professionalism. *The Chronicle of Higher Education,* B7–B9,

Russell, P. (1998). *Waking up in time.* Novato, CA: Origin Press.

Saito, N. (2005). *The gleam of light: Moral perfectionism and education in Dewey and Emerson.* New York: Fordham University Press.

Sanchez, A. (2010, November). Creating space for LGBT students and literature. Paper presented at the annual meeting of the National Council of Teachers of English, Orlando, FL.

Schiller, F. (1967). *On the aesthetic education of man in a series of letters.* New York: Oxford. (Original work published 1795)

Scholes, R. (1998). *The rise and fall of English: Reconstructing English as a discipline.* New Haven, CT: Yale University Press.

Schwehn, M. (ed.) (2000). *Everyone a teacher.* South Bend, IN: University of Notre Dame Press.

Schweitzer, A. (1965). *Reverence for life.* New York: Holt, Rinehart, & Winston.

Shamlin, M. (1997, April). The Center for Inquiry: The power, possibility, and vulnerability of university-public school partnership. Contribution to panel at the spring conference of the National Council of Teachers of English, Charlotte, NC.

Shannon, P. (2005). Wondering about NCLB. *Journal of Language and Literacy Education, 1*(1), 20–31. Available at: http://www.coe.uga.edu/jolle/2005_1/wondering.pdf

Shelley, P.B. (1820). *A defense of poetry.* Indianapolis: Bobbs-Merrill.

Slatoff, W. (1970). *With respect to readers: Dimensions of literary response.* Ithaca, NY: Cornell University Press.

Smith, H. (1991). *The world religions: Our great wisdom traditions.* New York: HarperCollins. (Original work published 1958)

Smith, M. W., & Wilhelm, J. D. (2002). *"Reading don't fix no Chevys": Reading in the lives of young men.* Portsmouth, NH: Heinemann.

Smith, M. W., & Wilhelm, J. D. (2006). *Going with the flow: How to engage boys (and girls) in their literacy learning.* Portsmouth, NH: Heinemann.

Smith, M. W., & Wilhelm, J. D. (2010). *Fresh takes on teaching the literary elements.* Urbana, IL: National Council of Teachers of English.

Smuts, J. C. (1926). *Holism and evolution.* New York: Macmillan.

Snow, C. P. (1959). *The two cultures and the scientific revolution.* New York: Cambridge University Press.

Stevenson, L. M., & Deasy, R. J. (2005). *Third space: When learning matters.* Washington, DC: Arts Education Partnership.

Stuart, M. (Director). (2006). *The Hobart Shakespeareans* [Motion picture]. New York: Stuart Productions and Thirteen/WNET.

Suskind, R. (1999). *A hope in the unseen: An American odyssey from the inner city to the Ivy League.* New York: HarperCollins.

Suskind, R. (2008). *The way of the world: A story of truth and hope in an age of extremism.* New York: HarperCollins.

Tannen, D. (1998). *The argument culture: Stopping America's war of words.* New York: Random House.

Tharp, R., & Gallimore, R. (1988). *Rousing minds to life: Teaching, learning, and schooling in social context.* Cambridge: Cambridge University Press.

Thurman, R. (1998). *Inner revolution: Life, liberty, and the pursuit of real happiness.* New York: Riverhead Books.

Tocqueville, A. (2000). *Democracy in America.* Chicago: University of Chicago Press. (Original work published 1835)

Tompkins, J. (1997). *A life in school.* New York: Perseus Books.

Valenzuela, A. (1999). *Subtractive schooling: U.S.-Mexican youth and the politics of caring.* Albany: State University of New York Press.

Vipond, D., & Hunt, R. (1984). Point-driven understanding: Pragmatic and cognitive dimensions of literary reading. *Poetics 13,* 261–267.

Voegelin, E. (1987). *The new science of politics: An introduction.* Chicago: University of Chicago Press. (Original work published 1952)

Vygotsky, L. (1978). *Mind in society: The development of higher psychological processes.* Cambridge: Harvard University Press.

Wallis, J. (1994). *The soul of politics.* New York: The New Press.

Warr, M. (Ed.). (2007, Summer) *Lessons outside: JOT writers on formal and informal education. The Journal of Ordinary Thought,*

Westbury, I., Hopmann, S., Carlgren, I., Connelly, F. M., Xu, Y., & Doyle, W. (2010). *Curriculum theory: Dead man walking? An international dialogue.* Symposium at the annual meeting of the American Educational Research Association, Denver, CO.

Whitcomb, J., Borko, H., & Liston, D. (2008). Why teach? *The Journal of Teacher Education, 59,* 3–10, 267–273.

Whitman, W. (1982). *Democratic vistas.* In *Complete Poetry and Collected Prose.* New York: Library of America. (Original work published 1871)

Wilhelm, J. D. (1991). The apostle of education. *Wisconsin State Reading Association Journal, 35*(3).

Wilhelm, J. D. (2007). *Engaging readers and writers with inquiry: Promoting deep understandings in language arts and the content areas with guiding questions.* New York: Scholastic.

Wilhelm, J. D. (2008). *You gotta BE the book: Teaching engaged and reflective reading with adolescents* (2nd ed.). New York: Teachers College Press. (Original work published 1997)

Wilhelm, J. D. (2010). Creating "third spaces": Promoting learning through dialogue. *Voices in the Middle, 18*(2), 55–58.

Wilhelm, J. D. (2011a). *Action strategies for deepening comprehension: Using drama strategies to improve reading performance* (2nd ed.). New York: Scholastic. (Original work published 2002)

Wilhelm, J. D. (2011b). *Improving comprehension with think-alouds: Modeling what good readers do* (2nd ed.). New York: Scholastic. (Original work published 2001)

Wilhelm, J. D. (2011c). *Reading is seeing: Learning to visualize scenes, characters, ideas, and text worlds to improve comprehension and reflective reading* (2nd ed.). New York: Scholastic. (Original work published 2004)

Wilhelm, J. D., Baker, T. N., & Dube, J. (2001). *Strategic reading: Guiding students to lifelong literacy, 6–12.* Portsmouth, NH: Heinemann.

Wilhelm, J. D., & Edmiston, B. (1998). *Imagining to learn: Inquiry, ethics, and integration through drama.* Portsmouth, NH: Heinemann.

Wilhelm, J.D. & Smith, M. W. (in press). *Let them read trash.* New York: Scholastic.

Wilhelm, J. D., Wilhelm, P. J., & Boas, E. (2009). *Inquiring minds learn to read and write.* Toronto: Rubicon.

Willinsky, J. (1991). *The triumph of literature/ the fate of literacy: English in the secondary curriculum.* New York: Teachers College.

Wilson, E. O. (1978). *On human nature.* Cambridge, MA: Harvard University Press.

Wilson, E. O. (1998). *Consilience: The unity of knowledge.* New York: Vintage.

Wilson, E. O. (2006). *The creation: An appeal to save life on earth.* New York: Norton.

Winnicott, D. W. (1953). Transitional objects and transitional phenomena: A study of the first not-me possession. *International Journal of Psycho-Analysis, 34,* 89–97.

Winnicott, D. W. (1965). Ego distortion in terms of True and False Self. In *The maturational process and the facilitating environment.* New York: International Universities Press. (Original work published 1960)

Winnicott, D. W. (1971). *Playing and reality.* New York: Basic Books.

Wittgenstein, L. (1953). *Philosophical investigations.* New York: Macmillan.

Woodruff, P. (2001). *Reverence: Renewing a forgotten virtue.* New York: Oxford University Press.

Woolf, V. (1929). *A room of one's own.* New York: Harcourt, Brace.

Wright, R. (2000). *Nonzero: The logic of human destiny.* New York: Vintage.

Zuckert, C. (1996). *Postmodern Platos.* Chicago: University of Chicago Press.

Zuckert, C. (2009). *Plato's philosophers.* Chicago: University of Chicago Press.

Index

Abrams, M.H., 45
Action, 13, 32, 107, 111, 122, 129, 143, 156, 158, 161, 167, 172
  cosmopolitanism and, 206, 208, 211–213
  drama and, 163–167, 179
  inter- (Dewey), 13–14, 30, 48, 73, 104, 187, 228–229
  self- (Dewey), 13–14, 72–73, 104, 192, 214, 229
  social, 12, 129–130, 175–177, 179, 229. See also Transaction
Adams, Hal, 117
Adams, John, 185
Addams, Jane, 160
AEPL (NCTE Assembly for Expanded Perspectives on Learning), v, xi, 10, 105, 199–200, 204, 226, 252
Alchemist, The, 131–132
Alexander, Thomas (*John Dewey's Theory of Art, Experience, and Nature: The Horizons of Feeling*), 13
Alloparenting (Hrdy), 58–59, 104, 136, 214
Anarchy, 33, 52, 88, 100, 129, 140–141
Angel (student), 151, 156, 159, 195, 202, 208
Anna Karenina (Tolstoy), 133–135
Anonymous student, Bruce's, 14, 17, 154
Antigone (Sophocles), 131
Appiah, Anthony, 152
Applebee, Arthur, 25, 43
Appleman, Deborah, xv, 12, 157, 164, 225
  Critical Encounters in High School English, 53, 83, 90, 99
Arendt, Hannah, 122, 204
Aristotle, xii, 98, 143
Armstrong, Karen, vii, 204–206
Arnold, Matthew, xi, 229, 230
  best self, 45, 136
  Culture and Anarchy, 45–46
  "Dover Beach," 46–47, 128–129, 222, 228
  as founder of "English," 45, 73
Arts Education Partnership, 179, 182
Ascesis (self-discipline), 46–47
  submissive, 46
  creative, 47,122–144, 190–223. *See also* Self, False; Self, True
Attachment, 57–59, 103–104, 136

ambivalent, anxious, 103, 128–129, 155, 181
  avoidant, 103
  cultural, 57, 70, 120–121, 141, 126, 176
  secure, 58–59 103–104, 121, 128–129, 145, 152, 180, 191, 197, 214
Austen, Jane (*Pride and Prejudice*), 134, 159
Author Chair, 107, 179
Authority, 128
  moral, 193
  personal, 46, 99
  professional, 43, 52
  repressive, 42–44, 82, 103, 129–132, 181
  transactional, 99–101, 129
Avery, Carol ("Laura"), 37–40, 43
Awakeness, 8–9, 55, 61, 67, 75, 94, 123–127, 136, 146, 156, 158, 161, 168, 181, 202, 208–212, 230
Awakening, The (Chopin), 130
Axial Age (Jaspers), 204–208, 213, 215

Bacon, A. (*The Nineteenth-Century History of English Studies*), 22
Baker, Tanya, xv, 77, 153
"Barrio Boy" (Garza), 135–136
Baumgarten, Alexander Gottlieb (*Aesthetics*), 15
Bayat, Asef (*Life as Politics*), 191, 210
Bear, Rachel, v, 2–9, 16, 45, 75–81, 88–89, 96, 114, 136, 143, 161–162, 168–171, 218–223
Beckett, Samuel (*Waiting for Godot*), 79
Bellow, Saul (*Mr. Sammler's Planet*), 184, 229
Best self
  Arnold, 136
  Bhabha ("becoming the others of our selves"), 182–189, 229
  Emerson, 41, 44–45, 160, 175
  Morrison ("acres of Edens within ourselves") vii, 19, 88
  possible (Schiller, Emerson, Arnold), 11, 13
  Ricoeur (*Oneself as Another*), 229
  Schiller, 44–46
  through art and aesthetic experience, 2, 90, 101, 103, 119, 135–138, 141–143

through classroom life, 5, 12, 119, 132–135, 140, 146, 159–162, 167, 171–172, 179–182, 194, 211–222
through democratic growing together, 45, 95, 121, 142–144, 146–147, 171, 175, 181–223, 229
Blau, Sheridan, xi-xiii, xv,
    The Literature Workshop, 178
Bloom, Harold, 203–204
Boesche, Roger, 187
Bollas, Christopher, 152
Booth, Stephen (*Shakespeare's Sonnets*), 128
Booth, Wayne, xv, 97
    Company We Keep, The, 92, 98–99
    Foreword, *Authorizing Readers* (Rabinowitz & Smith), 105
    Foreword, *Literature as Exploration* (Rosenblatt), 97, 225
    Modern Dogma and the Rhetoric of Assent, 99
    Rhetoric of Fiction, The 70, 97, 105. *See also* Implied author
Botstein, Leon, 152
Bowlby, John, 58, 103. *See also* Attachment
Brad (student), 133–135
"Bright Future of Everyone, The" (Albany Park Community Center), 117
Brodkey, Harold, 92
Brown, Stuart (*Play*), 88
Browning, Robert ("My Last Duchess"), 79
Bruner, Jerome ("The Narrative Construal of Reality"), 150
Bruns, Cristina, xvi, 96
    Why Literature?, 59, 69, 89–90, 96
Buber, Martin, 229. *See also* I-You relationship; I-It relationship
Buddhism, 93, 204, 206–208, 213
Bunscombe, Marie, 29, 33, 41–42, 140. *See also* Wye Conference, "holistic/Joy" subgroup

CAPE (Chicago Arts Partnerships in Education), 178–179
Care, 7, 16, 40, 44–47, 77, 103, 138, 150, 191, 217
    in art, 59, 70, 92, 95, 103–104, 109, 219, 221
    in evolution, 54–58
    in teaching, 78, 114, 137, 153–154, 164. *See also* Responsibility
Carlyle, Thomas, 45, 47, 229
Cavell, Stanley, 159, 229
Center for Inquiry (school), 180, 213
Change
    democratic, 14, 24–25, 51, 72, 106, 160, 166, 180, 182–188, 191, 200, 210
    educational, 23, 24, 28,153, 161, 166, 216, 227

global, 14, 72, 157
grassroots, 25, 117
personal, 4, 6, 14, 72, 106, 119, 122–125, 138, 166, 216, 227, 229
"the change we need," 24, 186, 216
transaction and, 13, 106–108, 122–125, 133.
Chaos, vii, 6, 14, 16, 73, 97, 129, 143, 183, 216
Christenbury, Leila (*Retracing the Journey*), 9
Coleridge, Samuel Taylor (*Biographia Literaria*), 48, 229
Colonizing relations, political and educational, 181–182, 207. *See also* Self, False
Commerce
    material, 185–186, 192, 227
    moral, xiii, 185, 227
Community, vii, xiii, 11, 102, 161, 206, 219, 231
    classroom, 38, 114–115, 119, 135, 140, 153, 160, 164–165, 173–180
    beloved, 182, 184, 230
    democratic, 102, 146, 173–189, 228
    Earth, 203–207
    literary, 42–43, 59–60, 65, 94, 102, 140, 185–186
    of possibility, 164, 190–209
    professional, 26, 157
    school, 159, 164, 179–182
    the human, 59
Confucianism, 205–207, 213
Connection, deep (Kessler), 96, 104, 173–175, 186
Consilience, 50–74
    defined, 51. *See also* Wilson, E.O.
Constructivism, 12–13, 228. *See also* Literacy, sociocultural
Conversation, 5–6, 25, 46, 94, 109, 138–142, 156–158, 165, 220–222
    classroom, 81, 140, 156–158
    literary, 65, 93, 105, 111, 123, 128, 138–142, 171, 177. *See also* Democracy
Copoiesis, 68, 166, 177, 179, 183, 181, 201, 222
Cora (student), 87–88, 92–93
Cormier, Robert, 99
Cosmopoiesis, 191
Cosmopolitanism, 180, 191–192, 198, 200, *206–208*, 231
Creger, John (*The Personal Creed Project and a New Vision of Learning*), xvi, 137, 194
Critical theory, xi, 51–53, 207, 226
Csikszentmihalyi, Mihalyi, 85, 231
Cultural studies, 21, 24
Curriculum, 8, 10, 22, 52, 132
    artful, 152–155, 161, 164–167
    arts-integrated, 178–179, 182
    fixed, xi, 3, 69, 91
    English, 9–10, 39, 159, 210–214

Curriculum, *continued*
  holistic, 48, 78, 116, 149, 194
  "issue-centered," 43, 46, 48, 88–90, 141,
    177, 226
  Social Studies, 71–72, 225
  "student-centered," 26, 42. *See also*
    Inquiry

Dalai Lama, 93, 199, 208
Dartmouth Seminar, 25–35, 39, 97, 175
Darwin, Charles, 54–56, 102, 190, 226
Deconstruction, 51–54, 77, 99, 155, 226
Deep connection (Kessler), 11, 96, 104, 159,
    173, 175, 186
De Man, Paul (*Allegories of Reading*), 52–53,
    155
Democracy, 33–34
  aesthetic, 69, 73, 141, 173–189, 213, 223
  conversation and, 171, 221–223
  classroom, 38, 135, 140–141, 173–174
  diverse, 29–31, 43, 59
  macrocosmic, 141, 181–189
  meaning-making and, 31, 41, 59
  microcosmic, 141, 173–182
  nurturant, 103, 227–228
  real, 6, 19, 26, 40, 90, 100, 160
  teaching for, 166–171
Democracy in America (Tocqueville), 187, 217,
    230
"Democracy through Language." *See* Wye
    Conference
Democracy Through Language (Lloyd-Jones &
    Lunsford), 28–35
Derrida, Jacques, 52, 225–227
  "The future of the profession," 53
  Of Grammatology, 52–53
Dewey, John, xii, 97, 229–230
  Art as Experience, 12–15, 129
  Democracy and Education, 13, 173
  Ethics, 222–223
  Experience and Nature, 13
  How We Think, 13
  Knowing and the Known, 12–16, 66–73, 96,
    100, 104, 129
  The Public and Its Problems, 229
Dialogue, xiii, 5, 40, 103, 133, 138–142, 154,
    174–189, 220–222, 228–229
Diamond, Jared, 157
Dickstein, Morris (*Dancing in the Dark*), 72
Discourse, xi, xiii, 12, 110, 194, 214, 226
  humanistic, 178
  living, 39–48, 52–57, 123
  of power, 181
  religious, 178
  vs. grammar, 39–41. *See also* Moffett
Dissanayake, Ellen, 48, 56–59, 66, 123, 176
  Art and Intimacy, 56

Homo Aestheticus, 48, 56–57
What Is Art For?, 56
Dominator culture (Eisler), 203–209
Donnelly, Amy, 180, 213
  From the Ground Up, 180
"Dover Beach" (Arnold), 48–49, 128–129,
    132, 156, 175, 222–223, 228
Drama, xii, 69, 123, 133, 150–151, 202
  classroom activities, 12, 39–40, 111–112,
    133–137, 140, 154, 156, 162–168, 171,
    219
  in student/teacher relationships, 69, 150–
    151

Each Person Drawn Forward, vii, 189, 198–
    201, 208
Edmiston, Brian (*Imagining to Learn*), 179
Edmundson, Mark (*Teacher*), 150
Educare, 8, 39–40, 60–61, 68, 73, 81, 96, 102,
    115, 119, 123, 197, 211–215. *See also*
    Each Person Drawn Forward.
Education, moral, xii, 24, 46–55, 67, 71,
    122–126, 178, 183–188, 193, 201, 217,
    223, 228–229.
Educational standardization. *See*
    standardization, educational
Efferent, 68, 73, 102, 115, 177
  and externalized educational goals, 77, 89,
    91, 149, 153, 173, 187, 191, 201
Einstein, Albert, 24, 73, 184, 216, 229
Eisler, Riane, xvi, 202–203, 231
Eisner, Eliot (*The Arts and the Creation of Mind*),
    179
Elbow, Peter, xv, 43, 199
  on the believing game, 99, 105
  What Is English?, 28–46, 59, 67, 79, 99, 105,
    225
Eliot, George (*Middlemarch*), 190–191
Emerson, Ralph Waldo, 47, 73, 229
  "American Scholar, The" 41, 44–45, 160,
    175
  "Experience," 175, 195, 222–223
  "Over-Soul, The," 160
Empire, 186, 192–194, 203–208, 213, 215
English Coalition Conference. *See* Wye
    Conference
Enron: The Smartest Guys in the Room (film), 142
Equality, 32, 120, 146, 184, 201, 215
Esquith, Rafe (teacher), 159–160
Essential questions, 11, 82, 105–106, 130
Evolution, 53–57, 66, 72, 157, 209, 225
  conscious, 70, 208
  Holism and (Smuts), 225
  human, 23, 34, 50–51, 54–60, 88, 143, 152,
    214
Evolutionary psychology, 47–48, 55–59, 123
Existential questions, existential inquiry, 11–

12, 69–71, 102, 105–106, 124, 132, 143, 175–179, 210, 214
External marks, 9, 15, 39–40, 43, 50, 112. *See also* Transubstantiation

Facing History and Ourselves, 200
Fantasy, 93, 217, 252
  in art, 91, 123
  in hope, 197
Feeling
  in art, 13, 15, 47, 57, 63, 70–73, 77, 80, 83, 91, 101, 109, 112, 118, 123–126, 191
  in democracy, 46, 97, 141–143, 181
  in English, 21, 28, 43
  in life, 13, 15–16, 47, 50, 57, 63, 66, 71, 91, 118, 191, 197
  in teaching, 73, 80, 83, 133, 139, 163, 165, 169–170, 194, 211, 219
Feight, Dan, 1–2, 14–17, 217
Fey, Tina (*Mean Girls*), 217, 228
Finn, Chester, 29, 32, 43
Fischer, Brian 151–152, 202
Flow, 55
  in and through art, 69–71, 89–91, 120, 127. *See also* Csikszentmihalyi, Mihaly; Immersion; Transaction
Foundation for Ethics and Meaning, v, 230, 252
Fox, Matthew, 202
Franzen, Jonathan, 122, 126
Freedom, 26, 43–47, 59, 62, 101–102, 126, 185, 209
  in teaching, xv, 105, 153
  new birth of, 100, 160, 167, 174, 185, 197
Freewriting, 180, 188–189, 222
Freedom Writers Diary (Gruwell), 180, 188–189, 222
Freedom (Franzen), 126
Freud, Sigmund (*The Ego and the Id*), 129, 136
Friendship, xv, xvi, 10, 38, 64, 124, 127–129. 153, 156, 158, 180, 184, 190–191, 195, 223
  authorial, 92–121
  circles, 180
  critical, 177
  for its own sake, 98–100, 143, 175
  for pleasure, 98, 143
  for use, 98, 143
  philosophy and, 190–191
From the Ground Up (Mills), 180
Frontloading, 77–82, 135, 162, 165, 169–170

Gallagher, Kelly (*Readicide*), 84
Gandhi, Mahatma, vii, 14, 129, 145, 202, 208, 213, 217
Gardner, Howard
  Frames of Mind, 67

Intelligence Reframed, 66–71
Garrison, Jim, xvi, 99
Gateway activities (Hillocks), 77, 175. *See also* Frontloading
Gendlin, Eugene, xvi, 200, 231
"Gestalt Prayer" (Perls), 26, 33
Gift, 22, 146, 222
  art as, 22, 32, 60, 65, 68–71, 96–98, 102–103, 107, 115, 122–123, 191
  economy, 140–144, 154, 192–193, 214–215, 219, 228, 231
  hope as (Obama), 197
  real democracy as interweaving of, 184–189, 193
  teaching as, 154, 157
Gift, The (Hyde), 141–142, 154
Great Gatsby, The (Fitzgerald), 166
Goethe, Johann Wolfgang von, xi
Good-enough mother (Winnicott), 150, 223
Good-enough teacher, 149–151, 162–164, 169–170, 181
Good-enough world (Lear), 155–150, 167, 191, 223
Goodwyn, Andrew, 8, 73, 211
Grammar, 21–24, 39–41, 48, 51–55, 77, 214
Grammatology, 51–54, 77, 226. *See also* Derrida, Jacques
Gray, Mary Kaye ("The Grandmother Course"), 117
Greene, Maxine (*Variations on a Blue Guitar*), 179
Grossman, Pam, 8, 73, 211
Growth, personal, xii, 30–35, 48, 64, 82, 86, 94, 124, 126, 149, 152–154, 177, 210–211, 217
Gruwell, Erin (*Freedom Writers Diary, The*), 180, 188, 222
Gutierrez, Carlos, xvi, 118, 137–138

Hahn, Thich Naht, 93
Handler, Daniel ("Lemony Snicket") (*Series of Unfortunate Events*), 84, 94–95
Hansen, David, xvi, *Exploring the Moral Heart of Teaching*, 178
  on cosmopolitanism and education, 231
Hanson, Sharon (teacher), v, 2, 7–9, 16, 45, 219–223
Haroutunian-Gordon, Sophie
  Art of Turning the Soul, The, 178
  Turning the Soul, 178
Harry Potter and the Deathly Hallows (Rowling), 95
Havel, Václav, 201
  "Democracy's Forgotten Dimension," 19, 213
Hawken, Paul, vii
Heart of Darkness (Conrad), 5

Heath, Shirley Brice (*Ways with Words*), 181
Hero's journey, 6, 16–17, 91, 106, 118, 120, 124, 126, 130–132, 136–138, 194–201
  in Carl Jung and Hermann Hesse, 94, 127–128
  the human, 209, 218
Hesse, Hermann, 93–94, 99, 127
  Glass Bead Game, The, 93–94, 127
  Narcissus and Goldmund, 93, 127
  Siddhartha, 93, 127–128
  Steppenwolf, 93, 127
Hilbert, Betsy, 41–42. *See also* Wye Conference, "wholistic/Joy" group
Hillocks, George, 97, 151, 157
  environmental teaching, 104
  inquiry methods, xv, 12, 66, 80
  teaching of, xvi, 77, 80, 153, 163, 217
Hirsch, E.D., 29, 32–33, 43, 140
History, nightmare of (Joyce), 200–202
Hobart Shakespeareans, The, (film), 159–160
Holding onto Good Ideas in a Time of Bad Ones (Newkirk), 86
Holism, 32–49, 58–59, 141, 153, 199, 214, 225. *See also* Wye Conference, "wholistic/Joy" group
Holistic Education Conference of the Ontario Institute for Studies in Education, 199
Holistic Education Special Interest Group (AERA), 199
Hope
  for America, 27, 120, 193–195
  for Dewey, 230
  for Fishman & McCarthy, 230
  for Fiona Wilhelm, 131
  for Marcel, 195–198
  for Obama, 197, 230
  for Wallis, 196
  for Wilhelm and Novak, xi, xvi, 9, 12, 15–17, 36, 50, 52, 64, 124–125, 145, 172, 230
  for the world, 167, 171–172, 193–198, 208–209
  history and, 201–209, 215
  in art, 70–71, 120–121
  in education, 116–120, 137, 194–195, 230
  in teaching, 3, 7, 134, 147, 159–160, 171–172, 187, 208, 217–218
  last, best (Lincoln), 193–195, 198
  mimesis, and, 197–198
  Politics of, The (Dauenhauer), 231
Hope in the Unseen, A (Suskind), 118–120, 137, 193, 194, 213
Hotseating, 111–113
Hrdy, Sarah Blaffer (*Mother Nature*), 58
Huckleberry Finn (Twain), 107, 111–113

Humanism, 55, 217
  democratic, 44–46, 128–129, 185–186, 215, 217
Humanities, the, xi, 17, 21, 28, 44, 51–53. 99, 130. *See also*, McGann, NEH, Nussbaum, Ruddick
Hunt, R. ("Point-driven Understanding"), 109

I-It relationship, 42, 149, 201, 226
Immersion, 47, 68, 77–78, 83–91, 96–100, 122–123, 127, 129
Implied author (Booth), 70–71, 92–121, 122, 129, 136, 141–143, 154, 161, 164, 177
Implied teacher, 149, 152–155, 161, 164–166, 170, 181
Inbetweenness, 182–183, 202. *See also* Third space
Inchausti, Robert, xv, xvi, 60, 102–103, 120, 129, 155, 215, 237
Inquiry, 4, 78, 82, 88, 110, 140, 153–154, 157–158, 164–168, 220, 226. *See also* Center for Inquiry; Essential questions; Existential questions
Inside Job (film), 142
Intentional fallacy, 5, 71, 109, 114, 227
Intercourse, 13, 39, 66, 149, 208
I-You relationship (Moffett, Buber), 39, 42, 55, 149, 154–155, 183, 201, 214, 226

Jaspers, Karl, 204
  "On the Conditions and Possibilities of a New Humanism," 217, 222
  Origin and Goal of History,The, 203–204. *See also* Axial Age
Jennings, Cedric, 118–120, 137–138, 194
Jesus, 47, 98, 206
Journal of Ordinary Thought, The, 116–117
Journal of Teacher Education, The, 199
Journey, education as, 16–17, 91, 195–201, 209, 218, 220. *See also* Hero's journey
Joy, 5, 7–9, 22, 36–49, 89, 141, 23
  ascesis and, 47
  disparagement and suppression of, 42–43, 48
  "Immortality Ode" (Wordsworth) and, 44
  Laura's, 38, 40
  literature and, 42, 59, 70, 79–81, 84–88, 94, 97, 104, 106, 108, 119
  "Ode to Joy" (Schiller), 44–46, 57, 102
  rationale for pedagogy of, 43
  teaching with and for, 8, 156–157, 163, 171, 201, 208, 219
  "The American Scholar" (Emerson) and, 41, 44. *See also* Wye Conference, "wholistic/Joy" group
Joyce, James, *Portrait of the Artist as a Young*

Man, 137.
Judaism, 178, 204, 206

Kant, Immanuel, 48, 228
Karen, Robert, 103
Kennedy, Robert F., 27
Kerr, Donna, 227
Kessler, Rachael, 11, 159, 173, 196, 199
King, Martin Luther, 27, 182, 207, 230
Kliebard, Herbert (*The Struggle for the American
    Curriculum, 1893–1958*), 72
Korten, David, 203

Lakoff, George, 103
Laura (first-grade student), 37–40, 43–44, 66,
    68, 114, 212
Leavis, F.R., xi
Lee, Harper, 99
Levertov, Denise ("Writing in the Dark"),
    61–65, 70, 72, 91, 101–104, 121–126, 142
Liberal education, 22, 30, 34, 51, 185, 215. *See
    also* Humanism
Life
    force, xvi, 39–47, 53, 129, 191, 197
    literacy for, 7, 10
Lin, J., 202
Lincoln, Abraham, 100, 160, 174, 193, 223
    Gettysburg Address, 100, 173–175 185
    Message to Congress, December 1, 1862,
        193, 195, 198
    Second Inaugural, 100, 160, 223
Listening, 5, 30, 33, 150, 163, 178, 200, 222
    literature and, 46–47, 52, 145, 191, 221
Literacy, xvi, 8,10, 12, 17, 72, 86, 132, 161,
    177, 215, 226
    boys and (Smith & Wilhelm), 130
    cultural (Hirsch), 29, 140
    holistic, 39–40
    in content areas, 2
    professional term, 21, 23, 24, 73, 157, 210,
        215
    sociocultural, 86, 153, 181, 209, 214, 228.
        See also Constructivism
    transactional, 100, 181
Literature, xi-xiii, 82–88, 203
    canonical, 22–25, 32, 34, 79
    care and, 55–59, 92–121
    defined, 42–43, 59, 118
    listening and (Ruddick), 47, 52
    Religion of modern life (Carlyle), 45
    transubstantiation through, 39–40, 60–66
    wisdom, 11, 159–160, 207
Lloyd-Jones, Richard, 28–29, 32–33
Lorax, The (Suess), 170
Love, teacherly, 7
Loye, David, xvi, 54

Lunsford, Andrea, 28–29, 32–33

Macrocosms, 127, 141
Marcel, Gabriel, 195, 197, 230
    Homo Viator, 195–198
    To Be and to Have, 159–160
    Royce's Metaphysics, 230
Marvy/Muddy sticky notes, 166, 179
Mazurski, George, 157
McCullough, David, 185
McGann, Jerome (Humanities teacher), 134,
    159
McKibben, Bill (*Eaarth*), 192
Meaning-making, xii-xiii, 11, 12, 48, 50–53
    aesthetic reflection and, 129, 131
    central to "English," 21–23, 31, 34–35, 43,
        46
    central to teachers' understanding of the
        goal of their teaching, 2, 4, 5, 164–166,
        218–220
    curriculum and, 152–153, 194–195
    democracy and, 183–189
    dialogical, 141–142, 150–152, 211
    diversity and, 30
    everyday life and, 191, 210
    history and, 202, 204, 206
    hope through 195–198
    inquiry and, 80–83, 90
    standardized writing tests and, 218
    third space and, 176–189
    transitional objects and, 58–72, 96, 145
    transactional authority and, 99, 166–167,
        214
    wisdom and, 126, 146–147, 207–208
Memes, 58–60, 66, 153
Metamorphosis, 138, 194
Microcosms, 102, 123, 126–127, 141, 174
Millard, E. ("Transformative Pedagogy),
    176–177
Miller, J. Hillis (*The Death of Literature*), 84
Miller, John P., 202
Mills, Heidi, 180, 213
    From the Ground Up, 180
Mimemes, 60–68, 123, 126, 153. *See also*
    Transaction
Mimesis (Ricoeur), 66–70, 98, 143–144, 197
Mind in Society (Vygotsky), 181
Moby Dick (Melville), 134
Moffett, James, xv, 194, 199
    Teaching the Universe of Discourse, 39–45, 48,
        52–55, 123, 149, 154, 194–195, 214,
        226, 229, 231
    Storm in the Mountains, 27
Moje, Elizabeth, 176, 181
Moral compass, 48, 51
Moral education. *See* Education, moral

Morris, Ian (*Why the West Rules—for Now*), 192,
    231
Morrison, Toni, 99
    Beloved, 92, 182, 230
    "The Future of Time," vii, 19, 88, 145, 147
Muller, Herbert J. (*The Uses of English*), vii,
    26–27
"Multeity in unity" (Coleridge), 48, 65,
    141–143, 175, 229. *See also* Transaction,
    connective dimension; Democracy,
    real; Natural supernaturalsim;
    Transubstantiation
Mystery questions (Kessler), 11, 95, 173, 177.
    See also Existential questions

Nagler, Michael, 202, 205
National Network for Educational Renewal,
    200
National Writing Project, v, xv, 2, 82, 107,
    149, 163, 168, 171, 200
Nation at Risk, A, 9, 28–29, 34, 187, 192, 198,
    201
Natural supernaturalism (Kant, Carlyle,
    Emerson, Whitman, Abrams), 45, 47,
    160, 186, 226, 228. *See also* Transaction;
    Transubstantiation
NCTE (National Council of Teachers of
    English, v, xi, 9–10, 21, 25, 96, 119, 194,
    199, 252
NEH (National Endowment for the
    Humanities), 213
Neighborhood Writing Alliance, 116–117
Newbolt Report (*The Teaching of English in
    England*), 22, 26, 29, 34, 45
New Criticism, 13, 114
Newkirk, Tom, 86
No Child Left Behind Act, 9, 187–188, 192–
    193, 201. *See also* Each Person Drawn
    Forward
Normotic (Bollas), 152
Novak, Bruce, 10–11
    "The Audacity of Thought," 217
    "Beyond 'English' and 'Literacy'," 10
    Humanism and Freedom, 45–46, 129
    "Humanizing Democracy," 129, 230
    learning of, 94, 101, 154–155, 158–159
    "'National Standards' vs the Free Standards
        of Culture," 45–46, 129
    "No Child Left Behind or Each Person
        Drawn Forward?," vii, 71–73, 189, 198,
        201, 208, 215
    philosophy and, xi, 10–11, 94, 137, 158–
        160, 173, 228
    "Reclaiming the Wisdom Tradition for
        Education" (Conference), 10, 199, 204
    "Reverence for Things Not Seen," 99
    "Seeing Student/Teacher Relationships

as Hidden Dramas of Personal
    Development," 150–152
    "Teachers, Students, and Authors Together,"
        96
    teaching of, 10–11, 14, 116–121, 132–138,
        154–155, 159–160, 194.
    "What If Education Is Not a Race?," 187,
        198
    "Words Before Morning" (poem), 64, 101,
        124
Nussbaum, Martha
    Cultivating Humanity, 180, 191
    Not for Profit, 228
    Upheavals of Thought, 228

Obama, Barack, 187–189, 192, 195–197, 207,
    222, 230
Odyssey, 118–120, 131, 137, 171, 193–195,
    198. *See also* Hero's journey
Odyssey, The (Homer), 118–120, 131, 137, 171,
    193, 195, 198
Oldenburg, Ray (*The Great Good Place*), 176
O'Reilley, Mary Rose
    The Peaceable Classroom, vii
    Radical Presence, 118–119

Palmer, Parker, 199
    The Courage to Teach, 199
    To Know as We Are Known, 199, 201
Parenting. *See* Alloparenting; Attachment
Partnership culture (Eisler), 202–209
Paterson, Katherine, 93
Perl, Sondra (*Felt Sense*), 200
Perls, Fritz ("Gestalt Prayer"), 26, 33
Personal Studies, vii, 71–73, 189, 211–217
Phillips, Christine, xvi, 158, 178
Philosophy, xi-xii, 10–14, 50–53, 94, 150–151,
    166–168, 190, 195, 198–204, 208, 213–
    217, 226, 228, 229
Plato, 51, 128, 225–226
    Gorgias, 228
    Phaedrus, 39–40, 43, 45, 48
    Seventh Letter, 208, 212
    Socrates's Defense, 160
    Tenth Letter, 190
Play, 58, 63, 69–70, 88–94. 99, 101, 103,
    112–113, 145–147, 153–154, 171, 176,
    181–183, 191, 202, 208, 219, 223
Play (Brown), 88
Point-driven understanding (Vipond & Hunt),
    109
Popular culture, 27, 79, 86, 93, 105–106, 112,
    177
Porter, Andrew (teacher), v, 2–4, 7–9, 45, 79,
    88–89, 161, 164–166, 179, 218–220, 223
Possibility. 11, 13, 51–52, 64, 68, 91, 101, 105,
    155, 218

community of, 164
democratic, 183–189, 192–195
human, 89, 118, 190–209
in art, 80, 87–88, 91, 101–102, 125, 131,
    142
in students, 1
in teaching, 9, 16, 48, 165, 167
pedagogy of (Halasek), 229
play and, 89
space of 214, *See also* Third space
vulnerability and (Shamlin), 141, 180
Postmodernism, xi, 6, 51–54, 201, 225–226
Pradl, Gordon (*Literature for Democracy*), 65,
    100, 154, 178
Preeminence (A Nation at Risk), 28, 192–193,
    198, 203
Pride and Prejudice (Austen), 134, 159
Professional Learning Communities, 163

Questioning the Author (Beck & McKeown),
    108

Rabinowitz, Peter (*Authorizing Readers*), 105,
    108, 114, 145
Race course, education as, 69, 103, 153,
    187–188, 193, 198, 201, 215. *See also*
    Curriculum
Race to Nowhere, The (film), 103, 187–188, 193,
    198, 201, 215
Race to the Top, 187, 193, 198, 201
Ravitch, Diane (*The Death and Life of the Great
    American School System*), 9
Reading Is Seeing (Wilhelm), 67
Reaching out, 150–156, 181, 193, 211, 223.
See also Good-enough mother; Good-enough
teacher; Good-enough world
Reciprocation (return of care), 57–59, 114–
    115
Re-creations, 42, 59–68, 116–121
    poetic pedagogy of (Rico), 60–68, 90, 100–
        104, 121, 124, 126, 142
Reflection, xii-xiii, 10, 54
    aesthetic, 124–144, 183
    vs. cogitation, 126
Remen, Rachel (*Kitchen Table Wisdom*), 75, 96,
    123, 136, 143
Renaud (student) 169–170
Renewal, 8, 10, 24, 55, 59, 66, 125, 130, 206,
    226, 230
Response, subjective, 12–13
Responsibility, 4–5, 11–12, 67, 71–72, 146,
    158, 170, 188–191, 197–200, 208–217,
    231
    resposiveness and, 15–17, 122–144, 189,
        191, 229
Rico, Gabriele, 60
    Re-creations, 60

Writing the Natural Way, 60
Ricoeur, Paul, 226–227, 230
    Time and Narrative, 10, 67–71, 77, 98, 137,
        195, 197
Rilke, Rainer Maria, xi
    "Archaic Torso of Apollo," 122–123
Rogers, Carl, 200
Ron (student), 84, 87, 90, 92
Roosevelt, Franklin Delano, vii, 72
Rosenberg, Marshall (*Nonviolent
    Communication*), 200
Rosenblatt, Louise, xv, 10–15, 57, 59, 66–69,
    90, 97–100, 210
    L'art pour l'art, 66
    Booth, Wayne, and, 97–100
    efferent/aesthetic distinction, xii-xiii, 15, 66,
        68, 152, 229
    life for life's sake, 66, 191
    Literature as Exploration, 97, 126
    The Reader, the Text, and the Poem, 13, 98, 229
    transaction, understanding of, xii-xiii, 10,
        12–14, 57, 66, 69, 97–98
Rousing Minds to Life (Tharp & Gallimore), 172
Rowling, J.K., 95, 132
Rud, A.G., 99
Ruddick, Lisa, xvi, 46–47, 51, 145, 191
Rugg, Harold, 72
Russell, Peter (*Waking Up in Time*), 16, 192,
    209

Sabovik, Stephen, xvi, 160–161
Saito, Naoko, 229
Sanchez, Alex, 119
Scarlet Letter, The (Hawthorne), 84, 167
Schiller, Friedrich, 73, 229
    Letters on the Aesthetic Education of Humanity,
        45–47
    "Ode to Joy," 44–46, 57, 65, 102
Scholes, Robert, 53
    Rise and Fall of English, The, 45
    Textual Power, 53.90
Schweitzer, Albert, 99
Secondary worlds (in art), 80–84, 87–88, 134
Secret Life of Bees, The (Kidd), 131
Self-action (Dewey). *See* Action, self-
Self, False (Winnicott), 150, 152, 176, 181–
    182, 188
Self, True (Winnicott), 150, 156, 160, 167,
    176, 181–182, 223. Shakespeare's Sonnets
    (Booth), 128
Shakespeare, William, xi, 43, 94, 99, 127–129,
    159–160, 222
    As You Like It, 94
    Hamlet, 94, 107, 160
    Macbeth, 207
    Othello, 94
    Romeo and Juliet, 79, 80, 165

Shakespeare, William, *continued*
  Sonnet 116, 94, 127–129, 143, 175, 222–223, 228–229
Shamlin, Michelle, 180, 213
Shannon, Patrick ("Wondering about NCLB"), 86
Shelley, Percy Bysshe, xi, 122
Sidney, Sir Philip, xi
Simpsons, The (television show), 79, 81
Slatoff, Walter (*With Respect to Readers*), 85
Smagorinsky, Peter, 157
Smith, Debra, v, 2, 6–9, 16, 45, 161, 166–168, 219–223
Smith, Huston, 202
Smith, Michael, 157
  Authorizing Readers, 104–105
  Going with the Flow, 85, 93, 130
  Reading Don't Fix No Chevys, 80, 84–85, 93, 130, 231
Smuts, Jan Christian (*Holism and Evolution*), 225
Snicket, Lemony. *See* Handler, Daniel
Snow, C. P. ("The Two Cultures"), 55
Social studies, 71–72, 225
Socratic dialogue, 5, 39, 158, 160, 178, 206, 212–213
Sonnet 116 (Shakespeare), 94, 127–129, 143, 175, 222–223, 228–229
Soul, xiii, 5, 160, 173, 182, 196–199, 202, 206–212, 216–217, 222, 230
Standardization, educational, xiii, 9, 22, 24, 48, 52, 55, 71, 77, 88, 103, 135, 140, 152, 162, 165. 192, 201, 207, 218–219
  related to strict parenting and morality, 129, 162
Stodolsky, Susan 8, 73, 211
Story time, 10, 12, 67–69, 75, 77, 89, 96, 122–123, 137, 141, 197, 214
Strom, William, xv, 156
Survival, human future, 16, 48, 56, 73, 157, 172, 183, 192–193
Survival value, evolutionary, 54–57, 88, 123
Superego (Over-I), 129, 136. *See also* Trans-ego (Beyond-me)
Suskind, Ron, 118–120, 137, 193–195, 213
Swift, Jonathan ("A Modest Proposal"), 79, 81

Tagore, Rabindranath, 145
  Home and the World, The, 89, 182
  "On the Seashore," 145–147, 181, 191
Teacher, real (Inchausti), 102–103, 129, 155
Teacher research, 5, 163–166, 171
Teaching. *See* Good-enough teacher; Implied teacher; Transaction, teaching and
Terror, Ages of, 45–46, 128–129, 204, 205
Theology, xi, xii. *See also* Natural supernaturalism

Things Fall Apart (Achebe), 5, 130–131
Think-alouds, 108–109, 163, 165–169, 219
Third places (Oldenburg), 176
Third space
  in Bhabha, 181–183, 208, 229
  in Moje, 176, 181
  in Wilhelm, 174–177
  in Winnicott, 89, 91, 122, 145
  political, 186–189
  psychological, 89, 91, 122, 145, 228
  social, 174, 178–179, 228. *See also* Democracy, aesthetic
Thoreau, Henry David, 159, 188, 190, 208
Thurman, Robert (*Inner Revolution*), 208
Tignor, Eleanor, 41–42. *See also* Wye Conference, "wholistic/Joy" group
Time, chronological, 77, 89, 96
  "The Future of" (Morrison), vii, 19, 145
  story, 10, 12, 67–69, 77, 89, 96, 122–123, 137, 141, 197, 214
To Be and To Have (film), 159–160
Tolstoy, Leo, 133–135, 213
Tocqueville, Alexis de, 187, 217, 230
To Kill a Mockingbird (Lee), 3–4, 84, 120, 164
Tompkins, Jane, xvi, 199
Transaction, xii-xiii, 10–16, 57–59, 66–75, 104, 145–147
  connective dimension, 12, 70, 78, 91, 92–122, 211
  democracy and, 16, 173–189, 222–223
  evocative dimension, 10–12, 15, 58, 70, 77–91, 96, 98, 101, 120, 122, 133, 141, 175, 184
  gift economy and, 140–144, 214–215
  reflective dimension, 10, 122–144
  teaching and, 15–16, 149–172, 210
  wisdom and, 16, 190–209, 212
Transactional mentality, 14, 69, 72–73, 100, 150–151, 183, 187, 192, 195, 200, 216. *See also* Tyrannical mentality
Trans-ego (Beyond-me), 129, 136, 229
Transitional objects, transitional space (Winnicott), 58–60, 66, 70, 88, 91, 98, 115–116, 129, 141–149, 161, 172–174, 191, 202
Transpersonal psychology, 71, 96, 123, 126, 129, 227
Transubstantiation, 40, 65–66. *See also* External marks; Transaction
Tyrannical mentality, 33, 52, 140–141, 150, 184, 204–206, 217, 228

United States, 22, 28, 71–72, 113, 118–120, 130, 160, 166, 175, 183–189, 192–194, 222–223, 226, 229, 230

Veigel, Sarah (teacher), v, 2–4, 7–9, 16, 45, 58,

161–63, 179, 218–223
Vipond, D. ("Point-driven Understanding"), 109
Voeglin, Eric, 205, 208
Voltaire (*Candide*), 79, 155–158
Vygotsky, Lev, 153, 181

Walden (Thoreau), 159, 190, 208, 217
Wallis, Jim (*The Soul of Politics*), 196–197
Way of the World, The (Suskind), 193–195
Westbury, Ian, 52
Where the Wild Things Are (Sendak), 170
Whitman, Walt, 188, 229–230
    Democratic Vistas, vii, 160, 185–186, 193, 210, 222, 229–230
Wilhelm, Fiona, x, xv, 94–95, 130–132
Wilhelm, Jasmine, v, xv, 2, 84, 94–95, 162, 169
Wilhelm, Jeff
    Action Strategies for Deepening Comprehension, 111–112, 163, 168, 179
    "Creating 'Third Spaces,'" 174–177
    Engaging Readers and Writers with Inquiry, 11, 108–109, 117, 140, 163, 179
    Going with the Flow, 85, 93, 130
    Imagining to Learn, 179
    Improving Comprehension with Think-Alouds, 163
    Inquiring Minds Learn to Read and Write, 180
    learning of, 93–94, 101, 124–125, 156–157
    Reading Don't Fix No Chevys, 80, 84–85, 93, 130, 231
    Reading Is Seeing, 67
    "Recreation," poem, 65, 101, 124–125
    Strategic Reading, 77, 153
    teaching of, 1–2, 14–17, 106–115, 157–158, 217
    "*You Gotta BE the Book*," 2, 14, 15, 57, 59, 69, 84, 87, 89, 92, 95–96, 139–140, 150, 252
Wilhelm, Peggy Jo, xv, 93, 24–125, 138, 180
Wilson, E. O., 51, 67, 157
    Creation, The, 192
    Consilience, 51
    On Human Nature, 51
Winnicott, D. W., 58, 228
    "Ego Distortion in Terms of the True and False Self," 150, 156
    Playing and Reality, 88, 181
    Third space, 174, 181
    "Transitional Objects and Transitional Phenomena," 58–59. *See also* Play; Self, False; Self, True; Third space; Transitional objects, transitional space
Wisdom
    Debra Smith on, 6, 166–168
    democracy and, 10
    loving, 10, 122, 126, 143, 206

practical, 143
revolution, vii, 16, 17, 144, 202, 204, 209, 213, 215
teacherly, 7
theoretical, 143
Wittgenstein, Ludwig (*Philosophical Investigations*), 134, 159, 227
Woodruff, Paul, 99
Woolf, Virginia (*A Room of One's Own*), 26
Worldview, democratic, transactional, 23, 48–49, 143–146, 156, 191–192, 226, 231
Wright, Robert (*Nonzero*), 190
Wye Conference (English Coalition Conference of 1987), 27–31
    College Section, 32–35, 42–44, 53, 59, 141
    Elementary Section, 32, 34, 36–39
    "wholistic/Joy" group, 32, 34, 36, 41–44, 59, 117, 141, 225

Zajonc, Arthur, 211
Zone of proximal development (Vygotsky), 153–154

About the Authors

Jeffrey D. Wilhelm is an internationally known teacher, author, and presenter. A classroom teacher for 15 years, Dr. Jeffrey Wilhelm is currently Professor of English Education at Boise State University. He works in local schools as part of the Professional Development Site Network, teaching middle and high school students each spring. He is the founding director of the Maine Writing Project and the Boise State Writing Project.

He has authored or coauthored 18 books about literacy teaching. He has won the two top research awards in English Education: the NCTE Promising Research Award for *You Gotta BE the Book* (Teachers College Press) and the Russell Award for Distinguished Research for *Reading Don't Fix No Chevys* (Heinemann).

He has worked on numerous materials for students and has edited a series of 100 books for reluctant readers entitled *The Ten*. Jeff enjoys speaking, presenting, and working with students and schools. He is currently researching how students read and engage with nontraditional texts like video game narratives, manga, horror, fantasy, and so on, as well as the effects of inquiry teaching on teachers, students, and learning.

His Web site can be found at jeffreywilhelm.com.

Bruce Novak is currently Director of Educational Projects for the Foundation for Ethics and Meaning, undertaking research and arranging gatherings promoting educational life that will support full-bodied democracy: education with meaning for a politics of meaning. From 1998–2008 he was instrumental in the leadership of the NCTE Assembly for Expanded Perspectives on Learning, and he has staged five of its national conferences. His twenty-year teaching career has given him a wide range of experiences: teaching English and Social Studies, grades 6–12, in diverse settings in and around Chicago; assisting the English Education program at the University of Chicago; and teaching Psychoanalysis and Education for DePaul University and the Chicago Institute for Psychoanalysis, Humanities and Social Science Core courses at the University of Chicago, Writing at the University of Chicago and Truman College, and Philosophy and Foundations of Education at the University of Chicago and Northern Illinois University. Among his many scholarly publications, his "Humanizing Democracy" was the lead article in the Fall 2002 edition of the American Educational Research Journal, and has been broadly acclaimed. Currently, he is seeking to help lead a program for English Education that will embody the ideas of that article and this book. He can be contacted at brucenovak@mac.com.